P9-DVD-006

AN ANALYTICAL INDEX
TO THE WORKS OF
Nathaniel Hawthorne

WITH A SKETCH OF HIS LIFE

By EVANGELINE M. O'CONNOR

With an Introduction by

C. E. FRAZER CLARK, JR.

ORIGINALLY PUBLISHED, BOSTON:
HOUGHTON, MIFFLIN AND COMPANY
1882

Republished by Gale Research Company, Book Tower, Detroit, 1967

Library of Congress Catalog Card Number 66-27844

PAPER USED IN THIS EDITION IS
A FINE ACID FREE PERMANENT/DURABLE PAPER
COMMONLY REFERRED TO AS "300-YEAR" PAPER

PREFACE

An Analytical Index To The Works Of Nathaniel Hawthorne With A Sketch Of His Life, by Evangeline Maria O'Connor, was another of the numerous publications resulting from the popular and profitable "Little Classics" Series originated and edited by Rossiter Johnson.

According to a *Buffalo Courier* review, incorporated by Houghton, Mifflin, in the prefatory advertisements to volumes in the series, the "Little Classics" Edition was "a series of exquisitely printed little volumes in flexible binding and red edges, which gather up the very choicest things in our literature in the way of short tales and sketches."

Results were encouraging. Readers seemed ready to accept the convenience of the handy pocket size, or, most likely, they responded to the new concept in price. The "Little Classics" were offered at $1.00 each, about one half the price of the traditional octavo publication.

Within the first year, Johnson had Volume 16 of the original "Little Classics" Series, *Authors,* off the press and the busy editor-author was already preparing to capitalize on the initial success of the series. Johnson reveals, in his capsule biography of Hawthorne, one of the selected *Authors,* that "a 'Little Classic' edition, with a volume of biography by his son-in-law, George P. Lathrop, is in the course of publication."

In addition to his biography, *A Study of Hawthorne,* (Boston: James R. Osgood and Company, 1876), Lathrop was commissioned to edit the "Little Classic" Edition of Hawthorne's Works. There is a letter in the Clark Collection dated July 12, 1901, from Houghton, Mifflin, to Mr. P. K. Foley, the Boston book dealer and bibliographer, identifying G. P. Lathrop as editor of the "Little Classic" Edition of Hawthorne and responsible for various textual alterations.

The E. M. O'Connor *Analytical Index (and) Sketch* appeared in 1882—followed in 1883 by a compiled *Sketches and Studies,* to complete a final 25-volume "Little Classic" Edition.

Precisely whose idea the *Analytical Index* was may remain a mystery, but we can suspect it to have been a family affair. Johnson, with many editorial irons in the fire, needed help and he drew on many sources, as his continued interest in the career of Joseph O'Connor indicates.

O'Connor had served in an editorial capacity on the Rochester, New York, *Democrat and Chronicle* only two years after Johnson had been an associate editor on the same paper. On November 20, 1877, O'Connor married Johnson's niece, Evangeline Maria (Johnson). In 1898 and 1900, Joseph O'Connor contributed two pieces to *The World's Great Books,* a 40-volume series for which Rossiter Johnson served as Editor-in-Chief.

Evangeline M. O'Connor had translated *Fire and Flame,* a novel by Levin Schücking, in 1877, and her next effort appears to have been the *Analytical Index (and) Sketch.* Five years later (1887), she undertook *An Analytical Index To The Works Of Shakespeare.* She also contributed numerous poems to the periodicals—the most important of which was "Daughters of Toil."

The O'Connor sketch of Hawthorne's life is primarily a biographical profile and provides only a superficial examination of Hawthorne's work. Following close on the heels of the substantial Lathrop and James biographies, the O'Connor sketch is perhaps best viewed as an Introduction popularizing Hawthorne and his work. O'Connor's view of Hawthorne is revealed in her summary statement: "Some critics have seen in the subjects of Hawthorne's art proofs of morbidness of mind, have written of him as a 'weird,' malarious genius,' and wondered that the works most 'lurid' should have sprung from his happiest years. This is simply to wonder that a man's imagination should be strongest and free-est when his affections are most at rest, and his ideal of life most nearly satisfied. It is to confuse the art of the author with the creed of the man."

Johnson was busy enough and Lathrop's help was undoubtedly welcome. Curiously, the Lathrop biography, although issued at the same time and in the same format, was never formally identified as part of the "Little Classic" Edition.

Considerable Hawthorne family bitterness was caused by the publication of Lathrop's biography. Julian Hawthorne felt he had staked out a claim in this area and resented being anticipated by his brother-in-law. Since Osgood certainly anticipated future Hawthorne publications, including Julian's follow-up biography, the firm may have found itself somewhat "in the middle" of the family quarrel and omitted the Lathrop biography from the "Little Classic" advertising as a matter of discretion.

The series prospered and was continued during the transition from James R. Osgood as publisher to the immergence of Houghton, Mifflin and Company. Although Rossiter Johnson, who continued as editor-in-chief, had identified the series title as early as 1876, the 23-volume set of Hawthorne's Works became officially designated in the publisher's advertisements as the "Little Classic" Edition only after the establishment of the Houghton, Mifflin, name.

The popularity of the Hawthorne "Little Classic" Edition grew as Hawthorne's stature gained increasing recognition. Johnson undoubtedly made a wise and fortunate choice in selecting Hawthorne as a logical candidate for the expanded "Little Classic" format. It may well have been Johnson who selected the appropriate excerpt used as a new advertising blurb for the Houghton, Mifflin, "Little Classic" reprints of the *Writings of Nathaniel Hawthorne:* "We are beginning to arrive at some faint sense of Hawthorne's greatness—immeasurably vaster than that of any other American who ever wrote"—*The Nation* (New York).

The rising tide of contemporary Hawthorne comment and certainly the influential Henry James biography contributed to a growing market for Hawthorne material. Undoubtedly sensitive to this potential, Rossiter Johnson cast about for additional publishable material for the successful "Little Classic" Edition of Hawthorne's Work and two supplementary volumes were brought out.

Hawthorne scholarship has come some distance, with interest in the Hawthorne canon undiminished, and little new will be found in the O'Connor *Sketch*. The fact of its existence may prove more of a discovery than its substance. It does serve as contemporary evidence of the sudden rise in Hawthorne's popular appreciation. The general reading public for whom Lathrop's *Study* or James's *Hawthorne* may have seemed overwhelming could easily "discover" Hawthorne in the O'Connor *Sketch*.

Evangeline O'Connor's *Analytical Index* rediscovered can prove greatly convenient. The *Index* includes both proper names and topics and is a useful tool. References are generally to volume, chapter, and in Hawthorne's *Note-Books,* to dates, which makes the *Index* useful with any standard works or separate volume. The *Index* is comprehensive and can prove rewarding.

Detroit. August, 1966

C. E. Frazer Clark, Jr.

SKETCH OF THE LIFE

OF

NATHANIEL HAWTHORNE.

THE family to which Hawthorne belonged, originally English, was one of the oldest of Salem, Mass., his native town. His journals mention some of the early records and incidents of the family, both in England and this country. In the "American Note-Books" he speaks of memorials in the village of Dundry, Somersetshire, England, and the family seat as being Wigcastle, Wigton (Wilton?), Wiltshire; and "Hawthorne Hall" is mentioned in the "English Note-Books," under date of December 1, 1853.

The first Hawthorne — or Hathorne, the earlier spelling — to come to America was William, a younger son in the English family, who came over with Winthrop in 1630, going first to Dorchester, but afterwards settling in Salem, attracted by the offer of grants of land. He filled many offices of trust in the town, and in 1676 was a major in a campaign against the Indians in Maine. He figured in the Quaker persecutions: first as an opponent of severity, but afterwards, having been made a magistrate, as a persecutor, at least in one instance, — that of "Anne Coleman and four of her friends." Of him Hawthorne says, in the chapter on the Salem Custom-House prefixed to "The Scarlet Letter:" —

"The figure of that first ancestor, invested by family tradition with a dim and dusky grandeur, was present to my boyish imagination as far back as I can remember. It still haunts me, and induces a sort of home-feeling with the past, which I scarcely claim in reference to the present phase of the town. I seem to have a stronger claim to residence here on account of this grave, bearded, sable-cloaked, and steeple-crowned progenitor, who came so early with his Bible and his sword, and trode the unworn street with such a stately port, and made so large a figure, as a man of war and peace, — a stronger claim than for myself, whose name is seldom heard and my face hardly known. He was a soldier, legislator, judge; he was a ruler in the church; he had all the Puritanic traits, both good and evil. He was likewise a bitter persecutor; as witness the Quakers, who have remembered him in their histories, and relate an incident of his hard severity toward a woman of their sect, which will last longer, it is to be feared, than any record of his better deeds, though these were many."

The son of this William was John, who bore the title of Colonel, and was a judge during the famous witch-trials of Salem. In this capacity he is recorded to have been bitter and stern, and an instance of his severity toward a woman, as related by her husband, is quoted from Upham's account of the witchcraft delusion: —

"She was forced to stand with her arms stretched out. I requested that I might hold one of her hands, but it was declined me; then she desired me to wipe the tears from her eyes and the sweat from her face, which I did; then she desired that she might lean herself on me, saying she should faint. Justice Hathorne replied she had strength enough to torment these persons, and she should have strength enough to stand. I repeating something against their cruel proceedings, they commanded me to be silent, or else I should be turned out of the room."

Another anecdote of him is told in the "American Note-Books," vol. i., August 27, 1838, the *dénoûment* of which suggests the ending of "The House of the Seven Gables." His grave in the old Charter-Street burial-ground is mentioned under date of July 4, 1838, in the same volume, and again in the introductory chapter of "The Scarlet Letter:" —

"His [William's] son, too, inherited the persecuting spirit, and made himself so conspicuous in the martyrdom of the witches that their blood may fairly be said to have left a stain upon him. So deep a stain, indeed, that his old dry bones in the Charter-Street burial-ground must still retain it, if they have not crumbled utterly to dust! I know not whether these ancestors of mine bethought themselves to repent, and ask pardon of Heaven for their cruelties; or whether they are now groaning under the heavy consequences of them, in another state of being. At all events, I, the present writer, as their representative, hereby take shame upon myself for their sakes, and pray that any curse incurred by them — as I have heard, and as the dreary and unprosperous condition of the race, for many a long year back, would argue to exist — may be now and henceforth removed."

It is interesting to trace the family through these slight records, not only because of the common interest in the antecedents and early associations of men of genius, but because they have passed into some of Hawthorne's best work. "The Gentle Boy," one of the most tender and beautiful of the short stories, evidently sprang from that blot on the family history left by the unhappy zeal of William Hathorne; and "The House of the Seven Gables" is built upon the curse invoked upon John Hathorne by the husband of the fainting witch.

Another slight reminder of the Hawthorne records may be found in "Lady Eleanore's Mantle," one of the "Legends of the Province House." The name of the insane lover of the proud English girl is Jervase Helwyse, a name which appears in the family records as Gervase Elwes, Holles, or Holwyse (see "English Note-Books," vol. i., May 30, 1854; vol. ii., July 30, 1857), though, as no foundation appears for the character or incidents, the name was probably taken merely for its picturesqueness, and its giving to the character in the author's mind a slight hold on reality.

Possibly, also, some association with the estate of Wigcastle, and the transplanting of a branch of the family to Massachusetts, may have been joined with the tradition of the bloody footprint in Smithell's Hall to suggest the concluding part of "Septimius Felton."

It was, no doubt, the Puritan element in the family associations, and the early surroundings of Hawthorne, as well as his inherited Puritan sense, or, perhaps one would better say, his inherited comprehension of the Puritan character and philosophy of life, that united with his genius to give him his imaginative control over New England's early history, and the insight that produced those studies of conscience that form his best and most characteristic work.

For the hundred years following the death of the witch-judge, the Hathornes were not prominent in the public affairs of Salem. Whether the judge suffered the unpopularity common to leaders of popular extravagances after the fever has subsided, when the "great popular heart" casts about for some one to bear the blame of its madness, and sank into an obscurity from which his descendants could not rally, or from whatever cause, the family history ran along as described by the author in "The Custom-House:"—

"Planted deep, in the town's earliest infancy and childhood, by these two earnest and energetic men, the race has ever since subsisted here; always, too, in respectability; never, so far as I have known, disgraced by a single unworthy member; but seldom or never, on the other hand, after the first two generations, performing any memorable deed, or so much as putting forward a claim to public notice. Gradually, they have sunk almost out of sight; as old houses, here and there about the streets, get covered half-way to the eaves by the accumulation of new soil. From father to son, for above a hundred years, they followed the sea; a gray-headed shipmaster in each generation, retiring from the quarter-deck to the homestead, while a boy of fourteen took the hereditary place before the mast, confronting the salt spray and the gale, which had blustered against his sire and grandsire. The boy, also, in due time, passed from the forecastle to the cabin, spent a tempestuous manhood, and returned from his world-wanderings to grow old and die, and mingle his dust with the natal earth."

This answers in some slight degree, at least far enough to have suggested it, to the description of the Maules in "The House of the Seven Gables."

It is worthy of note, however, that one of these sailors, Daniel Hathorne, grandfather of the author, enjoyed some local celebrity during the Revolution as the commander of a privateer.

NATHANIEL HAWTHORNE was born in Union Street, Salem, Mass., July 4, 1804. His father, Nathaniel also, was a sea-captain, and died of fever at Surinam in 1808, leaving a widow and three children, Nathaniel and his two sisters. Forty years afterward the son was recognized from his resemblance to his father by a sailor who had known the captain at the time of his death in Surinam.

Mrs. Hathorne, whose maiden name was Elizabeth Manning, now removed with her family to a house of her brother's in Herbert Street, and it was here that Hawthorne's early boyhood was spent.

At about the age of seven he went to a school

taught by Dr. Worcester, of dictionary fame. The most noteworthy fact recorded of his boyhood was that an accident lamed him when he was nine years old, thus keeping him in the house and shutting him up to books for more than two years. During this time Dr. Worcester came to the house to teach him, and there are traces of an affectionate regard kept up between them into later years.

When he was fourteen Hawthorne went with his mother to Raymond, Maine, near Sebago Lake, and lived in a house belonging to his uncle, Robert Manning, and called, from some attempt at grandeur, perhaps, "Manning's Folly." His life here is described by Mr. Fields, in his "Yesterdays with Authors," partly in Hawthorne's own words, as he talked over his life near its close:—

"'I lived in Maine,' he said, 'like a bird of the air, so perfect was the freedom I enjoyed. But it was there I first got my cursed habits of solitude.' During the moonlight nights of winter he would skate until midnight all alone upon Sebago Lake, with the deep shadows of the icy hills on either hand. When he found himself far away from his home and weary with the exertion of skating, he would sometimes take refuge in a log-cabin where half a tree would be burning on the broad hearth. He would sit in the ample chimney and look at the stars through the great aperture through which the flames went roaring up. 'Ah,' he said, 'how well I recall the summer days, also, when, with my gun, I roamed at will through the woods of Maine. How sad middle life looks to people of erratic temperaments! Everything is beautiful in youth, for all things are allowed to it then.' "

Possibly this idle life had as much to do in ripening the genius of Hawthorne as any of his studies, if his discursive, desultory reading may be called study. Among his early favorites in books were Bunyan, Spenser, Shakespeare, Sir Philip Sydney, Milton, Thomson, and Gray; and there are traces of familiarity with some of them in his books, the allusions to Bunyan being perhaps more frequent than those to any other author. "The Celestial Railroad" is a satire founded on "The Pilgrim's Progress," and his tendency to allegory is due, no doubt, to his early love for Spenser and Bunyan. Judging from "Fanshawe," his earliest novel, he must have read Scott with care and admiration. Voltaire, and Rousseau, also, are said to have been early read, and "The Newgate Calendar" was a favorite of his boyhood.

It is by no means to be supposed, because he is remarkably free from quotations and allusions, that he read little, or that he owed little to reading. It may be that his genius found comparatively little congenial to it in books, and that that little was so appropriated and transformed by his own originality that it became a different thing and would have been no longer represented by the original form. The matter of his best work, much of it, is elaborated from the annals of early historians, and from slight incidents in his own experience minutely observed and noted.

An early tendency toward literature is shown by some boyish journals and copies of a paper, "The

Spectator," which have been preserved, and a few rhymes of his young manhood. These fragments are noticeable for careful observation and a clear style, with now and then a passage indicating that the boy has brooded over some little incident, some ghost-story, or other tale, and has seen it in more varied lights and drawn from it a deeper meaning than it would bear to the understanding of the ordinary boy.

Hawthorne stayed only a year in Maine, returning to Salem in 1819, to prepare for college under the tuition of a lawyer, Benjamin L. Oliver. In 1821 he entered Bowdoin College, Brunswick, Maine, being in the same class with Henry W. Longfellow. He had at college the reputation of unusual excellence in writing; his poetic translations are remembered as remarkably good, and the Professor of Rhetoric was in the habit of taking home young Hawthorne's essays to read to his family. A college friend's prophecy of his fame as a romance-writer is alluded to in the dedication to "The Snow Image."

One of his most intimate friends at college was Franklin Pierce, of the class next higher, with whom his friendship continued through life, and to whom he owed his consulship at Liverpool. Another was Horatio Bridge, afterward an officer in the United States Navy, for whom Hawthorne edited a volume, and to whom he dedicated "The Snow Image." Still another classmate and intimate was Jonathan Cilley, who, after rapid success in political life, was killed in a duel, while a member of Congress, in 1838, by a Kentucky member. Hawthorne wrote a sketch of his life the same year, which is published in the volume with "Fanshawe."

From the time of his graduation in 1825 till 1838 Hawthorne lived mostly in Salem, presumably in the Herbert Street house, which seems to have had a face toward Union Street as well. It is to a chamber in this house, and to this period of his life, that the often-quoted sentence in the "Note-Books" refers, "In this dismal chamber FAME was won," and the passage dated October 4, 1840: —

"Here I sit in my old accustomed chamber where I used to sit in days gone by. Here I have written many tales, — many that have been burned to ashes, many, doubtless, that deserved the same fate. This claims to be called a haunted chamber, for thousands upon thousands of visions have appeared to me in it; and some few of them have become visible to the world. If ever I should have a biographer he ought to make great mention of this chamber in my memoirs, because so much of my lonely youth was wasted here, and here my mind and character were formed; and here I have been glad and hopeful, and here I have been despondent. And here I sat a long, long time, waiting patiently for the world to know me, and sometimes wondering why it did not know me sooner, or whether it would ever know me at all, — at least till I were in my grave. And sometimes it seemed as if I were already in the grave, with only life enough to be chilled and benumbed. But oftener I was happy, — at least, as happy as I then knew how to be, or was aware of the possibility of being. By and by the world found me out in my lonely chamber, and called me forth, — not, indeed, with a loud roar of acclamation, but rather with a still small voice, — and forth I went, but found nothing in the world that I thought preferable to my old solitude till now. . . . And now I begin to understand why I was imprisoned so many years in this lonely chamber, and why I could never break through the viewless bolts and bars; for if I had sooner made my escape into the world, I should have grown hard and rough, and been covered with earthly dust, and my heart might have become callous by rude encounters with the multitude. . . . But living in solitude till the fullness of time was come, I still kept the dew of my youth and the freshness of my heart."

His first published work was "Fanshawe" (Boston, 1828). This is a novel, very unlike his later work, and showing strong traces of the study of Scott, in both characters and incidents, though there may be in the character of Fanshawe that little of the autobiographical which creeps into nearly all first work in fiction, — a young author's character, as he himself understands it. The scene is laid at "Harley College," standing for Bowdoin, at about the middle of the eighteenth century. The plot is somewhat involved, and gives occasion for the development of the character of Fanshawe, a close and ambitious student, fitted for the life of a recluse, who gives up the heroine to Edward Walcott, a fellow-student, as better suited than himself to make her happy in the ordinary walk of life to which her temperament would lead her.

Dr. Melmoth, the president of the college, is a simple-minded and gullible old pedant, very well brought out in the scenes of chapters v. and vii.

This book Hawthorne afterward tried to suppress, very naturally, as his views and aims in romance developed later into an originality with which it has nothing in common. But it was republished in 1879, as being of interest to students of his genius.

During this residence in Salem, Hawthorne made some journeys by carriage with an uncle, about New England and perhaps New York. These journeys probably suggested and furnished material for the "Passages from a Relinquished Work," the "Sketches from Memory," describing Burlington, Rochester, Niagara, and the White Mountains, "The Seven Vagabonds," "Chippings with a Chisel," located in Martha's Vineyard, and the description of Fort Ticonderoga. A letter written on one of these expeditions in 1831 describes a visit to the Shaker settlement at Canterbury, N. H., which must have suggested "The Canterbury Pilgrims" and "The Shaker Bridal."

His quiet and almost solitary life at this time, and his lonely walks about the town and its vicinity, gave rise, no doubt, to those sketches of Salem, "Footprints on the Sea-shore," "Night-Sketches," "The Toll-Gatherer's Day," and "The Village Uncle." The "Journal of a Solitary Man" may represent his feeling about his own career during this period. How it looked to him afterward is indicated in the passage already quoted, and, from another mood, in the following from the "English Note-Books," at Christmas, 1854: —

"I think I have been happier this Christmas than ever before, — by my own fireside, and with my wife and children about me, — more content to enjoy what I have, less anxious for anything beyond it, in this life. My early life was perhaps a good preparation for the declining half of life; it having been such a blank that any thereafter would compare favorably with it. For a long, long while I have occasionally been visited with a singular dream; and I have an impression that I have dreamed it ever since I have been in England. It is, that I am still at college, — or, sometimes even at school, — and there is a sense that I have been there unconscionably long, and have quite failed to make such progress as my contemporaries have done; and I seem to meet some of them with a feeling of shame and depression that broods over me as I think of it, even when awake. This dream, recurring through all these twenty or thirty years, must be one of the effects of that heavy seclusion in which I shut myself up for twelve years after leaving college, when everybody moved onward and left me behind. How strange that it should come now, when I may call myself famous and prosperous! — when I am happy, too!"

The next attempt in literature was a set of stories called "Seven Tales of my Native Land," and bearing the motto, "We are Seven." These, after many discouragements in looking for a publisher, Hawthorne gave to a Salem printer, who intended to bring them out at a favorable opportunity. But, wearied by his long delay, the author recalled the manuscript and burned it. On this incident is founded "The Devil in Manuscript."

About 1836 Hawthorne was engaged by the "Bewick Publishing Company," in which S. G. Goodrich ("Peter Parley") was prominent, to go to Boston as editor of "The American Magazine of Useful and Entertaining Knowledge," a post in which he did a great deal of work at a salary of five or six hundred dollars a year. Many of the articles were written by his sister, who also helped him in the "Universal History" which he wrote for Goodrich, and for which he received one hundred dollars.

Meantime, contributions of his were appearing, sometimes under assumed names — Oberon, A. A. Royce, and others, — in various periodicals, — the *Salem Gazette*, the *New England Magazine*, the *Boston Token and Atlantic Souvenir*, — the latter edited by Goodrich. These attracted some notice and favorable criticism, some of them being copied into London periodicals.

Through the intervention of Horatio Bridge, they were collected early in 1837, and published under the title, "Twice-Told Tales." They include two of the stories founded on early New England annals, — "The Gray Champion," based on a tradition of one of the judges of Charles I., and "The Maypole of Merry Mount," in which Endicott appears as the embodiment of the Puritan spirit. Besides these are the allegories "Fancy's Show Box," "The Great Carbuncle," and "The Prophetic Pictures;" "The Hollow of the Three Hills," one of the typical stories of witchcraft, foreshadowing some of his later and more powerful work; the curious study, "Wakefield;" the popular "Rill from the Town Pump;" the pretty fantasy, "David Swan," in which the light-hearted boy goes on his pilgrimage unconscious of the shadows of possibilities that have fallen across his sleeping face; the pathetic story of Quaker suffering, "The Gentle Boy;" "Dr. Heidegger's Experiment," touching a subject which recurs again in "Septimius Felton" and "The Dolliver Romance;" and the light humor of "Mr. Higginbotham's Catastrophe," — thus including almost every class of subject on which he afterward touched, though in all he rose to higher levels in his later work.

Six or seven hundred copies of the book were sold, and it was favorably criticised, noticeably by Longfellow in the *North American Review*. This led to interesting letters between the classmates. Some extracts from one of Hawthorne's give his own view of his work: —

"For the last ten years I have not lived, but only dreamed of living. It may be true that there have been some unsubstantial pleasures here in the shade, which I might have missed in the sunshine, but you cannot conceive how utterly devoid of satisfaction all my retrospects are. I have laid up no treasure of pleasant remembrances against old age; but there is some comfort in thinking that future years can hardly fail to be more varied, and therefore more tolerable, than the past.

2

"You give me more credit than I deserve in supposing that I have led a studious life. I have indeed turned over a good many books, but in so desultory a way that it cannot be called study, nor has it left me the fruits of study. As to my literary efforts, I do not think much of them, neither is it worth while to be ashamed of them. They would have been better, I trust, if written under more favorable circumstances. I have had no external excitement, — no consciousness that the public would like what I wrote, nor much hope, nor a passionate desire, that they should do so. Nevertheless, having nothing else to be ambitious of, I have been considerably interested in literature; and if my writings had made any decided impression I should have been stimulated to greater exertions; but there has been no warmth of approbation, so that I have always written with benumbed fingers. I have another great difficulty in the lack of materials; for I have seen so little of the world that I have nothing but thin air to concoct my stories of, and it is not easy to give a life-like semblance to such shadowy stuff. Sometimes through a peep-hole I have caught a glimpse of the real world, and the two or three articles in which I have portrayed these glimpses please me better than the others.

"I have now, or shall soon have, a sharper spur to exertion, which I lacked at an earlier period; for I see little prospect but that I shall have to scribble for a living. But this troubles me much less than you would suppose. I can turn my pen to all sorts of drudgery, such as children's books, etc., and by and by

I shall get some editorship that will answer my purpose.

"Frank Pierce, who was with us at college, offered me his influence to obtain an office in the Exploring Expedition; but I believe he was mistaken in supposing a vacancy existed. If such a post were attainable I should certainly accept it; for, though fixed so long to one spot, I have always had a desire to run round the world."

In the same year, 1837, Hawthorne made a visit to Horatio Bridge, in Maine, full details of which are recorded in the "American Note-Books," vol. i.

In 1838 he began writing for the *Democratic Review*, a magazine of high standing, published first in Washington, afterward in New York from 1838 to 1851. Many of his best tales and sketches were contributed to it during the few years following. In the same year George Bancroft, who had been made collector of the port of Boston, gave Hawthorne an appointment as weigher and gauger, — a post which he took in January, 1839. His work here was tedious and tiresome. An interesting fact about it is noted by Mr. Lathrop, — that he made a point of getting to his duties as early in the morning as possible, — earlier than he was required to do, — for the benefit of the wharf-laborers, whose wages depended on the number of hours they worked in a day.

He had by this time become engaged to Miss Sophia Peabody, his future wife, and some extracts from his letters to her, bearing on his custom-house work, are given at the close of the first volume of the "American Note-Books."

With the change of administration, two years later (Hawthorne was a Democrat), this position was lost. About this time the first part of "Grandfather's Chair" was written, and published in Boston and New York; the second part not being brought out till 1842. This is a series of stories for children, in which some of the striking and picturesque events in early American history are connected by association with an old chair, originally given by the Earl of Lincoln to his daughter, Lady Arabella Johnson, from whom it passed in succession to a long series of colonial worthies down to the time of the Revolution, — Roger Williams, Anne Hutchinson, Sir Henry Vane, President Dunster of Harvard, several governors of Massachusetts, Eliot, the Indian apostle, Cotton Mather, and others. "The Pine-Tree Shillings," which has been so widely copied in books for children, is one of the stories of "Grandfather's Chair."

In April, 1841, Hawthorne tried a new kind of life, — the life which gave us "The Blithedale Romance." Among the radical thinkers and enthusiasts of that day in Boston originated a scheme of social reform, a theory of communism which united some of the features of European socialism with American ideas; and under the leadership of the late George Ripley, formerly a Unitarian clergyman, afterwards known as editor of the "American Cyclopædia," and literary editor of the *New York Tribune*, a community was established in West Roxbury.

The design was to combine bodily labor with mental culture, and by giving all a share in the production of the necessaries of life, to give all a share of time for the pursuit of its higher objects. The name "Brook Farm" was given to the home of the community. Each had his allotted share of house or farm work, leaving some leisure for study, and the evenings were given to social discussions, readings, or amusements. Those families who chose had separate houses; and it was with some view to making his home there after his marriage that Hawthorne joined the community. His experience there and his reasons for leaving may be found in the "American Note-Books," the first part of the second volume. The principal one was, that the exhaustive bodily labor left him no strength for literary work and in no mood for it; so that, as far as he was concerned, the experiment of combining the two was a failure. He stayed only one year at Brook Farm. Observations on that kind of life, suggested by his residence there, are scattered through "The Blithedale Romance." Many members of the community are mentioned in the "Note-Books" and in the preface to "The Blithedale Romance."

The novel which grew out of this experience will be noticed hereafter, since it was not written till ten years later.

In July, 1842, Hawthorne was married and went to live in Concord, Mass., in the house well known to all his readers as the Old Manse. Notes of his residence here are included in the second volume of the "American Note-Books," and a description of the life he led in the chapter introductory to the "Mosses from an Old Manse." His time was now given up to writing, and his journals show that he had entered on a much more contented and satisfactory life, — a change marked by increased power and depth in his writings, as well as by greater activity and productiveness.

In 1845 the second volume of "Twice-Told Tales" was published. It opens with the four "Legends of the Province House." This old building, now gone, the residence of the royal governors, is described in the introduction to those charming romances founded on the slender annals of colonial times. "Endicott and the Red Cross" is drawn from the same source.

"The Seven Vagabonds" is a fantastic tale whose allegorical significance is more delicately conveyed than that of perhaps any other of the stories of this character, — by an impression brought away from the reading, rather than by any definite applications one is forced to make of it as metaphor.

Among the other more noticeable tales are "The White Old Maid," "The Ambitious Guest," and "The Threefold Destiny." "The Haunted Mind," "Snow-Flakes," "The Sister Years," "Night Sketches," and "Footprints on the Sea-Shore" are essays or musings.

In the same year Hawthorne edited the "Journals of an African Cruiser," for Horatio Bridge, and the "Papers of an Old Dartmoor Prisoner," the latter published in the *Democratic Review.*

In 1846 the "Mosses from an Old Manse" was published in New York in two volumes, which contain, on the whole, his best work in short stories, and are prefaced by one of his most delightful essays, "The

Old Manse." In some of them, it may be, the allegory is too apparent, but in general they are very deep and searching studies of the heart and conscience. Among the best are "Young Goodman Brown," "Roger Malvin's Burial," "Rappaccini's Daughter," which is usually placed highest, and "Drowne's Wooden Image." "The Birthmark" and "The Artist of the Beautiful" also rank high in the estimation of critics.

"The Celestial Railroad" is a clever satire on modern religion; "The Intelligence Office," "The Procession of Life," and "Earth's Holocaust" are conceits with a burden of symbolic meaning. "The Old Apple-Dealer" is a study of a character with the least possible amount of coloring. "P.'s Correspondence" is mainly interesting, perhaps, for the curious speculation, under the guise of a lunatic's vagaries, on what age might have made of those early poets of the century who died young or in middle life, — especially of what its sobering and conservative tendencies would have done for Byron, Burns, Shelley, and Keats. "The Hall of Fantasy," "A Select Party," and "A Virtuoso's Collection" are ingeniously executed fancies. "Mrs. Bullfrog" is a light, humorous sketch, and "Fire Worship" and "Buds and Bird Voices" are delightful essays.

In 1846 Hawthorne was appointed surveyor in the Salem Custom-House, an office which he filled till 1849. There are no records of these years in the "Note-Books," but it was during them that the first draught of "The Scarlet Letter" was written, designed at first to be the leading story in a collection made up in part of the tales afterward included in the volume "The Snow Image and Other Twice-Told Tales," the collection to be called "Old-Time Legends: together with Sketches, Experimental and Ideal." The following extract from Mr. Fields's "Yesterdays with Authors" gives an account of the first appearance of the novel which made Hawthorne's fame: —

"In the winter of 1849, after he had been ejected from the Custom-House, I went down to Salem to see him and inquire after his health, for we heard he had been suffering from illness. He was then living in a modest wooden house in Mall Street, if I remember rightly the location. I found him alone in a chamber over the sitting-room of the dwelling; and as the day was cold he was hovering near a stove. We fell into talk about his future prospects, and he was, as I feared I should find him, in a very desponding mood. 'Now,' said I, 'is the time for you to publish; for I know during these years in Salem you must have got something ready for the press.' 'Nonsense,' said he, 'what heart had I to write anything, when my publishers [M. and Company] have been so many years trying to sell a small edition of the "Twice-Told Tales?"' I still pressed upon him the good chances he would now have with something new. 'Who would risk publishing a book for me, the most unpopular writer in America?' 'I would,' said I, 'and would start with an edition of two thousand copies for anything you might write.' 'What madness!' he exclaimed; 'your friendship for me gets the better of your judgment. No, no,' he continued; 'I have no money to indemnify a publisher's losses on my account.'

"I looked at my watch and found that the train would soon be starting for Boston, and I knew there was not much time to lose in trying to discover what had been his literary work during these last few years in Salem. I remember that I pressed him to reveal to me what he had been writing. He shook his head, and gave me to understand that he had produced nothing. At that moment I caught sight of a bureau or set of drawers near where we were sitting; and immediately it occurred to me that hidden away somewhere in that article of furniture was a story or stories by the author of the 'Twice-Told Tales;' and I became so positive of it that I charged him vehemently with the fact. He seemed surprised, I thought, but shook his head again; and I rose to take my leave, begging him not to come into the cold entry, saying I would come back and see him again in a few days. I was hurrying down the stairs when he called after me from the chamber, asking me to stop a moment. Then, quickly stepping into the entry with a roll of manuscript in his hands, he said: 'How in Heaven's name did you know this thing was there? As you have found me out, take what I have written, and tell me, after you get home and have time to read it, if it is good for anything. It is either very good or very bad, — I don't know which.' On my way up to Boston I read the germ of 'The Scarlet Letter'; before I slept that night I wrote a note all aglow with admiration of the marvelous story he had put into my hands, and told him that I would come again to Salem the next day and arrange for its publication. I went on in such an amazing state of excitement when we met again in the little house, that he would not believe I was really in earnest. He seemed to think I was beside myself, and laughed sadly at my enthusiasm. However, we soon arranged for his appearance again before the public with a book."

The introductory chapter to this book, "The Custom-House," gives a picture of the life of the surveyor there, with some sketches of his brother officials, which very naturally excited grievous indignation in Salem. Its allusions to the Hathornes have been already referred to. The account of the finding of the old embroidered letter and the manuscript is, of course, fictitious. But the punishment which gives the story its name is actually prescribed in the old colonial regulations, and was referred to by the author long before, in the picture of a Puritan town in the story "Endicott and the Red Cross."

Like all of Hawthorne's novels, "The Scarlet Letter" has but a slender plot and but few characters with an influence on the development of the story. Its great dramatic force depends entirely on the mental states of the actors and their relations to one another, — relations of conscience, — relations between wronged and wrongers. Its great burden is the weight of unacknowledged sin as seen in the remorse and cowardice and suffering of the Rev. Arthur Dimmesdale. Contrasted with his concealed agony is the constant confession, conveyed by the letter, which is forced upon Hester, and has a double effect, — a healthful one, working beneficently, and making her helpful and benevolent, tolerant and thoughtful; and an unhealthful one, which by the great emphasis placed on her transgression, the keeping her forever under its ban and isolating her from her fellows, prepares her to break away from the long repression and lapse again into sin when she plans her flight. Roger Chillingworth is an embodiment of subtle and refined revenge. The most striking situation is perhaps "The Minister's Vigil," in chapter xii.

The book, though corresponding in its tone and burden to some of the shorter stories, had a more startling and dramatic character, and a strangeness, which at once took hold of a larger public than any of those had attracted. Though imperfectly comprehended, and even misunderstood in some quarters, it was seen to have a new and unique quality; and Hawthorne's reputation became national.

The book was published by Ticknor, Reed, and Fields, in 1850. The first edition of five thousand copies was rapidly exhausted, and it was reprinted in England.

In the summer of 1850 Hawthorne went for change and country air to Lenox, Berkshire County, Massachusetts, where he lived until the autumn of 1851. There are some slight notes of this residence in the latter part of the second volume of the "American Note-Books," and references to the scenery and the literary residents of the place may be found in the prefatory and concluding chapters to the stories of the "Wonder-Book."

"The House of the Seven Gables" was begun at Lenox in the autumn of 1850, finished in January, 1851, and published in the same year. It met with great success in both America and England.

This book, which the author himself preferred to his previous novel, is of quieter tone than "The Scarlet Letter." It is more minutely elaborated, and its pathos depends more on the peculiar temperaments of its characters. The scene is laid in Salem, and the house, which much effort has been made to identify, corresponds in many points to an old dwelling formerly standing there, known as the Curwen House, and sometimes called "the old witch-house." Engravings from a picture of it are used as illustrations of the book. Some points in the story corresponding to the history of the Hawthornes were noted in the beginning of this sketch. A hint of the grant of land in Maine may be seen in the account of the estate of General Knox, a visit to which is described in the "American Note-Books," vol. i., August 12, 1837.

The character of Clifford and the problem of his strange destiny, the mockery of fate, which, having adapted him so delicately to an existence of sensuous refinement, stripped him in his youth, at one brutal stroke, of everything fair in life, and threw him among the lowest and coarsest surroundings, is the great study of the book. Its pervading thought is the theory of inheritance, the repetition of an original type now and then down a family line, and the curse of wrong-doing, blasting innocent lives when wronger and wronged are dust.

The characters of Hepzibah and Phœbe are beautiful types, strongly contrasted on the surface, but having at bottom an intimate kinship in moral uprightness and capacity for devotion. That of Judge Pyncheon also is exquisitely worked out in the subtle self-deception of the hypocrite, — no character being so great a favorite in fiction, and none so often badly drawn, as that of the hypocrite, because it looks so much more easy and uncomplicated than it is. The most admired scene of the book is that of chapter xviii., where the judge sits waiting for Clifford in the ancestral chair.

The use of the name Pyncheon drew down a shower of indignation on the author from Pyncheons who felt themselves aggrieved by it, one of them demanding that some other be substituted for it in the book. Another, with curious inconsistency, while complaining of the desecration of his ancestral name, asked that it be spelled in the novel without the *e*, that being the orthography in use in his family.

During six weeks of the summer of 1851 the "Wonder-Book" was written in Lenox. This is a children's book, made up of classic legends, re-told for them, and set in a slight frame-work, as entertainment given to a company of children at Tanglewood, a family residence in Berkshire.

In November, being wearied with inland life, Hawthorne went back to the east, and settled for the winter in West Newton, Massachusetts, where he wrote

"The Blithedale Romance." This book is founded on his experience at Brook Farm, ten years before, though the incidents, he says, are purely imaginary, and the characters are but slightly related, if at all, to any of the participants in that scheme. That of Hollingsworth grew, no doubt, out of thoughts suggested by his residence among reformers as to the tendencies of all-absorbing theories of reform, though it needed a strong and narrow nature like that of Hollingsworth to exhibit them in all their force. There are many observations scattered through the book, regarding communistic life, which evidently resulted from his experience there.

Miles Coverdale, who tells the story, of course represents the author in many points, if not intended as a portrait. A story told in the first person in a contemplative and analytic style like that of Hawthorne must necessarily reproduce the author to some extent in the mental structure of the narrator. Coverdale is a type of the men who do nothing because they see too much and too widely. Hollingsworth's narrowness is the great source of his power, and in the end becomes his destruction.

The character of Zenobia, which is said to have some traits of Margaret Fuller, is one of the strongest ever drawn by Hawthorne, and one of the most unique in literature. Literary women have had but a slender showing in fiction, most of the portraits of them being feeble caricatures. But this one, whose literary work is secondary to her impressive personality, is the type of a class, not large, who have gone into literature because of their abounding vitality and the scarcity of outlets for it; who stand for very little to readers beyond the reach of their social influence.

The character of Priscilla, strongly contrasted with that of Zenobia, may stand for the purely womanly ideal, — the creature of weaknesses and intuitions, — morbidly exaggerated in her case to clairvoyance, — whose only strength is in the affections.

In the same year, 1851, "The Snow Image and Other Twice-Told Tales" was prepared, and in 1852 it was published. It is dedicated in an interesting preface to Horatio Bridge, and is made up of tales and sketches gathered from periodicals. It is a little inferior in general to the other collections, though the title story is done with a wonderfully fine and delicate touch, and "Ethan Brand" has a great deal of power. This is written from the hint for a story on the unpardonable sin, which occurs in the "Note-Books," the setting being suggested by the lime kilns in Berkshire, alluded to in the first volume of the "American Note-Books," September 7, 1838.

The other noticeable sketches of the book are "The Canterbury Pilgrims," a story of the Shakers, "The Great Stone Face," a tale of the Profile in the Franconia Notch, and the curious sketch "Major Molineux." "Old News" is made up from some old Boston newspapers, issued before and during the Revolution. "Old Ticonderoga" is one of the slight reminiscences of travel. "A Bell's Biography" and "Main Street" have the peculiar touch that marks all the sketches of Puritan life.

In the summer of 1852 Hawthorne removed to a house which he had bought of A. B. Alcott in Concord, changing the name "The Hillside," which Mr. Alcott had given it, to "The Wayside." This is the house described in "Septimius Felton" as the home of Robert Hagburn. In a letter to George William Curtis he mentions a story of it told him by Thoreau, — that it was once inhabited by a man who believed he should never die, — another suggestion of that book.

In this year Franklin Pierce, after his nomination for the presidency, asked Hawthorne to write his biography, to be used as a campaign document. This Hawthorne felt that he could not refuse to do, on account of their old friendship, though he did it somewhat reluctantly, as being out of his chosen line of work. It drew on him some censure by its dealing with the slavery question, of which, of course, it took the democratic view.

In the following winter the "Tanglewood Tales." a series of stories like the "Wonder-Book," was written. The introductory chapter has some interesting observations on the adaptation of the classic myths to children.

After the inauguration of President Pierce, Hawthorne, who had declined taking office under him, was persuaded to accept the post of consul at Liverpool, one of the best paid offices his friend had to bestow; and in the summer of 1853 he removed to England, where he lived till the close of 1857. During this time he made many short journeys about the country, to London often, and into Wales and Scotland; notes of these trips will be found in the "English Note-Books" and "Our Old Home."

On leaving England Hawthorne went to France, Switzerland, and Italy, returning to England in 1859. Full records of his residence on the Continent are given in the "French and Italian Journals." His criticisms on art are noticeable for their frankness, his failure to appreciate many famous works being freely confessed, while he sets out to study them and discover the source of their fame; so that his admiration, when it is awakened, has a flavor of originality and independence. The observations on art in "The Marble Faun" embody his more matured judgments, while those of the "Note-Books" exhibit them in a formative state.

"The Marble Faun" was sketched in Italy and prepared for publication mainly in Redcar, England, in 1859–60. It was published by Ticknor & Fields, in 1860, and simultaneously by Smith & Elder, in London, under the title "Transformation," chosen by the publishers. The Castle of Monte Beni, the ancestral home of Donatello, the human faun, stands for Villa Montanto, where the author made his home for a time in the summer of 1858; and the original of Hilda's tower is described in the "French and Italian Note-Books," May 15, 1858.

This romance, which is generally held to be somewhat inferior to the novels of American life, though in an entirely different setting, does not differ greatly from them, or from some of the best short stories, in the nature of its topic and the handling of its characters. Like them it has for its theme a subject of conscience, — the influence of the consciousness of sin and its penalty, in elevating the life of a soul. Donatello's resemblance to the sculptured faun is typical of his spirit, unawakened, and looking neither before nor after, until his crime puts an end forever to his joyous holiday existence, and remorse for it develops his intellect and his soul.

Kenyon is a good type of a cultivated American, quietly enthusiastic, tolerant and not cynical, loving art and not despising America. Hilda is remarkable for the great moral strength united with her delicacy and sensibility. Her suffering on account of the crime of which she has been merely a witness is strongly contrasted with the attitude of Miriam, whose conscience needs to be brought to a full awakening even after participation in it; her free and strong nature having been bewildered in a maze of wrong, the one escape from which has offered itself in sudden temptation.

There has been much speculation on the subject of the relationship between Miriam and the mysterious character known in the book as "Miriam's Model," "The Spectre of the Catacombs," and "Brother Antonio." The relationship is left unexplained; but the use made in the book of the picture of Beatrice Cenci, Miriam's remarks on it, and her intense desire to penetrate to the consciousness of Beatrice, seem to point to some similarity of situation between them.

In the summer of 1860 Hawthorne returned to America and took up his residence again at "The Wayside," in Concord. A single note written on a trip to Maine, in 1862, appears at the end of the "French and Italian Journals," and shows his feeling about the civil war. He prepared for the *Atlantic Monthly* some sketches of England, which appeared in that magazine in 1862 and 1863, and with others were published in book form in 1863, under the title "Our Old Home."

The opening article, "Consular Experiences," gives some curious incidents in his office at Liverpool, and describes queer Americans who came for the consular help. The closing one, "Civic Banquets," affords a glimpse at some of the public social intercourse to which his position introduced him. "Lichfield and Uttoxeter" is devoted largely to Dr. Johnson. Long before, Hawthorne had written for children the story of Johnson's penance in Uttoxeter market. The offense taken by the Uttoxeter people at an article published in *Harper's Magazine* is mentioned in the "English Note-Books," vol. ii., August 2, 1857. "Recollections of a Gifted Woman" gives some notes on Stratford, together with reminiscences of Delia Bacon. In "Yesterdays with Authors" Mr. Fields says: "One of the most difficult matters he had to manage while in England was the publication of Miss Bacon's singular book on Shakespeare. The poor lady, after he had agreed to see the work through the press, broke off all correspondence with him in a storm of wrath, accusing him of pusillanimity in not avowing full faith in her theory; so that, as he told me, so far as her good-will was concerned, he had not gained much by taking the responsibility of her book upon his shoulders. It was a heavy weight for him to bear, in more senses than one, for he paid out of his own pocket the expenses of publication."

The other articles of the book describe Warwick, Oxford, Leamington, Boston, Lincoln, some parts of London, and the haunts of Burns. This book Hawthorne dedicated to Franklin Pierce, against the advice of friends, who feared it might be injured by the unpopularity which the ex-President suffered during the war. The following extract from a letter on the subject is worthy of note: —

"I find that it would be a piece of poltroonery in me to withdraw either the dedication or the dedicatory letter. My long and intimate personal relations with Pierce render the dedication altogether proper, especially as regards this book, which would have had no existence without his kindness; and if he is so exceedingly unpopular that his name is enough to sink the volume, there is so much the more need that an old friend should stand by him. I cannot, merely on account of pecuniary profit or literary reputation, go back from what I have deliberately felt and thought it right to do; and if I were to tear out the dedication I should never look at the volume again without remorse and shame. As for the literary public, it must accept my book precisely as I think fit to give it, or let it alone."

In the spring of 1859 Pierce was in Italy, at a time of great trial in Hawthorne's family, — the dangerous illness of his daughter with Roman fever; and his kindly offices and sympathy, mentioned in the "Note-Books," under date of April 18, 1859, had drawn closer the old bonds of friendship, and no doubt added to Hawthorne's desire to make a public expression of his regard at a time when his friend was being publicly disparaged. Possibly the anxiety of the publishers about the dedication was suggested by the reception of an article published in the *Atlantic Monthly* for July, 1862, — an account of a visit to Washington the previous April, which has not been reprinted. Its views of war-matters were not strong enough for the tone of feeling then prevailing at the North; though, looked at from this distance, there would seem to be nothing in it inconsistent with the purest patriotism. In "Yesterdays with Authors" Mr. Fields gives a description of President Lincoln which was omitted from the article at his request, as being too personal for publication during the life of the subject.

"Our Old Home" was published with the dedication; and, notwithstanding the publisher's fears, was highly successful. Its judgments on the English were naturally not appreciated in England, and it was criticised in no amiable spirit by many English journals. On this subject Hawthorne wrote to Mr. Fields: —

"The English critics seem to think me very bitter against their countrymen, and it is perhaps natural that they should, because their self-conceit can accept nothing short of indiscriminate adulation; but I really think that Americans have more cause than they to complain of me. Looking over the volume, I am rather surprised to find that whenever I draw a comparison between the two peoples I almost invariably cast the balance against ourselves. It is not a good nor a weighty book, nor does it deserve any great amount of either praise or censure. I don't care about seeing any more notices of it."

"I received several private letters and printed notices of 'Our Old Home,' from England. It is laughable to see the innocent wonder with which they regard my criticisms, accounting for them by jaundice, insanity, jealousy, hatred, on my part, and never admitting the least suspicion that there may be a particle of truth in them. . . . But they do me great injustice in supposing I hate them. I would as soon hate my own people."

About 1861, it is supposed, Hawthorne wrote "Septimius Felton," the incomplete romance discovered among his papers after his death. It is founded on a search for the elixir of life. This idea as a subject for a romance had evidently been in his mind for a long time. It is alluded to in the "Note-Books," and, under the form of a youth restoring cordial, was the subject of "Doctor Heidegger's Experiment." With this was united the legend of the "Bloody Footprint," in Smithell's Hall, which he had seen in England. The reader's sympathy in the story is apparently not intended to go with Septimius, the seeker for the cordial. He exhibits the coldness, narrowness, and hardness of heart that result from an absorbing, selfish purpose, though he disguises the selfishness to himself, and excuses his disregard for those about him by visions of the good to be wrought out in his endless earthly future. The characters of Rose Garfield and Sybil Dacy are quite clearly sketched, — the first gentle, practical, and healthful; the other full of fire and daring, with an air of mystery that chimes with the exaggerated mood of Septimius. What the story might have been with full elaboration, we can only conjecture; but it would seem that the author must have seen in it some inherent defect, which induced him to give it up after so full an outline was made, and begin again on the same theme with a plan so essentially altered.

"The Dolliver Romance" was begun as a serial for the *Atlantic Monthly*, but only one part was finished for publication. This appeared in the magazine for July, 1864. Two other scenes, not revised by the author, were found among his papers after his death. The story opens with the figures of an old man and a child, — gentle and simple old Grandsir Dolliver, who has seen all his family fall about him except his little great-grandchild, Pansie. Some of the passages regarding the illusions of age in connection with the old man are very pathetic: —

"This weight of years had a perennial novelty for the poor sufferer. He never grew accustomed to it, but, long as he had now borne the fretful torpor of his waning life, and patient as he seemed, he still retained an inward consciousness that these stiffened shoulders, these quailing knees, this cloudiness of sight and brain, this confused forgetfulness of men and affairs, were troublesome accidents that did not really belong to him. He possibly cherished a half-recognized idea that they might pass away. Youth, however eclipsed for a season, is undoubtedly the proper, permanent, and genuine condition of man; and if we look closely into this dreary delusion of growing old, we shall find that it never absolutely succeeds in laying hold of our innermost convictions. A sombre garment, woven of life's unrealities, has muffled us from our true self, but within it smiles the young man whom we knew; the ashes of many perishable things have fallen upon our youthful fire, but beneath them lurk the seeds of inextinguishable flame. So powerful is this instinctive faith, that men of simple modes of character are prone to antedate its consummation. And thus it happened with poor Grandsir Dolliver, who often awoke from an old man's fitful sleep with a sense that his senile predicament was but a dream of the past night; and hobbling hastily across the floor to the looking-glass, he would be grievously disappointed at beholding the white hair, the wrinkles and furrows, the ashen visage and bent form, the melancholy mask of age, in which, as he now remembered, some strange and sad enchantment had involved him in years gone by. . . .

"He longed to be gazed at by the loving eyes now closed; he shrank from the hard stare of them that loved him not. Walking the streets seldom and reluctantly, he felt a dreary impulse to elude the people's observation, as if with a sense that he had gone irrevocably out of fashion, and broken his connecting links with the net-work of human life; or else it was that nightmare-feeling which we sometimes have in dreams, when we seem to find ourselves wandering through a crowded avenue, with the noonday sun upon us, in some wild extravagance of dress or nudity."

In contrast with this is the fierce malice of Colonel Dabney, an age-stricken old scoundrel, who is plotting to rob Grandsir Dolliver of the supposed draught of immortality which has been left in his care: "I hate everything young. As for young people, let me be one of them, and they may exist, — otherwise not. It is a cursed bad arrangement of the world that there are young and old here together."

The character of Grandsir Dolliver is said to have been suggested by Mr. Kirkup, an old Englishman, an antiquarian and spiritualist, whom Hawthorne visited in Florence. He is alluded to in "The Marble Faun," and the visit is detailed at length in the "French and Italian Journals." A little girl of four years, Imogen, who lived with him, made an impression on Hawthorne's mind, and is no doubt the original of Pansie. The correspondence between Mr. Kirkup, who held high converse with Dante and other great spirits, and simple old Grandsir Dolliver, is hardly apparent.

By this time Hawthorne's health had begun to fail rapidly, and it was with great difficulty that he applied himself to literary work. Mr. Fields gives some extracts from his letters: —

"I can't tell you when to expect an instalment of the Romance, if ever. There is something preternatural in my reluctance to begin; I linger at the threshold, and have a perception of very disagreeable phantasms to be encountered if I enter. I wish God had given me the faculty of writing a sunshiny book."

"I don't see much probability of my having the first chapter of the Romance ready so soon as you want it. There are two or three chapters ready to be written, but I am not yet robust enough to begin, and I feel as if I should never carry it through. Besides I want to prefix a little sketch of Thoreau to it, because, from a tradition which he told me about this house of mine, I got the idea of a deathless man, which is now taking a shape very different from the original one. It seems the duty of a live literary man to perpetuate the memory of a dead one when there is such fair opportunity as in this case; but how Thoreau would scorn me for thinking that *I* could perpetuate him! And I don't think so.

. . . .

"Those verses entitled 'Weariness,' in the last magazine, seem to me profoundly touching. I, too, am weary, and begin to look ahead for the Wayside Inn."

"I have not yet had courage to read the Dolliver proof-sheet, but will set about it soon, though with terrible reluctance such as I never felt before. . . . I am most grateful to you for protecting me from that visitation of the elephant and his cub. . . . If you happen to see Mr. ——, of L——, a young man who was here last summer, pray tell him anything that your conscience will let you, to induce him to spare me another visit, which I know he intended. I really am not well, and cannot be disturbed by strangers without more suffering than it is worth while to endure."

"I am not quite up to writing yet, but shall make an effort as soon as I see any hope of success. You ought to be thankful that (like most other broken-down authors) I do not pester you with decrepit pages, and insist upon your accepting them as full of the old spirit and vigor. That trouble, perhaps, still awaits you, after I shall have reached a further stage of decay. Seriously, my mind has, for the present, lost its temper and its fine edge, and I have an instinct that I had better keep quiet. Perhaps I shall have a new spirit of vigor if I wait quietly for it; perhaps not."

In April, 1864, Hawthorne started on a southern journey with Mr. Ticknor, in search of health. They went only as far as Philadelphia, where Mr. Ticknor died after a few hours' illness. Hawthorne returned, in great grief and depression, to Concord. After this his health failed very rapidly. In May Franklin Pierce planned a journey with him to the White Mountains. It was hoped that the mountain air, together with the coming of warm weather, might restore him. In Boston, at Mrs. Hawthorne's request, Dr. Oliver Wendell Holmes saw him. The following is an extract from his report: —

"His aspect, medically considered, was very unfavorable. . . . He was very gentle, very willing to answer questions, very docile to such counsel as I offered him, but evidently had no hope of recovering his health. He spoke as if his work were done, and he should write no more. With all his obvious depression there was no failing noticeable in his conversational powers. . . . The calm despondency with which he spoke about himself confirmed the unfavorable opinion suggested by his look and history."

On the 18th of May the friends reached Plymouth, N. H., on their way to the Franconia Mountains. Hawthorne retired early to rest in his room at the Pemigewassett House, and before morning passed quietly and painlessly out of life. On the 24th of May he was laid in the Sleepy Hollow Cemetery, at Concord. The manuscript of his unfinished romance was borne upon the coffin. Longfellow, who stood beside his grave with Emerson, Lowell, Holmes, Whipple, Hillard, Pierce, Channing, and many others with whom he was associated in life, wrote of the occasion: —

How beautiful it was, that one bright day,
  In the long week of rain!
Though all its splendor could not chase away
  The omnipresent pain.

The lovely town was white with apple-blooms,
  And the great elms o'erhead
Dark shadows wove on their aerial looms,
  Shot through with golden thread.

Across the meadows, by the gray old manse,
  The historic river flowed;
I was as one who wanders in a trance,
  Unconscious of his road.

The faces of familiar friends seemed strange;
  Their voices I could hear,
And yet the words they uttered seemed to change
  Their meaning to the ear.

For the one face I looked for was not there,
  The one low voice was mute;

Only an unseen presence filled the air,
And baffled my pursuit.

Now I look back, and meadow, manse, and stream
Dimly my thought defines;
I only see — a dream within a dream —
The hill-top hearsed with pines.

I only hear above his place of rest
Their tender undertone,
The infinite longings of a troubled breast,
The voice so like his own.

There in seclusion and remote from men
The wizard hand lies cold,
Which at its topmost speed let fall the pen,
And left the tale half told.

Ah, who shall lift that wand of magic power,
And the lost clue regain?
The unfinished window in Aladdin's tower
Unfinished must remain!

"Septimius Felton" was found among Hawthorne's manuscripts, and published serially in the *Atlantic Monthly.* In 1872 it appeared in book-form, with a preface from the hand of his daughter Una, acknowledging the aid received from Mr. Robert Browning in reading the manuscript. In 1876 the three fragments of "The Dolliver Romance" appeared in a volume that included also some sketches of travel, two fragments of the "Journal of a Solitary Man," which seem to have been parts of the same design as the "Passages from a Relinquished Work," and some other tales and sketches not before collected. The journals were edited by Mrs. Hawthorne, published first in the *Atlantic Monthly*, and afterward in six volumes in book-form. The "American Note-Books" are especially interesting as giving the first suggestions of many of the author's works, as well as showing his mode of observing minutely. Much of the "English Note-Books" went into "Our Old Home," and much of the Italian into "The Marble Faun," though there is personal matter of interest in all of the journals.

Some critics have seen in the subjects of Hawthorne's art proofs of morbidness of mind, have written of him as a "weird, malarious genius," and wondered that the works most "lurid" should have sprung from his happiest years. This is simply to wonder that a man's imagination should be strongest and freeest when his affections are most at rest, and his ideal of life most nearly satisfied. It is to confuse the art of the author with the creed of the man. No doubt the choice of subjects which Hawthorne made for imaginative handling was due to several contributing causes, — causes lying partly in his surroundings, partly in his intellectual inheritance, not at all in his affections or in his disposition toward the world in general. First, his inheritance and associations as a son of Puritans, which gave him an understanding of the Puritan view of life, — a thing wholly different from a historic knowledge of the Puritan theology and formulated ethics, — the difference between a system in theory and a system applied to life by generations till it has become not rules but instincts. This inheritance made him at home in the Puritan mind and conscience. Second, perhaps, of the influences acting on his choice of subjects was the lack, of which he himself complained, of material for romance in the new and monotonous life of America. The field for romance, which in any case would have been most productive and was most untried, was almost the only one in American life which offered material for strong effects. Added to these was his own inexperience of life, — an inexperience, indeed, which was largely voluntary, but which prevented him from gaining material for original work in the more ordinary lines of romance.

Hawthorne left a widow and three children. Mrs. Hawthorne, who edited his "Note-Books," and published a volume of her own, "Notes in England and Italy," died in London in 1871. Una, the eldest daughter, died unmarried. Julian is well known as a novelist and essayist. Rose, who has had considerable success as an artist, is the wife of Mr. George P. Lathrop, author of "A Study of Hawthorne."

E. M. O'C.

ROCHESTER, *November* 1, 1881.

INDEX

TO THE

WORKS OF NATHANIEL HAWTHORNE.

Abbeys: Battle, *English Note-Books*, vol. i., end; Dryburgh, *ibid.*, vol. ii., May 10, 1856; Furness, *ibid.*, vol. i., July 13, 1855; Grondale, *American Note-Books*, vol. ii., 1842; Melrose, *English Note-Books*, vol. ii., May 10, 1856, July 11, 1857; Westminster, *ibid.*, vol. i., September 10, 26, 30, October 5, 1855, vol. ii., August 7, 1856, November 12, December 27, 1857, *Our Old Home*, Up the Thames.

Abbotsford, *English Note-Books*, vol. ii., May 10, 1856; July 11, 1857.

Abbott, Eliakim. See FELLOW-TRAVELLER.

Abercrombie, General, *Twice-Told Tales*, vol. ii., Edward Randolph's Portrait; *The Snow Image and Other Twice-Told Tales*, Old Ticonderoga.

Aberfoyle, *English Note-Books*, vol. ii., May 10, 1856.

About Warwick, an article in *Our Old Home*, describing Warwick Town and Castle, Leicester's Hospital, Redfern's Curiosity Shop, and St. Mary's Church with Beauchamp Chapel, the burial-place of the Earls of Warwick.

Abraham, the cave of Machpelah, *The Snow Image and Other Twice-Told Tales*, The Man of Adamant.

Absorption in the fortunes of others, *The Blithedale Romance*, chapter xxiv., near the beginning.

Absurdity, as distinguished from heroism, *The Blithedale Romance*, chapter xix., near the end; in sensible people, *Our Old Home*, Consular Experiences, after the middle.

Abuses, converted to uses, *English Note-Books,* vol. ii., September 13, 1857.

Abyssinians, the, a custom of, *American Note-Books,* vol. i., October 25, 1836.

Academies, country, *American Note-Books,* vol. i., August 31, 1838.

Academy of Fine Arts, Florence. See PICTURE-GALLERIES.

Academy of St. Luke, Rome. See PICTURE-GALLERIES.

Acadia, expedition against, *Grandfather's Chair,* part i., chapter xi.

Acadian Exiles, the, a sketch in *Grandfather's Chair,* part ii., chapter viii.; subject for a drawing, *American Note-Books,* vol. ii., September 14, 1841; subject for a story, see EVANGELINE.

Accuracy, infrequency of, *American Note-Books,* vol. ii., May 1, 1841.

A'Combe, John, friend of Shakspeare, tomb of, *Our Old Home,* Recollections of a Gifted Woman.

Acquapendente, *French and Italian Journals,* vol. ii., October 15, 1858.

Actor, suggestion for pictures of an, *American Note-Books,* vol. i., October 25, 1836.

Actors, some English, *Mosses from an Old Manse,* vol. ii., P.'s Correspondence.

Actress, an insane, *Our Old Home,* Outside Glimpses of English Poverty.

Actual, the, necessity and charm of returning to, from among ideal schemes, *The Blithedale Romance,* chapters xvi., xvii.

Adage, a modern Jewish, *American Note-Books,* vol. i., September, 1836.

Adam, one disadvantage of, *American Note-Books,* vol. ii., August 24, 1842; interest of in gardening, *ibid.,* August 10, 1842.

Adam and Eve, fantasy about a new, *American Note-Books,* vol. i., October 25, 1836, see NEW ADAM AND EVE; supposition concerning, *ibid.;* the faces looked back at by, *Our Old Home,* Outside Glimpses of English Poverty.

Adams, John, *Grandfather's Chair,* part iii., chapter vi.; letters of, *The Dolliver Romance and Other Pieces,* A Book of Autographs.

Adams, North, Mass., *American Note-Books,* vol. i., July 26 to September 9, 1838.

Adams, Samuel, *Grandfather's Chair,* part iii., chapters vi., x.; letter from, *The Dolliver Romance and Other Pieces,* A Book of Autographs.

Addison, Joseph, an essay of, *English Note-Books,* vol. i., September 30, 1855; early home of, *Our Old Home,* Lichfield and Uttoxeter; grave of, *ibid.,* Up the Thames; residence of, *English Note-Books,* vol. i., March 22, 1856.

Admiral, the son of a Scotch, *English Note-Books,* vol. ii., May 10, 1856, Melrose.

Adolphus, John Leycester, and his niece, *English Note-Books,* vol. ii., August 30, 1857.

Adventurer, an American, *Our Old Home,* Consular Experiences.

Advice, the giving of, *Our Old Home,* Consular Experiences.

Æetes, King, *Tanglewood Tales,* Circe's Palace, The Golden Fleece.

Ægeus, King, *Tanglewood Tales,* The Minotaur.

Æolus, King, *Tanglewood Tales,* Circe's Palace.

Æschylus, tortoise that killed, *Mosses from an Old Manse,* vol. ii., A Virtuoso's Collection.

Æson, King, *Tanglewood Tales,* The Golden Fleece.

Æsop, *Mosses from an Old Manse,* vol. i., the Hall of Fantasy.

Æthra, mother of Theseus, *Tanglewood Tales,* The Minotaur.

Affectation in death, *The Blithedale Romance,* chapter xxvii, near the end.

Affection, influence of, *The Blithedale Romance,* chapter xxii.; absorption by one, *ibid.,* chapter xxviii.

Affections, danger of making a chasm in the, *Twice-Told Tales,* vol. i., Wakefield; desire to shake off, *The Blithedale Romance,* chapter xxiii.

Agawam, the cobbler of. See Ward, Nathaniel.

Age, crickety humor of, *Mosses from an Old Manse,* vol. ii., P.'s

Correspondence; repugnance to, *The Dolliver Romance and Other Pieces*, Journal of a Solitary Man, i.

Age, the, men in advance of, *Mosses from an Old Manse*, vol. i., The Hall of Fantasy.

Aged, the, fancying the youth of, *Twice-Told Tales*, vol. ii., Edward Fane's Rosebud; follies of, *ibid.*, vol. i., The Wedding Knell; great number of in England, *Our Old Home*, Recollections of a Gifted Woman; infirmities of to themselves, *The Dolliver Romance*, first fragment; in solitude, *Twice-Told Tales*, vol. i., Fancy's Show Box; latter spring of, *The Dolliver Romance*, third fragment; mirth of, *The Scarlet Letter*, The Custom-House; sleep of, *The Dolliver Romance*, third fragment.

Agenor, King, *Tanglewood Tales*, The Dragon's Teeth.

Agent, a newspaper, *American Note-Books*, vol. i., August 31, 1838.

Agnews, shop of the, *English Note-Books*, vol. ii., May 24, 1856, Manchester.

Agrippa, legend of, in connection with the Fountain of Trevi, *The Marble Faun*, vol. i., chapter xvi.

Aiken, Mr., Liverpool, *English Note-Books*, vol. i., October 3, 1853.

Ailsa Crag, *Our Old Home*, Some of the Haunts of Burns, end.

Airey Force, *English Note-Books*, vol. i., July 21, 1855.

Akers, Paul, American sculptor at Rome, *The Marble Faun*, vol. i., preface, chapter xiii.

Aladdin's Lamp, *Mosses from an Old Manse*, vol. ii., A Virtuoso's Collection.

Alban Hills, the, *French and Italian Journals*, vol. i., February 19, 1858; *The Marble Faun*, vol. i., chapter i.

Albani Villa, *French and Italian Journals*, vol. i., May 12, 1858.

Albany, Countess of, monument to Alfieri by, *French and Italian Journals*, vol. ii., June 28, 1858.

Albemarle, Duke of, *Grandfather's Chair*, part i., chapter x.

Albert, Prince, *English Note-Books*, vol. i., September 17, 1855.

Albertus Magnus, *Mosses from an Old Manse,* vol. i., The Birthmark, vol. ii., The Artist of the Beautiful.

Alchemist, house of an, *The Snow Image and Other Twice-Told Tales,* Main Street.

Alchemists in Salem, *American Note-Books,* October 24, 1838.

Alchemy, *Mosses from an Old Manse,* vol. i., The Birthmark, near the middle.

Alcott, A. B., *The Scarlet Letter,* The Custom-House, middle; article on mentioned, *American Note-Books,* vol. ii., April 9, 1843; house of in Concord, *Septimius Felton,* p. 5 (12mo), *Tanglewood Tales,* introduction.

Aldershott Camp, *English Note-Books,* vol. i., April 1, 1856.

Ales in England, *Our Old Home,* Near Oxford.

Alexander of Scotland, tomb of, *English Note-Books,* vol. ii., May 10, 1856, Melrose, July 11, 1857.

Alexander II., of Russia, his father's opinion of, *English Note Books,* vol. i., September 26, 1855.

Alexander the Great, a story of, *Mosses from an Old Manse,* vol. i., Rappaccini's Daughter.

Alexanders, the, of Ballochmyle, *Our Old Home,* Some of the Haunts of Burns.

Alfieri, tomb of, *French and Italian Journals,* vol. ii., June 28, 1858.

Allegoric Figures in sculpture, *French and Italian Journals,* vol. ii., June 28, 1858.

Allegories of the Heart, perhaps a title for an intended collection of stories which were to be put into the mouth of Roderick Elliston, the hero of the story Egotism, and of which The Christmas Banquet was to form one.

Allen, Ethan, *The Snow Image and Other Twice-Told Tales,* Old Ticonderoga.

Allen, Rev. Thomas, tomb of, *American Note-Books,* vol. i., July 27, 1838.

Allen, William, *American Note-Books,* vol. ii., April 28, September 27, October 9, 1841.

Allingham, William, meeting with, *English Note-Books,* vol. i., February 23, 1854.

Allori, Alessandro, Judith by, *French and Italian Journals*, vol. ii., June 13, 1858.

Allston, Washington, *Mosses from an Old Manse*, vol. ii., The Artist of the Beautiful; autograph of, *The Dolliver Romance and Other Pieces*, A Book of Autographs.

Almanacs, old, *Mosses from an Old Manse*, vol. i., The Old Manse, near the middle.

Alms-Boxes in England, *Septimius Felton*, p. 180 (12mo).

Almshouse, visit to an, *Our Old Home*, Outside Glimpses of English Poverty.

Alnaschar, *English Note-Books*, vol. i., December 26, 1855.

Alphabet, the invention of, *Tanglewood Tales*, The Dragon's Teeth.

Alsatia, *English Note-Books*, vol. i., September 25, 1855.

Alva, Duke of, leading-staff of, *English Note-Books*, vol. ii., July 26, 1857.

Amazon, the, statue in Rome, *The Marble Faun*, vol. i., chapter i.

Ambition, *The Dolliver Romance and Other Pieces*, Rochester; a solitary, not good, *Twice-Told Tales*, vol. i., The Prophetic Pictures; literary, *ibid.*, preface; of youth the fate of age, *ibid.*, The Great Carbuncle.

Ambitious Guest, the, a sketch in *Twice-Told Tales*, vol. ii., founded on the incident of the destruction of the Willey Family, in 1826, by a slide from the mountain now called Mt. Willey, of the White Mountain group.

Ambleside, *English Note-Books*, vol. i., July 16, 1855.

America, art in, *French and Italian Journals*, vol. ii., September 29, 1858; as a field for romance, *The Marble Faun*, preface; defective dinners in, *Our Old Home*, Civic Banquets; during the civil war, *French and Italian Journals*, vol. ii., August 15, 1862; girls of, *Our Old Home*, Outside Glimpses of English Poverty; incidents in the early history of, *Grandfather's Chair*; primitive statesmen of, *The Scarlet Letter*, chapter xxii.; ruin of, *Our Old Home*, About Warwick, near the end; treatment of officials by the government of, *French and Italian Journals*, vol. i., January 11, 1858; women of, *The Scar-*

let Letter, chapter ii., *Our Old Home*, Civic Banquets, near the end.

American, a typical, *The House of the Seven Gables*, chapter xii.

American Dinner, an, *English Note-Books*, vol. i., January 16, 1856.

American Learning, the only trace of seen in Oxford, *English Note-Books*, vol. ii., August 31, 1856, Ratcliffe Library.

American Note-Books, the, in two volumes, edited by Mrs. Hawthorne, were published in book form in 1868, having previously appeared in "The Atlantic Monthly." The entries extend from 1835 to 1853.

American Taste, satire on, *The Marble Faun*, vol. i., chapter xvi.

Americans, abroad, *Our Old Home*, Consular Experiences, beginning; adventurousness of, *The House of the Seven Gables*, chapter xii.; artistic criticisms of, *French and Italian Journals*, vol. i., February 14, 1858; attraction of to England, *Our Old Home*, Consular Experiences; charge of ill health against, *English Note-Books*, vol. ii., July 9, 1856; claims of to English estates, *Our Old Home*, Consular Experiences; curious specimens of, *ibid.*; digestion of, *English Note-Books*, vol. i., March 6, 1856; English opinion of, *ibid.*, vol. ii., September 21, 1856; excitements of, *Our Old Home*, Civic Banquets, near the end; feeling of toward the English, *ibid.*, Leamington Spa, end; in public positions in Europe, *English Note-Books*, vol. i., October 19, 1853; love of antiquity of, *Our Old Home*, About Warwick, Leamington Spa; love of change of, *ibid.*, Leamington Spa; manners of, *English Note-Books*, vol. ii., September 13, 1857; patriotism of, *French and Italian Journals*, vol. ii., October 11, 1858; physique of, *Septimius Felton*, page 7 (12mo); recognition of genius by, *English Note-Books*, vol. ii., January 3, 1858; refinement of, *ibid.*, vol. i., September 17, 1855; reverence of, *The Scarlet Letter*, chapter xxii; self-made, *English Note-Books*, vol. ii., April 8, 1856; tracing English ancestry by, *ibid.*, July 13, 1856; vagabond habits of, *Our Old Home*, Consular Experiences, beginning.

Amherst, Sir Jeffrey, *The Snow Image and Other Twice-Told Tales,* Old News, part ii., Old Ticonderoga.

Amiens, town and cathedral, *French and Italian Journals,* vol. i., January 6, 1858.

Aminadab, assistant of the scientist in The Birthmark, *Mosses from an Old Manse,* vol. i.

Amonoosuck River, the, *Twice-Told Tales,* vol. i., The Great Carbuncle.

Analysis of character and motives, *The Blithedale Romance,* beginnings of chapters xviii. and xix.; of individual character, unhealthy, *ibid.,* chapter ix.

Ancient Roman Life, seemingly not so distant as the intervening ages, *The Marble Faun,* vol. i., chapter xviii.

André, Major, a favorite walk of, *Our Old Home,* Lichfield and Uttoxeter.

Andros, Sir Edmund, Governor of Massachusetts, *Grandfather's Chair,* part i., chapter ix.; *The Dolliver Romance and Other Pieces,* Dr. Bullivant, *Twice-Told Tales,* vol. i., The Gray Champion, vol. ii., Howe's Masquerade.

Angelico, Fra. characteristics of his pictures, *The Marble Faun,* vol. ii., chapter ix.; devoutness of, *ibid.,* chapter xii.; pictures by, *French and Italian Journals,* April 12, May 29, June 17, July 4, 10, 1858

Anger of Heaven, instance of the, *Fanshawe and Other Pieces,* Mrs. Hutchinson, sixth paragraph.

Angler, quotation applicable to an, *English Note-Books,* vol. i., March 16, 1854.

Anglesea, island of, *English Note-Books,* vol. i., July 19, 1854.

Angling, *Fanshawe,* chapter iii.

Animals, famous, *Mosses from an Old Manse,* A Virtuoso's Collection; forbearance of wild, *American Note-Books,* vol. i., September 4, 1838; the lower, *ibid.,* vol. ii., December 19, 1850.

Anne, Queen, portrait of, *English Note-Books,* vol. ii., July 1, 1857; relic of, *ibid.,* vol. i., March 24, 1856; statues of, *ibid.,* September 8, October 14, 1855, *Our Old Home,* Near Oxford.

Annihilation, a character deserving, *The Blithedale Romance,* chapter xxviii.

Antæus, the giant, *Wonder-Book*, The Three Golden Apples, *Tanglewood Tales*, The Pygmies.

Anthony-à-Wood, tomb of, *English Note-Books*, vol. ii., August 31, 1856, Merton College.

Antinous, the, *The Marble Faun*, vol. i., chapters i. and ii.; bas-relief of, *French and Italian Journals*, vol. i., May 12, 1858.

Antique, the, imitations of, *Our Old Home*, About Warwick

Antique dresses (about 1690), *American Note-Books*, vol. ii., 1842.

Antique Ring, the, a story in the volume *The Dolliver Romance*.

Antiquities, *English Note-Books*, vol. i., September 29, 1855; of the British Museum, *ibid.*, March 27, 1856.

Antiquity, charm and impressiveness of, to Americans, *Our Old Home*, dedication and Leamington Spa; ideas of, in Rome, *French and Italian Journals*, vol. i., February 7, 1858; one charm of, *English Note-Books*, vol. i., July 13, 1855; relics of, *ibid.*, vol. ii., July 26, 1857; smell of, *ibid.*, vol. i., August 24, 1854; superior taste of, in minor things, *Our Old Home*, About Warwick, end; tediousness of, *ibid.*, Leamington Spa.

Antoninus, Marcus Aurelius, column of, *The Marble Faun*, vol. i., chapter vi.; statue of, *ibid.*, chapter xviii.; *French and Italian Journals*, vol. i., February 23, April 25, 1858.

Antonio, Brother, a character in *The Marble Faun*, introduced at the close of chapter ii., vol. i. He is doing penance as a Capuchin monk for a crime with which Miriam also is mysteriously connected, and in consequence of which she is to some extent in his power.

Antwerp, incident concerning the siege of, *American Note-Books*, vol. i., October 25, 1836.

Apathy before realizing anticipations, *The Dolliver Romance and Other Pieces*, My Visit to Niagara.

Apollo Belvedere, the, *French and Italian Journals*, vol. i., March 10, 1858.

Apollo, the Lycian, *The Marble Faun*, vol. i., chapters i. and ii.

Apollyon, *Mosses from an Old Manse*, vol. i., The Celestial Railroad.

Appian Way, the, *French and Italian Journals*, vol. i., March 3, May 9, 1858, *The Marble Faun*, vol. ii., chapter xxi.

Appledore, Isles of Shoals, *American Note-Books*, vol. ii., August 30, 1852; traces of old habitations on, *ibid.*, September 13, 1852.

Appleton, Miss, of Bangor, *American Note-Books*, vol. i., July 15, 1837.

Appleton, Mr., *English Note-Books*, vol. i., September 13, 1855.

Apple-trees, *Mosses from an Old Manse*, vol. i., Buds and Bird Voices, The Old Manse, near the middle.

Arabella Johnson, Lady, story of, *Grandfather's Chair*, part i. chapter ii.

Arabian Nights, the, *Our Old Home*, Lichfield and Uttoxeter.

Ararat, Mt., fancy about, *American Note-Books*, vol. i., January 4, 1839.

Arbutus, trailing, *Wonder Book*, The Hill-Side.

Arcadia, a cold, *The Blithedale Romance*, chapter v., end.

Arc de Triomphe, the, *French and Italian Journals*, vol. i., January 9, 1858.

Arch, a natural, in Charlemont, *American Note-Books*, vol. i., August 31, 1838.

Archbishop of Paris, relics of, *French and Italian Journals*, vol. i., January 11, 1858.

Archdeacon ale, the, *Our Old Home*, Near Oxford.

Archer, Mr., anecdote told by, *English Note-Books*, vol. i., October 14, 1855.

Architects, American, *Mosses from an Old Manse*, vol. i., The Hall of Fantasy.

Architecture, compared with music, *American Note-Books*, vol. i., January 4, 1839; domestic, *English Note-Books*, September 9, 1855, vol. i.; Gothic and Grecian, *ibid.*, July 1, 1855, vol. ii., August 31, 1856, Ratcliffe Library, *French and Italian Journals*, vol. ii., September 3, 1858; imitations of ancient, *ibid.*, February 5, 1860; Italian, *ibid.*, June 28, 1858; prototypes of, *American Note-Books*, vol. i., September, 1836; secrecy in Gothic, *English Note-Books*, vol. ii., April 13, 1857; suggestion concerning, *Our Old Home*, A London Suburb.

Arctic, loss of the, *English Note-Books*, vol. i., October 16, 1854.

Arctic gentleman, a celebrated, *English Note-Books*, October 5, 1854.

Arden, forest of, *The Blithedale Romance*, chapter xi.

Arethusa, *Twice-Told Tales*, vol. i., Sights from a Steeple.

Arethusa, the (flower), *American Note-Books*, vol. ii., June 23, 1843.

Arezzo, town and cathedral, *French and Italian Journals*, vol. i., May 30, 1858.

Argo, the, **Argonauts**, and **Argus**, *Tanglewood Tales*, The Golden Fleece.

Argyle family, an old mansion of the, *English Note-Books*, vol. ii., July 7, 1857.

Ariadne, *Tanglewood Tales*, The Minotaur.

Ariosto, *Mosses from an Old Manse*, vol. i., The Hall of Fantasy.

Aristocracy, an, *Our Old Home*, About Warwick, near the end; an old, worm-eaten, *American Note-Books*, vol. i., August 22, 1837; advantages of an, *Mosses from an Old Manse*, vol. ii., Earth's Holocaust; in America, illustration of, *American Note-Books*, vol. i., August 12, 1837; of wretchedness, *Mosses from an Old Manse*, vol. ii., The Christmas Banquet.

Aristocrats of a summer day, *Twice-Told Tales*, vol. i., The Toll-Gatherer's Day.

Arkwright family, seat of the, *English Note-Books*, vol. ii., June 7, 1857.

Armada, Spanish, the, instruments of torture carried by, *English Note-Books*, vol. i., September 10, 1855.

Armboth House, *English Note-Books*, vol i., July 21, 1855.

Armor, famous, *Mosses from an Old Manse*, vol. ii., A Virtuoso's Collection; of the age of chivalry, *English Note-Books*, vol. ii., July 26, 1857; old, *ibid.*, vol. i., September 10, 1855.

Army, the provincial, appearance of, *Fanshawe and Other Pieces*, Sir William Pepperell, fourth paragraph.

Arno, the, *French and Italian Journals*, vol. i., May 30, June 7, 1858, vol. ii., August 4, September 7, 1858.

Arnold, Benedict, descendants of, *English Note-Books,* vol. i., March 23, 1854; note from, *The Dolliver Romance and Other Pieces,* A Book of Autographs.

Arnold, William Fitch, *English Note-Books,* vol. i., March 23, 1854.

Arrangement, the talent for, *The House of the Seven Gables,* chapter v., near the beginning.

Arroquhar, *English Note-Books,* vol. ii., May 10, 1856.

Art, appreciation of, *French and Italian Journals,* vol. i., April 12, vol. ii., June 10, 15, 1858; apostrophe to, *Twice-Told Tales,* vol. i., The Prophetic Pictures; a second nature, *Mosses from an Old Manse,* vol. ii., The New Adam and Eve; Catholic, not satisfying to the finest artistic sense, *The Marble Faun,* vol. ii., chapters xiii., xvi; English, *English Note-Books,* vol. ii., July 28, 1857; enjoyment of, *French and Italian Journals,* vol. i., May 28, 1858; impression to be judged from, *ibid.,* vol. ii., June 11, 1858; in Italy, its pervasiveness, *The Marble Faun,* preface; in ships, *English Note-Books,* vol. i., October 5, 1854; in the Middle Ages, *French and Italian Journals,* vol. ii., June 17, 1858; love of, compared with love of nature, *The Marble Faun,* vol. ii., chapter xii.; productions of the present in, *French and Italian Journals,* vol. i.; March 11, 1858; quality necessary to works of, *Mosses from an Old Manse,* vol. ii., Drowne's Wooden Image; seen best by the united power of dissimilar intelligences, *The Marble Faun,* vol. ii., chapter xviii.; suggestiveness its highest merit, *ibid.,* vol. ii., chapter xvi.; what adequate appreciation of demands, and what might be done for religious truth by, *ibid.,* vol. ii., chapter xii.; works of, in human shape, *Mosses from an Old Manse,* vol. i., Feathertop, near the end.

Arthur, King, legends of, *English Note-Books,* vol. i., June 30, September 20, 1854.

Artist, gift of the, *Twice-Told Tales,* vol. i., The Prophetic Pictures.

Artist-life in Italy in summer, *The Marble Faun,* vol. i., chapter xxiv.; in Rome, its freedom, *ibid.,* chapter vi.

Artist of Stonehenge, the, *English Note-Books,* vol. ii., June 17, 1856.

Artist of the Beautiful, the, a story in *Mosses from an Old Manse,* vol. ii., of a sensitive artist in contact with the discouragements from unsympathetic and worldly minds. It was first published in "The Democratic Review."

Artists, character of, *French and Italian Journals,* vol. ii., June 16, 1858; distaste of for their finished work, *The Marble Faun,* vol. ii., chapter xvi.; fascination of Rome for, *French and Italian Journals,* vol. i., February 15, 1858; force of character necessary to, *Mosses from an Old Manse,* vol. ii., The Artist of the Beautiful; implements of, *ibid.,* A Virtuoso's Collection; in Rome, *The Marble Faun,* vol. i., chapter xv.; in society, *ibid.;* jealousies of, *ibid.;* loss of faith in the ideal by, *Mosses from an Old Manse,* vol. ii., The Artist of the Beautiful; rewards of, *ibid.;* rooms of, *American Note-Books,* vol. ii., May 6, 1850.

Arts' Exhibition, Manchester, *English Note-Books,* vol. ii., July 22 to September 6, 1857.

Arts in another world, *American Note-Books,* vol. ii., 1842.

Ash-Wednesday in Rome, *French and Italian Journals,* vol. i., February 19, 1858.

Assabeth River, the, *Mosses from an Old Manse,* vol. i., The Old Manse, near the middle.

Assisi, town, convent, and church, *French and Italian Journals,* vol. i., May 28, 1858.

Astley, Sir Jacob, relic of, *English Note-Books,* vol. ii., July 26, 1857.

Aston, Sir Arthur, death of, *English Note-Books,* vol. i., October 22, 1853.

Atalanta, *Tanglewood Tales,* The Golden Fleece.

Athenæum Library, Boston, the, *American Note-Books,* vol. ii., May 5, 1850.

Athol, Colonel, monument to, *English Note-Books,* vol. i., August 10, 1854.

At Home, first of the Passages from a Relinquished Work, in *Mosses from an Old Manse,* vol. ii. It gives a sketch of the life of the supposed author, under the guardianship of Parson Thumpcushion.

Atlas, *Wonder Book,* The Three Golden Apples.

Atropos, scissors of, *Mosses from an Old Manse,* vol. ii., A Virtuoso's Collection.

Attorney, characteristic answer of an, *English Note-Books,* vol. i., October 14, 1855.

Aubépine (Hawthorn), a *nom de plume* used in "The Democratic Review," *American Note-Books,* vol. i., July 13, 1837; writings of, *Mosses from an Old Manse,* vol. i., Rappaccini's Daughter.

Auchinleck, estate of the Boswells, *Our Old Home,* Some of the Haunts of Burns.

Auctioneers, *American Note-Books,* vol. i., August 15, 1838; English and American, *English Note-Books,* vol. i., July 1, 1855.

Audience, an, in a New England Village, *The Blithedale Romance,* chapter xxiii.

Augustine, St., legend of, *American Note-Books,* vol. i., September 7, 1835.

Augustus, the Emperor, dying question of, *American Note-Books,* vol. i., October 25, 1836.

Auld, Captain, *English Note-Books,* vol. i., August 22, 1853.

Aurelius, Marcus. See ANTONINUS.

Author, an, estimate of his last work by, *Tanglewood Tales,* introduction; punishment for, *The Snow Image and Other Twice-Told Tales,* The Devil in Manuscript.

Authors, not done in wax, *The Blithedale Romance,* chapter xxiii.; peculiarly suited to adventurers like those of Blithedale, *ibid.,* chapter vii., middle; opinions of their own work, *Twice-Told Tales,* preface; reading MSS. to friends, *Mosses from an Old Manse,* vol. i., The Old Manse, end; unsuccessful, *The Snow Image and Other Twice-Told Tales,* The Devil in Manuscript; works planned by, *Mosses from an Old Manse,* vol. i., A Select Party; writings as measures of the men, *The Snow Image,* dedication.

Autobiography, *The Scarlet Letter,* The Custom-House.

Autograph Collector, the original, *Septimius Felton,* page 173 (12mo).

Autographs, *English Note-Books,* vol. ii., December 7, 1857; price of, *ibid.,* vol. i., August 10, 1853; reading character from, *The Dolliver Romance and Other Pieces,* A Book of Autographs, end. See BOOK OF AUTOGRAPHS.

Autumn, air of, *American Note-Books,* vol. ii., September 23, 1843; *Mosses from an Old Manse,* vol. i., The Old Manse, after the middle; first hints of, *ibid., American Note-Books,* vol. ii., August 22, 1842; foliage of, *ibid.,* vol. i., October 17, 1835, October 7, 14, 1837, vol. ii., September 26, 27, October 8, 9, 12, 13, 18, 22, 1841, October 6, 1843; scenery of, *ibid.,* vol. ii., September 18, October 10, November 8, 24, 1842; sunshine of, *ibid.,* October 7, 1841; the time to give up civilized life, *Mosses from an Old Manse,* vol. i., The Old Manse, after the middle.

Avignon, *French and Italian Journals,* vol. ii., June 1, 1859.

Avon River, the, *Our Old Home,* Recollections of a Gifted Woman, About Warwick.

Aylmer, hero of the story The Birthmark, *Mosses from an Old Manse,* vol. i.

Ayr, town and river, *Our Old Home,* Some of the Haunts of Burns.

B——, Colonel, engineer, *American Note-Books,* vol. i., July 20, 1837.

B——, H. A., *English Note-Books,* vol. i., August 9, 15, November 29, 1853.

B——, Mr., of the American Chamber of Commerce, *English Note-Books,* vol. i., August 4, 5, 1853.

B——, Mr., of Coventry, *French and Italian Journals,* vol. ii., February 5, 1860.

B——, Mr., of Poulton Hall, *English Note-Books,* vol. i., August 8, 1853.

B——, Mr., sculptor, *French and Italian Journals,* vol. i., April 22, 1858.

B——, Mrs., of Brook Farm, *American Note-Books,* vol. ii., April 13, 1841.

Bab, Old. See KIDD.

Baby's smile, a, *American Note-Books,* vol. ii., October 13, 1851.

Bachelors, *The Blithedale Romance,* chapter vi.

Back Windows, picturesqueness of, *The Blithedale Romance,* chapter xvii.

Bacon, Delia, *English Note-Books,* vol. ii., July 13, 1856 ; theory of the authorship of Shakspeare's plays, and visit to Stratford of, *Our Old Home,* Recollections of a Gifted Woman. Miss Bacon died in Hartford in 1859.

Bacon, Francis, letters of, *Our Old Home,* Recollections of a Gifted Woman.

Bacon, Roger, *Septimius Felton,* pages 92, 94 (12mo) ; the Brazen Head of, *Mosses from an Old Manse,* vol. i., The Birthmark, vol. ii., The Artist of the Beautiful.

Baglioni, Professor Pietro, a character in Rappaccini's Daughter, *Mosses from an Old Manse,* vol. i.

Bahama Islands, royalists of the, *English Note-Books,* vol. i., May 18, 1855.

Bailey, Judge, of Maine, *Fanshawe and Other Pieces,* Jonathan Cilley.

Bailey, Philip James, *English Note-Books,* vol. ii., July 6, 1856.

Bailey, Samuel, author of "The Philosophy of Necessity," *French and Italian Journals,* vol. ii., February 5, 1860.

Bainbridge, Commodore, *American Note-Books,* vol. i., August 27, 1837.

Baker, tomb of a, *French and Italian Journals,* vol. ii., October 23, 1858.

Balaam, *Mosses from an Old Manse,* vol. ii., A Virtuoso's Collection.

Bald Mountain, Berkshire County, Mass., *American Note-Books,* vol. i., September 3, 1838 ; subject of a chapter in *The Wonder-Book, Tanglewood Tales,* introduction.

Ball, Mr., house of, *English Note-Books,* vol. i., July 19, 1855.

Balloch, Scotland, *English Note-Books,* vol. ii., May 10, 1856.

Ballochmyle, the Lass of, *Our Old Home,* Some of the Haunts of Burns.

Bancroft, George, allusions to, *American Note-Books,* vol. i., letter, November, 1840, *Mosses from an Old Manse*, The Old Manse, near the beginning.

Bangor, Wales, *English Note-Books*, vol. i., July 19, 1854.

·**Banks**, *Mosses from an Old Manse*, vol. ii., The New Adam and Eve.

Bannockburn, battle of, *English Note-Books*, vol. ii., July 7, 1857.

Banqueting Halls in England, *Our Old Home*, Civic Banquets.

Banquets, at a castle in the air, *Mosses from an Old Manse*, vol. i., A Select Party; of the Mayors of Liverpool and London, *Our Old Home*, Civic Banquets.

Barberini Palace, picture gallery of the, *French and Italian Journals*, vol. i., February 20, March 25, 1858.

Barber-Surgeons' Hall, London, *English Note-Books*, vol. i., March 25, 1856, *Our Old Home*, Civic Banquets.

Bardone, Judith by, *French and Italian Journals*, vol. ii., June 15, 1858.

Barings, bank of the, *English Note-Books*, vol. i, October 6, 1855.

Barker's Tavern, scene at, *American Note-Books*, July 26, 1837.

Barlow, Joel, *Mosses from an Old Manse*, vol. i., A Select Party, vol. ii., P.'s Correspondence.

Barnaby Rudge, raven of, *Mosses from an Old Manse*, vol. ii., A Virtuoso's Collection.

Barnard, D. D., Minister at Berlin, *English Note-Books*, vol. i., October 19, 1853.

Baronet, the first American, *Fanshawe and Other Pieces*, Sir William Pepperell, last paragraph.

Bartlett, N. H., *Mosses from an Old Manse*, vol. ii., Sketches from Memory, The Notch of the White Mountains, *Twice-Told Tales*, vol. ii., The Ambitious Guest.

Barton, Sir Roger, *English Note-Books*, vol. i., August 25, 1855.

Bartram, a lime-burner in the story Ethan Brand, in *The Snow Image and Other Twice-Told Tales*, a rude, clownish fellow.

Bastile, site of the, *French and Italian Journals*, vol. i., January 15, 1858.

Bath, *French and Italian Journals*, vol. ii., April 23, 1860.

Battle Abbey, church, and village, *English Note-Books*, vol. i., end.

Battlefields, *French and Italian Journals*, vol. i., May 30, 1858; of Scotland, *English Note-Books*, vol. ii., May 10, 1856.

Baucis, *Wonder-Book*, The Miraculous Pitcher.

Beach-Birds, *Twice-Told Tales*, vol. ii., Footprints on the Sea-Shore.

Beacon Street, scene in, *American Note-Books*, vol. i., October 24, 1838.

Bear and Ragged Staff, the, *Our Old Home*, About Warwick.

Bearhaven, Comte de, *Mosses from an Old Manse*, vol. i., Rappaccini's Daughter.

Beatrice, heroine of the story Rappaccini's Daughter, *Mosses from an Old Manse*, vol. i., a character of great purity and beauty.

Beatrice Cenci. See CENCI.

Beauchamp Chapel, *French and Italian Journals*, vol. ii., March 17, 1860, *Our Old Home*, About Warwick.

Beauchamp, Richard, Earl of Warwick, tomb of, *Our Old Home*, About Warwick.

Beauchamp Tower, *English Note-Books*, vol. i., September 10, 1855.

Beaumaris, *English Note-Books*, vol. i., July 19, 1854.

Beautiful, the, why sought, *Twice-Told Tales*, vol. i., The Great Carbuncle.

Beautiful Young Lady, a, *English Note-Books*, vol. ii., April 8, 1856, *Our Old Home*, Civic Banquets.

Beauty, descriptions of, never satisfactory, *Fanshawe*, chapter i.; never a delusion, *Mosses from an Old Manse*, vol. i., Buds and Bird Voices; relation of, to size, *ibid.*, vol. ii., The Artist of the Beautiful; worthy of immortality, *ibid.*, vol. i., Buds and Bird Voices.

"**Beaux' Stratagem**," the (Farquhar), locality of a scene of, *Our Old Home*, Lichfield and Uttoxeter.

Bebbington, *English Note-Books,* vol. i., August 29, 1853, February 20, 1854, June 11, 1855 ; a memorial in the churchyard of, *Our Old Home,* Leamington Spa.

Beckford, Mayor of London, *English Note-Books,* vol. ii., July 13, 1856.

Bedlam, a kind of, *The Blithedale Romance,* chapter xvi.

Bedouins, coins of the, *English Note-Books,* vol. i., February 18, 1856.

Beelzebub, compromise with, *Mosses from an Old Manse,* vol. i., The Celestial Railroad.

Beer, effects of, *English Note-Books,* vol. i., May 31, 1855.

Beggars, in England, *English Note-Books,* vol. i., December 10, 31, 1853, October 19, 1854, September 30, 1855, *Our Old Home,* Outside Glimpses of English Poverty ; in Italy, *French and Italian Journals,* vol. i., February 7, 15, 1858, *The Marble Faun,* vol. ii., chapter viii.

Bekkers, the, *American Note-Books,* vol. ii., September 11, 1852.

Belcher, Jonathan, Governor of Massachusetts, *Grandfather's Chair,* part ii., chapter vi., *Twice-Told Tales,* vol. i., The Minister's Black Veil, *ibid.,* vol. ii., Howe's Masquerade, Old Esther Dudley.

Belhaven, Lord, tomb of, *English Note-Books,* vol. ii., May 10, 1856, Holyrood.

Bell, the great, of Lincoln. See GREAT TOM.

Bell's Biography, a, the story of a church-bell in *The Snow Image and Other Twice-Told Tales.*

Bellamont, Earl of, Governor of Massachusetts, *Twice-Told Tales,* vol. ii., Howe's Masquerade.

Bellerophon, *Wonder-Book,* The Chimæra.

Bellingham, Richard, Governor of Massachusetts, *Twice-Told Tales,* vol. ii., Howe's Masquerade, *The Scarlet Letter,* chapters iii., vii., xii.

Bellowspipe, the (mountain notch), *American Note-Books,* vol. i., September 9, 1838.

Belvedere, Villa, *French and Italian Journals,* vol. ii., October 4, 1858.

Benedict, Saint, bridge founded by, *French and Italian Journals*, vol. ii., June 1, 1859.

Benedictions, cheapness of, in Italy, *The Marble Faun*, vol. ii., chapter viii.

Ben Lomond, *English Note-Books*, vol. ii., May 10, 1856, July 2, 1857, *Our Old Home*, Some of the Haunts of Burns, end.

Bennett, Wm. Cox, *English Note-Books*, vol. i., September 13, 30, 1855. (Name not given.)

Bennoch, Francis, of London, a friend of the author to whom the *English Note-Books* were dedicated by Mrs. Hawthorne, mentioned in those books under the dates March 22, 25, April 1, 4, May 24 (Manchester), July 10, August 31, 1856, July 8, 1857, January 3, 1858, in the *French and Italian Journals*, June 14, 1859, and in *Our Old Home*, near the end of Civic Banquets. His home, where Hawthorne spent a summer, is described in *Our Old Home*, A London Suburb. Bennoch is a silk merchant. He published a book of poems in 1849.

Bentley, William, tomb of, *English Note-Books*, vol. i., November 29, 1853.

Benton, Colonel, quarrel of, with Jackson, *English Note-Books*, vol. i., February 19, 1855.

Beppo, old Roman beggar, *The Marble Faun*, vol. i., chap. xii.

Bequeathing of property to relatives, the, *The House of the Seven Gables*, chapter i., toward the end.

Berkshire County, Mass., *American Note-Books*, vol. i., July 26, 27, 1838, *Tanglewood Tales*, preface. It is the location of Tanglewood, the home of the children to whom the stories of *The Wonder-Book* and *Tanglewood Tales* were told.

Bernard, Sir Francis, Governor of Massachusetts, *Grandfather's Chair*, part ii., chapter x., part iii., chapter iv., *Twice-Told Tales*, vol. ii., Howe's Masquerade.

Bernardo Luini, allusion to his John the Baptist in Florence, *The Marble Faun*, vol. i., chapter v.

Bernini, statues of, *French and Italian Journals*, vol. i., February 21, March 26, April 18, 25, 1858.

Berwick-on-Tweed, *English Note-Books*, vol. ii., May 10, 1856, July 11, 1857.

Better times to come, the sense of, *The House of the Seven Gables,* chapter xii., middle.

Betty Moody, story of, *American Note-Books,* vol. ii., September 5, 1852.

Beulah, the land of, *Mosses from an Old Manse,* vol. i., The Celestial Railroad.

Beverly, Mass., a walk through, *American Note-Books,* vol. i., October 14, 1837.

Bias, vase of, *Mosses from an Old Manse,* vol. ii., A Virtuoso's Collection.

Bible, the, *Mosses from an Old Manse,* vol. ii., Earth's Holocaust; double use of, *Fanshawe and Other Pieces,* Sir William Pepperell, second paragraph.

Bickley Hall, *English Note-Books,* vol. i., October 22, 1853.

Bigotry, religious, represented by the Man of Adamant in the story of that name in *The Snow Image and Other Twice-Told Tales.*

Billingsgate Market, *English Note-Books,* vol. i., September 10, 1855, vol. ii., November 15, 1857.

Biographical Sketches, of Mrs. Hutchinson, Sir William Phips, Sir William Pepperell, Thomas Green Fessenden, and Jonathan Cilley, are included in the volume with *Fanshawe,* and of Benjamin West, Sir Isaac Newton, Samuel Johnson, Oliver Cromwell, Benjamin Franklin, and Queen Christina, in the *True Stories from History and Biography.*

Biography, character of the knowledge it imparts, *Fanshawe and Other Pieces,* Sir William Phips, first paragraph.

Biography of Hawthorne, his feeling about, *English Note-Books,* Preface.

Birch, Mr., *American Note-Books,* vol. i., August 31, 1838.

Birch, Sir Thomas, *English Note-Books,* vol. i., March 23, 1854.

Birds, *American Note-Books,* vol. i., August 1, 1837, vol. ii., April 25, 27, 1843; famous, *Mosses from an Old Manse,* vol. ii., A Virtuoso's Collection; in spring, *Mosses from an Old Manse,* vol. i., Buds and Bird Voices.

Birkenhead Priory, *English Note-Books,* vol. i., September 7,

1853, February 27, 1854; old inscription regarding, and old sculpture from, *ibid.*, April 3, 1854; Park of, *ibid.*, August 12, 1854.

Birmingham, *English Note-Books*, vol. i., June 21, 1855.

Birthmark, the, one of the tales in *Mosses from an Old Manse*, vol. i. It is an allegorical story regarding the taint of imperfection essential to everything earthly. A suggestion of the story may be found in the last paragraph under date of January 4, 1839, in the *American Note-Books*. The story appeared originally in "The Pioneer," a magazine edited by J. R. Lowell and Robert Carter (Boston, 1843).

Blackbirds, *American Note-Books*, vol. ii., April 25, 1843; *Mosses from an Old Manse*, vol. i., Buds and Bird Voices.

Black Cross, the, of the Coliseum. See CROSS.

Blackheath, *English Note-Books*, vol. ii., July 6, 16, 1856, *Our Old Home*, A London Suburb.

Blacksmith's Shop, a, *Mosses from an Old Manse*, vol. ii., The Artist of the Beautiful.

Blackstone, Rev. Mr., *Twice-Told Tales*, vol. i., The Maypole of Merry Mount, *The Scarlet Letter*, chapter vii.

Black Swan Inn, *Our Old Home*, Lichfield and Uttoxeter.

Blagden, Miss, *French and Italian Journals*, vol. ii., June 27, August 12, 1858.

Blencathra, *English Note-Books*, vol. i., July 21, 1855.

Blenheim, palace of, *Our Old Home*, Near Oxford.

Blessings at table, *Twice-Told Tales*, vol. ii., Peter Goldthwaite's Treasure.

Blind Man's Walk, a, *American Note-Books*, vol. i., August 22, 1837.

Blithedale Romance, the, a novel in one volume, published in Boston in 1852, and simultaneously in London. It was written at West Newton, Mass., in 1851–2. The scene is laid at a farm held by a socialistic community, drawn from Brook Farm, in Roxbury, which was occupied by such a community, where Hawthorne spent nearly a year in 1841–2. How far the actual community served as a basis for the ideal one of the book is explained by the author in the preface. What the experiment was in its profoundest relation, chapter xvii.; the enthusiasm of visitors at Blithedale, chapter x., beginning.

Blockheads, respectable old, *The Blithedale Romance*, chapter xvi.

Blodgett, Mrs., boarding-house of, *English Note-Books*, vol. i., September 16, 24, 1855, vol. ii., June 25, 1857; euphemism of, *ibid.*, vol. i., March 6, 1856.

Blood, the instinct to shed, *Septimius Felton*, pp. 29, 51 (12mo).

Blood-and-Thunder, Old, a successful general in the story The Great Stone Face, in *The Snow Image, etc.*

Blood Stain, torture of a, *Mosses from an Old Manse*, vol. i, The Old Manse, near the beginning.

Bloody Brook, fight at, *The Snow Image, etc.*, Main Street.

Bloody Footstep, the, *English Note-Books*, vol. i., August 25, 1855, *Septimius Felton*, p. 111 *et seq.*, and last page (12mo).

Bluebeard, suggestions for a story about, *French and Italian Journals*, vol. i., March 25, 1858.

Bluebeard, a, *Our Old Home*, Civic Banquets.

Blue Eye, name given to one of the children to whom the stories of *The Wonder-Book* and *The Tanglewood Tales* were told.

Blue Hill, Milton, Mass., *American Note-Books*, vol. ii., October 13, 1841.

Blunder, an English, *Our Old Home*, Up the Thames.

Boarding-House, a, *The Blithedale Romance*, chapters xvii. and xviii.

Boats on the Kennebec, *American Note-Books*, vol. i., July 13, 1837.

Boboli Gardens, the, *French and Italian Journals*, vol. ii., June 10, 21, September 10, 1858.

Boccaccio, a character of, *French and Italian Journals*, vol. ii., October 14, 1858; a locality of, *ibid.*, July 4, 1858; incident of the plague described by, *ibid.*, June 30, 1858; a well associated with, *ibid.*, vol. i., May 30, 1858.

Bodleian Library, the, *English Note-Books*, vol. ii., August 31, 1856.

Bologna, John of, Mercury by, *French and Italian Journals*, vol. ii., July 4, 16, 1858; tomb of, *ibid.*, July 8, 1858.

Bolsena, Lake, Town, and Castle, *French and Italian Journals*, vol. ii., October 15, 1858.

Bolt Court, *English Note-Books*, vol. i., March 22, 1856.

Bolton, *Our Old Home*, Pilgrimage to Old Boston.

Bolton le Moors, *English Note-Books*, vol. i., August 25, 1855.

Bolton Priory, *English Note-Books*, vol. ii., April 11, 1857.

Bonapartes, the, memorials of, *French and Italian Journals*, vol. ii., June 28, 1858; statue of Pauline, *ibid.*, vol. i., April 18, 1858.

Bonfire, of all symbols of evil, a, *American Note-Books*, 1840; the world's, *Mosses from an Old Manse*, vol. ii., Earth's Holocaust.

Boniface, Mr., inn of, in Farquhar's time, *Our Old Home*, Lichfield and Uttoxeter.

Booby, a complete, *Our Old Home*, Consular Experiences.

Book, a stupid, suited to a certain mood, *The Blithedale Romance*, chapter xvii.

Book of Autographs, A, notes on a collection of letters, chiefly from historical characters of America, in the volume *The Dolliver Romance*. It was first published in "The Democratic Review."

Books, ancient, *French and Italian Journals*, vol. ii., September 17, 1858; collection of old, *English Note-Books*, vol. ii., April 8, 1856; famous ancient, *Mosses from an Old Manse*, vol. ii., A Virtuoso's Collection; lifelessness of, *Septimius Felton*, p. 16 (12mo); old, *Mosses from an Old Manse*, vol. i., The Old Manse, at the middle.

Bookseller, a traveling, *Twice-Told Tales*, vol. ii., The Seven Vagabonds.

Bookworms, *Mosses from an Old Manse*, vol. ii., Earth's Holocaust.

Borghese Palace, the, *French and Italian Journals*, vol. i., February 25, 1858.

Borghese Villa, the, *French and Italian Journals*, vol. i., April 18, 1858, *The Marble Faun*, vol. i., chapter viii.

Borghetto, *French and Italian Journals,* vol. i., May 25, 1858.

Borrow, George, descent of, *English Note-Books,* vol. ii., May 24, 1856.

Boston, England. See PILGRIMAGE TO OLD BOSTON.

Boston, Mass., the scene of *The Scarlet Letter* and many of the short stories, — the four Legends of the Province-House, The Gray Champion, The Prophetic Pictures, and others. Many of the incidents in its early history are told in *Grandfather's Chair;* a scene at night in the harbor of, *American Note-Books,* vol. i., July 10, 1838; the Common, *English Note-Books,* vol. i., September 8, 1855; contrasted with the English Boston, *Our Old Home,* Pilgrimage to Old Boston; dismal aspect of, *Fanshawe, etc.,* Mrs. Hutchinson, last paragraph, great fire of, *The Snow Image, etc.,* Old News, part ii., in 1760, *ibid.;* scene during the siege of, *Twice-Told Tales,* vol. ii., Howe's Masquerade; Snow's History of, engraving in, *American Note-Books,* vol. ii., September 14, 1841.

Boswells, the, *Our Old Home,* Some of the Haunts of Burns.

Bothwellhaugh, shooting of Murray by, *English Note-Books,* vol. ii., July 8, 1857.

Bourne, Reuben and Cyrus, characters in Roger Malvin's Burial, *Mosses from an Old Manse,* vol. ii.

Bowdoin College, Brunswick, Maine, the scene of the story, *Fanshawe,* under the name "Harley College."

Bower, Ralph, *English Note-Books,* vol. i., December 1, 1853.

Bowles, William Lisle, tablet to, *English Note-Books,* vol. ii., June 17, 1856.

Bowman, Mr., *English Note-Books,* vol. i., March 25, 1856, vol. ii., May 10, 1856.

Bowness, *English Note-Books,* vol. i., July 16, 1855.

Bowring, Sir John, *English Note-Books,* vol. i., August 5, 1853.

Boyd, Rev. Dr. Zachary, bust of, *English Note-Books,* vol. ii., July 1, 1857.

Boylston, Dr. Zabdiel, *Grandfather's Chair,* part ii., chapter v., *Twice-Told Tales,* vol. i., The Prophetic Pictures.

Boys, choirs of, *English Note-Books,* vol. ii., December 6, 1857;

insensibility of, *The House of the Seven Gables*, chapter xvi., middle; plays of as compared with those of girls, *The Blithedale Romance*, chapter ix.

Brackett, **Master**, a jailor mentioned in *The Scarlet Letter*, chapters iv., xxi.

Bradford, **George P.**, *American Note-Books*, vol. ii., June 1, September 28, 1841, August 27, 1842, *English Note-Books*, vol. i., August 24, 1854.

Bradford, **William**, Governor of Plymouth Colony, baby-linen of, *American Note-Books*, vol. i., August 22, 1837.

Bradstreet, **Colonel John**, march of, *The Snow Image, etc.*, A Bell's Biography.

Bradstreet, **Simon**, Governor of Massachusetts, *Grandfather's Chair*, part i., chapter ix., *Twice-Told Tales*, vol. i., The Gray Champion, vol. ii., Howe's Masquerade, *The Dolliver Romance*, first fragment; funeral of, *The Snow Image, etc.*, Main Street.

Brand, **Ethan**, the hero of a story of that name in the volume *The Snow Image*. He becomes a monomaniac on the subject of the unpardonable sin, and wanders about the world with the idea of finding out what it is.

Brattleboro Reporter, the, a political newspaper, *Fanshawe, etc.*, Thomas Green Fessenden.

Brazen Head, the prophetic, *Mosses from an Old Manse*, vol. i., The Birthmark.

Brazer, **Mr.**, sermon of, *American Note-Books*, vol. i., October 17, 1835.

Breach of Promise of Marriage, trial for, *Mosses from an Old Manse*, vol. i., Mrs. Bullfrog.

Breakfast, *The House of the Seven Gables*, chapter vi.

Bremer, **Fredrika**, *French and Italian Journals*, vol. i., April 22, May 22, 1858.

Brewers, draymen of, *English Note-Books*, vol. i., May 31, 1855.

Brick, use of, *English Note-Books*, vol. i., March 23, 1854, September 8, 1855.

Bridge, **Horatio**, a classmate and life-long friend of Hawthorne, at one time in the United States Navy, and author of the

"Journals of an African Cruiser," which Hawthorne edited. He was active in procuring the publication of *The Snow Image* and the first volume of *Twice-Told Tales*, the former of which is dedicated to him. The *American Note-Books* give details of a visit to him in Maine, July, 1837, where he is frequently mentioned by initial, as well as under dates of September 7, 1835 (?), and June 16, 1838, and in *Mosses from an Old Manse*, vol. i., near the end of The Old Manse. His friendship with and prophecy concerning Hawthorne are spoken of in the dedication of *The Snow Image*.

Bridgton, Maine, visit to, *American Note-Books*, vol. i., July 5, 1837.

Brig of Allan, the, *English Note-Books*, vol. ii., July 6, 1857.

Bright, Eustace, a college student, character introduced into the *Wonder-Book*, and the *Tanglewood Tales*, as the narrator of the stories.

Bright, Henry, *English Note-Books*, vol. i., February 23, July 19, 1854, February 19, November 14, 1855, *French and Italian Journals*, vol. ii., June 14, 1859, May 17, 1860.

Brighton, Mass., fair at, *American Note-Books*, vol ii., September 27, 1841.

British Coffee-House, Boston, *Grandfather's Chair*, part iii., chapter iv.

British Museum, the, *English Note-Books*, vol. i., September 29, 1855, March 27, 1856, vol. ii., December 7, 1857.

British soldiers, contempt of for provincials, *The Snow Image, etc.*, Old News, part ii.; graves of the first who fell in the American Revolution, *Mosses from an Old Manse*, vol. i., The Old Manse, near the beginning; tradition respecting one of them, *ibid.*

Brobdingnag, location of, *American Note-Books*, vol. ii., 1842; portable mansion in, *Twice-Told Tales*, vol. ii., The Seven Vagabonds.

Bronté, Charlotte, looks of, *English Note-Books*, vol. ii., August 2, 1857; marriage of, *ibid.*, April 19, 1857; Mrs. Gaskell's life of, *ibid.*

Bronté Sisters, scenery described by, *Our Old Home*, Pilgrimage to Old Boston.

Brook, description of a, *American Note-Books,* vol. i., July 8, 24, 1837 ; a plaything for children, *ibid.*, vol. ii., March 31, 1851.

Brook Farm, Roxbury, *The Blithedale Romance,* Preface, *Mosses from an Old Manse,* vol. i., The Old Manse, near the middle ; elected to office at, *American Note-Books,* vol. ii., September 27, 1841 ; letters from, *ibid.*, vol. ii. ; prospects of the community, *ibid.*, August 22, 1841 ; residence at, *The Scarlet Letter,* The Custom-House, middle ; return to, *American Note-Books,* vol. ii., September 22, 1841 ; seclusion of, *ibid.*, April 28, 1841 ; Spanish boys at, *ibid.*, September 28, 1841 ; talk with Emerson about, *ibid.*, April 8, 1843 ; vicinity of, *ibid.*, September 26, 27, 1841.

Brooke, Lord, death of, *Our Old Home,* Lichfield and Uttoxeter, About Warwick.

Brookhouse's Villa, beach near, *American Note-Books,* vol. i., October 16, 1837.

Brotherhood of men, the intimate, *Our Old Home,* Outside Glimpses of English Poverty.

Brothers' Water, *English Note-Books,* vol. i., July 21, 1855.

Brown, Capability, landscape gardening of, *Our Old Home,* Near Oxford.

Brown, Charles Brockden, *Mosses from an Old Manse,* vol. ii., P.'s Correspondence.

Brown, Dr., *English Note-Books,* vol. i., September 13, 1855.

Brown, John, a character in Peter Goldthwaite's Treasure, *Twice-Told Tales,* vol. ii., a prosperous, matter-of-fact merchant.

Brown, Mr., paintings of, *French and Italian Journals,* vol. i., April 22, 1858.

Brown, Zechariah, *Mosses from an Old Manse,* vol. i., The Old Manse, near the beginning.

Browne, Mr., free library of, *English Note-Books,* vol. ii., April 19, 1857.

Browne, Mr. William, dinner with, *English Note-Books,* vol. i., January 9, 1855.

Browne, Sir Anthony, and his lady, statues of, *English Note-Books,* end of vol. i., article Battle Abbey.

Browne, Sir Thomas, quotation from, *American Note-Books,* vol. i., January 4, 1839.

Browne's Folly, the title of the last article in the volume *The Dolliver Romance.* It is a description of a hill in Salem where the author had once purposed to locate a story. The article was written for the Essex Institute in Salem, in 1860. See *American Note-Books,* vol. i., October 14, 1837.

Browne's Hill. See title above.

Browning, Elizabeth B., *English Note-Books,* vol. ii., July 13, 1856, *French and Italian Journals,* vol. ii., June 8, 9, 1858, *The Marble Faun,* vol. i., chapter xiii.

Browning, Robert, *French and Italian Journals,* vol. ii., June 8, 9, 1858, *The Marble Faun,* vol. i., chapter xiii.; conversation of, *French and Italian Journals,* vol. ii., June 27, 1858; help of in reading manuscript, *Septimius Felton,* Preface; portrait of, *French and Italian Journals,* vol. ii., June 27, 1858; scene of a poem of, *ibid.,* July 8, 1858.

Bruce, Robert, cave of, *English Note-Books,* vol. ii., July 4, 1857; heart of, *ibid.,* July 11, 1857.

Brutality of men turned brutes, *Tanglewood Tales,* Circe's Palace.

Brutes, sufferings of, *French and Italian Journals,* vol. ii., July 28, 1858.

Brutishness of brutish men, *American Note-Books,* vol. i., October 25, 1836.

Brutus, head of, by Michael Angelo, at Florence, *The Marble Faun,* vol. ii., chapter xvi.

Bryant, W. C., *French and Italian Journals,* vol. i., May 22, vol. ii., June 9, 1858, *Mosses from an Old Manse,* vol. ii., P.'s Correspondence.

Bucephalus, *Mosses from an Old Manse,* vol. ii., A Virtuoso's Collection.

Buchan, Earl of, *English Note-Books,* vol. ii., May 10, 1856, Dryburgh.

Buchanan, James, United States Minister to England, afterwards President, *English Note-Books,* vol. i., January 6, September 13, 25, 26, October 5, 1855, March 15, 1856, *Our Old Home,* Consular Experiences.

Buckingham, Duke of (I.), the dagger that killed the, *English Note-Books*, vol. ii., July 26, 1857.

Buckingham, Duke of (II.), quotation from, *American Note-Books*, vol. i., October 24, 1838.

Buckingham Palace, *English Note-Books*, vol. i., September 8, 1855.

Buckland, Dean, anecdote of, *Our Old Home*, Pilgrimage to Old Boston.

Buds and Bird Voices, an essay in *Mosses from an Old Manse*, vol. i., first published in "The Democratic Review."

Buff-and-blue, whom worn by, *American Note-Books*, vol. i., October 25, 1836.

Buffum, Joshua, punishment of, *The Snow Image and Other Twice-Told Tales*, Main Street.

Bulkely, Sir Richard, *English Note-Books*, vol. i., July 19, 1854.

Bull, the white, *Tanglewood Tales*, The Dragon's Teeth.

Bull-baiting in Liverpool, *English Note-Books*, vol. i., September 7, 1853.

Bullfrog, Mrs., a story in *Mosses from an Old Manse*, vol. i. It is a light, humorous sketch, and quite out of Hawthorne's usual style; the author's opinion of, *American Note-Books*, vol. ii., September 16, 1841.

Bullfrog, Thomas, hero of the story Mrs. Bullfrog, in *Mosses from an Old Manse*, vol. i., a lady-like man, in the dry-goods business.

Bullivant, Dr., a sketch in the volume *The Dolliver Romance*, laid in Boston in 1670–88, and later. Dr. Bullivant is also mentioned in The Gray Champion, *Twice-Told Tales*, vol. i.

Bulls, the brazen, *Tanglewood Tales*, The Golden Fleece.

Bulwer, Sir E. L., *English Note-Books*, vol. ii., April 4 and 5, 1856.

Bunker Hill, the battle of, *Grandfather's Chair*, part iii., chapter vii., *Twice-Told Tales*, vol. i., The Gray Champion, vol. ii., Howe's Masquerade; monument of, *Mosses from an Old Manse*, vol. ii., The New Adam and Eve; one in England, *Our Old Home*, Pilgrimage to Old Boston; relics of, *English Note-Books*, vol. ii., November 30, 1856.

Bunyan, John, allusions to, *American Note-Books,* vol. i., October 25, 1836, *English Note-Books,* vol. i., September 22, 1854, *French and Italian Journals,* vol. i., February 20, May 30, 1858, To Florence, *Mosses from an Old Manse,* vol. i, The Celestial Railroad, The Hall of Fantasy, vol. ii., A Virtuoso's Collection, *The Snow Image, etc.,* Ethan Brand, *The Blithedale Romance,* chapter xxviii., *The Scarlet Letter,* chapter x., *Our Old Home,* A London Suburb.

Buonarotti, Palazzo, *French and Italian Journals,* vol. ii., July 2, 1858.

Burghersh, Lord, *English Note-Books,* vol. i., February 18, 1856.

Burglary, a, *English Note-Books,* vol. ii., March 1, 1857.

Burgoyne, General, *The Snow Image, etc.,* Old Ticonderoga, Old News, part iii.

Burial, a custom of, *American Note-Books,* vol. i., August 11, 1838 ; a custom of the Capuchins, *The Marble Faun,* vol. i., chapter xxi. ; in churches, *Our Old Home,* Lichfield and Uttoxeter ; in England, *English Note-Books,* vol. i., August 24, 1853 ; regard for, of the early settlers of America, *Mosses from an Old Manse,* vol. ii., Roger Malvin's Burial.

Burial-grounds : at Ipswich, *American Note-Books,* vol. i., September 7, 1835 ; at Litchfield, *ibid.,* September 9, 1838 ; Charter Street, *ibid.,* July 4, 1838, *The Scarlet Letter,* The Custom-House ; Copp's Hill, Boston, *Twice-Told Tales,* vol. ii., Lady Eleanore's Mantle ; natural sites for, *American Note-Books,* vol. i., August 31, 1838. See, also, Cemeteries.

Burke, Bishop, *English Note-Books,* vol. i., February 19, 1855.

Burlington, Earl of, *English Note-Books,* vol. i., July 13, 1855.

Burlington, Vermont, the subject of the sketch The Inland Port, included in the volume with *The Dolliver Romance.*

Burnet, William, Governor of Massachusetts, *Grandfather's Chair,* part ii., chapter v., *Twice-Told Tales,* vol. i., The Prophetic Pictures, vol. ii., Howe's Masquerade.

Burns, Robert, *Our Old Home,* Some of the Haunts of Burns, *Mosses from an Old Manse,* vol. i., The Procession of Life, *The Blithedale Romance,* chapter viii., near the end ; Chambers's edition of, *English Note-Books*, vol. i., October 3, 1853; manuscripts of, *ibid.*, vol. ii., April 8, 1856; old age of, imagined, *Mosses from an Old Manse*, vol. ii., P.'s Correspondence; songs of, *English Note-Books*, vol. i., October 3, 1853; two sons of, *ibid.*

Burr, Aaron, *Mosses from an Old Manse*, vol. ii., The Christmas Banquet.

Burr, Aaron, letter from, *The Dolliver Romance, etc.*, A Book of Autographs; mystery of the nature of, *ibid.*

Burritt, Elihu, "the learned blacksmith," *Mosses from an Old Manse*, vol. i., The Procession of Life.

Burroughs, Rev. George, *Grandfather's Chair*, part ii., chapter ii., *The Snow Image, etc.*, Main-Street.

Burton, Rev. Warren, *The Blithedale Romance*, Preface.

Bush, the, still the symbol of the wine-shop in Italy, *The Marble Faun*, vol. ii., chapter vii.

Busts, classic, *French and Italian Journals*, vol. ii., June 8, 1858; why should Americans want them, *The Marble Faun*, vol. i., chapter xiii.; more real than portraits, *American Note-Books*, vol. ii., May 5, 1850; rarity of good, *French and Italian Journals*, vol. i., June 7, 1858.

Butchers, names for, *American Note-Books*, vol. ii., June 1, 1842.

Bute, Earl of, hanging in effigy of the, *Grandfather's Chair*, part iii., chapter ii.

Butler, a character in *Fanshawe*, first appearing in chapter iii. He is a bold and evil character, working for the carrying out of his purposes by coarse and bald intrigue.

Butler, Bishop, tomb of, *English Note-Books*, vol. i., September 5, 1855.

Butler, Samuel, quotation from Hudibras, *Fanshawe*, head of chapter vi.

Butler, Widow, a character in *Fanshawe*, appears in chapter ii., the scene of her death, chapter viii.

Butter Cross, the Shrewsbury, *English Note-Books*, vol. i., September 5, 1855.

Buttercup, name given to one of the children to whom the stories of *The Wonder-Book* and *The Tanglewood Tales* were told.

Butterflies, *American Note-Books*, vol. i., letter October 4, 1840.

Butterfly, the ideal, *Mosses from an Old Manse*, vol. ii., The Artist of the Beautiful.

Byles, Rev. Mather, *Twice-Told Tales*, vol. ii., Howe's Masquerade.

Byron Hotel, Lake Geneva, *French and Italian Journals*, June 12, 14, 1859.

Byron, Lady, *English Note-Books*, vol. ii., July 13, 1856.

Byron, Lord, *Mosses from an Old Manse*, vol. i., The Procession of Life, vol. ii., Earth's Holocaust; description of the Coliseum by, *The Marble Faun*, vol. i., chapter xvii.; of Lake Thrasymene, *French and Italian Journals*, vol. i., May 30, 1858; of Mount Soracte, *ibid.*, May 24, 1858; expurgated works and imagined old age of, *Mosses from an Old Manse*, vol. ii., P.'s Correspondence; home of, *English Note-Books*, vol. ii., May 29, 1857; "Prisoner of Chillon," *French and Italian Journals*, vol. ii., June 12, 1859; tame bear of, *Mosses from an Old Manse*, vol. ii., A Virtuoso's Collection; temple immortalized by, *French and Italian Journals*, vol. i., May 26, 1858.

Byrons, the, ill fate of, *English Note Books*, vol. ii., May 29, 1857.

C——, H. L., suggestion of the poem of "Evangeline," *American Note-Books*, vol. i., October 24, 1838.

C——, Mr., a tutor, *English Note-Books*, vol. i., August 2, 1855.

Cacaphodel, Doctor, a character in The Great Carbuncle, *Twice-Told Tales*, vol. i. He is seeking the stone to gratify the vanity of an author.

Cade, Jack, *English Note-Books*, vol. i., March 25, 1856.

Cadmus, *Tanglewood Tales*, The Dragon's Teeth, *The Marble Faun*, vol. ii., chapter xxi.; a legend like that of, *English Note-Books*, vol. ii., July 11, 1857.

Cæsar, Julius, face of, *English Note-Books*, vol. i., September 29, 1855; site of the murder of, *French and Italian Journals*, vol. ii., March 23, 1859; statue of, *ibid.*, vol. i., May 12, 1858.

Cæsars, the, busts of, *French and Italian Journals*, vol. i., February 23, 1858; statues of, *ibid.*, March 1, 1858.

Caffarelli Palace, the, *The Marble Faun*, vol. i., chapter xviii.

Caius Cestius, pyramid of, *French and Italian Journals*, vol. i., March 27, 1858, vol. ii., March 23, 1859.

Calamities of life, the great, *American Note-Books*, vol. i., October 25, 1836.

Calhoun, John C., letter from, *The Dolliver Romance and Other Pieces*, A Book of Autographs.

Calixtus, St., the catacomb of, *The Marble Faun*, vol. i., chapter iii.

Callender, village of, *English Note-Books*, vol. ii., May 10, 1856.

Cambridge, the Duke of, *English Note-Books*, vol. i., April 1, 1856.

Cambridge, Mass., headquarters of Washington in, *Grandfather's Chair*, part iii., chapters viii., ix.

Campanile, the, of Florence, *French and Italian Journals*, vol. ii., September 3, 1858.

Campbell, Colonel, *English Note-Books*, vol. ii., April 19, 1857.

Campbell, General, consul at London, *English Note-Books*, vol. i., September 26, 1855.

Campbell, Mrs., *English Note-Books*, vol. i., September 2, 1853.

Campbell, Thomas, *Mosses from an Old Manse*, vol. ii., P.'s Correspondence.

Canaan, Conn., inscription in, *American Note-Books*, vol. i., September 9, 1838.

Canada, attempted conquest of, *Grandfather's Chair*, part ii., chapter iv; rebellion in, *Twice-Told Tales*, vol. ii., The Sister Years.

Canal Boat, the, one of the Sketches from Memory in *Mosses from an Old Manse*, vol. ii., a story of a ride on the Erie Canal.

Canaletto, pictures by, *English Note-Books*, vol. i., March 26, vol. ii., August 7, 1856.

Candide. See VOLTAIRE.

Candlestick, the seven-branched, *The Marble Faun*, vol. i., chapter xvii., vol. ii., chapter xv.

Caner, Rev. Dr., *The Snow Image, etc.*, Old News, part iii.

Canning, George, anecdote of, *English Note-Books,* vol. ii., April 4, 1856 ; imagined in the House of Lords, *Mosses from an Old Manse,* vol. ii., P.'s Correspondence ; portrait of, *English Note-Books,* vol. ii., August 31, 1856, Christ Church.

Cannon, made into church bells, *American Note-Books,* vol. i., September 7, 1835.

Canova, *English Note-Books,* vol. ii., August 7, 1856 ; statue of Pauline Bonaparte by, *French and Italian Journals,* vol. i., March 23, April 18, June 7, 1858.

Canterbury Pilgrims, the, a story in *The Snow Image and Other Twice-Told Tales.* It is located at Canterbury, N. H., the site of a Shaker settlement.

Canute, sceptre of, *Mosses from an Old Manse,* vol. ii., A Virtuoso's Collection.

Capital Punishment, *American Note-Books,* vol. ii., October 13, 1851 ; instruments of, *Mosses from an Old Manse,* vol. ii., Earth's Holocaust.

Capitol, the Roman, *French and Italian Journals,* vol. i., February 23, March 1, April 10, 15, 22, 1858.

Capitoline Hill, the, *The Marble Faun,* vol. i., chapter xviii.

Captain, a popular title, *American Note-Books,* vol. i., August 31, 1838.

Capuchin Cemetery, description and strange customs of, *The Marble Faun,* vol. i., chapter xxi.

Capuchin Monk, the. See Antonio.

Capuchins, church of the, funeral of a monk in, *French and Italian Journals,* February 17, 1858, *The Marble Faun,* vol. i., chapter xx.

Caracalla, the Emperor, busts of, *French and Italian Journals.* vols. i., ii., June 7, 8, 1858.

Caracci, famous picture by, *English Note-Books,* vol. ii., September 6, 1857.

Caravan, a, *American Note-Books,* vol. i., September 4, 1838.

Caravan-Man, the, *American Note-Books,* vol. i., August 18, 1838.

Carbuncle, The Great, *Mosses from an Old Manse,* vol. ii , A Virtuoso's Collection. See Great Carbuncle.

Cardinal-flower, the, *American Note-Books*, vol. ii., August 13, 1842; *Mosses from an Old Manse*, vol. i., The Old Manse, after the middle.

Caresses, *American Note-Books*, vol. ii., March 9, 1853.

Carleton Club-house, London, *English Note-Books*, vol. i., September 10, 1855.

Carlisle, City, Castle, and Cathedral, *English Note-Books*, vol. ii., June 28, 1857.

Carlyle, Thomas, dress of, *English Note-Books*, vol. i., August 12, 1855; one character of the works of, *The Blithedale Romance*, chapter vii.

Carnival in Rome, the, *French and Italian Journals*, vol. i., February 13, 14, 17, 27, 1858, vol. ii., March 7, 8, 9, 1859, *The Marble Faun*, vol. ii., chapters xxiii., xxiv.

Carrier, Martha, a character in the story Young Goodman Brown, *Mosses from an Old Manse*, vol. i., *The Snow Image and Other Twice-Told Tales*, Main Street.

Carriers, newspaper, addresses of, *The Dolliver Romance and Other Pieces*, Time's Portraiture.

Carroll, General, at New Orleans, *English Note-Books*, vol. ii., December 15, 1856.

Carven images, natural animosity against, *Our Old Home*, Pilgrimage to Old Boston, Lincoln.

Caryl, Edward, a young lawyer and *littérateur* in the story The Antique Ring, volume *The Dolliver Romance*.

Casa Guidi, residence of the Brownings in Florence, *French and Italian Journals*, vol. ii., June 9, 1858.

"**Caskets**," *Our Old Home*, About Warwick.

Cass, Lewis, an official reply of, *Our Old Home*, Consular Experiences.

Cassandra of the inner depths, the, *The Blithedale Romance*, chapter xvi.

Castagno, Andrea del, crime of, *French and Italian Journals*, vol. ii., August 19, 1858.

Castellani, jewel-shop of, *French and Italian Journals*, vol. i., April 27, 1858.

Castel Nuovo di Porta, *French and Italian Journals*, vol. i., May 24, 1858.

Castle, an American, at Gardiner, Maine, *American Note-Books,* vol. i., July 11, 1837.

Castle in the Air, a, *Mosses from an Old Manse,* vol. i., A Select Party.

Castle of Monte Beni, *The Marble Faun,* vol. i., chapters xxiv. and xxv.

Castle of St. Angelo, the, *French and Italian Journals,* vol. i., March 25, 1858.

Castle William, fortress of, Boston, *Twice-Told Tales,* vol. ii., Edward Randolph's Portrait.

Castor and Pollux, *Tanglewood Tales,* The Golden Fleece.

Caswell, Joe, *American Note-Books,* vol. ii., September 5, 1852.

Catacombs, the, *French and Italian Journals,* vol. ii., March 11, 1859, *The Marble Faun,* vol. i., chapter iii.

Catharine of Arragon, tomb of, *English Note-Books,* vol. ii., May 27, 1857.

Catharine, St., ancient picture of, *French and Italian Journals,* vol. i., May 8, 1858.

Cathedral, the world's, *The Marble Faun,* vol. ii., chapters xiii., xiv.

Cathedrals, attempts to describe, *English Note-Books,* vol. ii., June 17, 1856; closes of, *ibid.*, June 28, 1857, *Our Old Home,* Lichfield and Uttoxeter, Pilgrimage to Old Boston; need of antiquity of, *English Note-Books,* vol. ii., June 17, 1856; purpose of, evident, *Mosses from an Old Manse,* vol. ii., The New Adam and Eve. For descriptions of particular cathedrals, see under CHURCHES.

Catherine, a persecuted Quakeress in The Gentle Boy, *Twice-Told Tales,* vol. i.

Catholicism, its attractions, origin, and "infinite convenience," *The Marble Faun,* vol. ii., chapters xiii., xiv., xv.; kind of illumination it gives, *ibid.*, chapter xv.; symbol of, *French and Italian Journals,* vol. i., May 28, 1858.

Catholics, *English Note-Books,* vol. i., November 14, 1854; confiscated church property of, *Our Old Home,* About Warwick; worship of, *French and Italian Journals,* vol. i., January 9, February 21, 1858, vol. ii., July 4, 1858.

Cato, the Censor, bust of, *French and Italian Journals*, vol. i., April 10, 1858.

Catrine, the village of, *Our Old Home*, Some of the Haunts of Burns.

Cats, pet, *Mosses from an Old Manse*, vol. ii., A Virtuoso's Collection.

Caustic, Dr. Christopher, *nom de plume* of the author of the poem "Terrible Tractoration," *Fanshawe, etc*, T. G. Fessenden.

Caves in Derbyshire, *English Note-Books*, vol. ii., June 7, 1857.

Cecil, Mr., *English Note-Books*, vol. i., July 6, 1854.

Cecilia Metella, tomb of, *French and Italian Journals*, vol. i., May 9, 1858. See APPIAN WAY.

Cecilia, St., *The Marble Faun*, vol. i., chapter iii.

Celestial City, the, *Mosses from an Old Manse*, vol. i., The Celestial Railroad.

Celestial Railroad, the, a satire on modern religion, on the basis of Bunyan's allegory, in *Mosses from an Old Manse*, vol. i. It was first published in "The Democratic Review." It is alluded to in the *American Note-Books*, vol. ii., April 14, 1844.

Celeus, King, *Tanglewood Tales*, The Pomegranate Seeds.

Cellini Benvenuto, *American Note-Books*, vol. ii., December 19, 1850; figures by, *French and Italian Journals*, vol. ii., July 2, 1858; jewel-case of his time and school, *The Marble Faun*, vol. i., chapter xiii.; statue of Perseus by, *English Note-Books*, vol. ii., November 16, 1857, *French and Italian Journals*, vol. i., June 5, vol. ii., July 4, 1858; prison of, *ibid.*, vol. i., March 25, 1858; salamander seen by, *Mosses from an Old Manse*, vol. ii., A Virtuoso's Collection; scene in the autobiography of, *The Marble Faun*, vol. i., chapter xvii.; site of the workshop of, *French and Italian Journals*, vol. ii., September 7, 1858; vase made by, *Mosses from an Old Manse*, vol. i., Rappaccini's Daughter; other works of, *French and Italian Journals*, vol. ii., July 16, 1858.

Cemeteries, hint for an article on, *American Note-Books*, vol. ii., December 19, 1850; of Scotland, *Our Old Home*, Some of the Haunts of Burns; St. James's, Liverpool, *English Note-Books*, September 14, 1853. See, also, BURIAL GROUNDS.

Cenci, Beatrice, *French and Italian Journals*, vol. i., March 25, 1858, vol. ii., May 15, 1859; pictures of, *The Marble Faun*, vol. i., chapters vii., xxiii.

Cenci, Palace of the, *The Marble Faun*, vol. ii., chapter xvii.

Centaurs, the, *Tanglewood Tales*, The Golden Fleece.

Centre of the world, the, *Our Old Home*, A London Suburb.

Cerberus, *Tanglewood Tales*, The Pomegranate Seeds, *Mosses from an Old Manse*, vol. ii., A Virtuoso's Collection.

Ceremonies, antique, in London, *Our Old Home*, Civic Banquets.

Ceres, *Tanglewood Tales*, The Pomegranate Seeds.

Cervantes, *Mosses from an Old Manse*, vol. i., The Hall of Fantasy.

Chabbiquidick, an Indian of, *Twice-Told Tales*, vol. ii., Chippings with a Chisel.

Chad, St., legend of, *Our Old Home*, Lichfield and Uttoxeter.

Chairs, *Grandfather's Chair*, part i., chapter xi.

Chalk-cliffs of England, the, *French and Italian Journals*, vol. i., January 6, 1858.

Chamber, in Union Street, Salem, *American Note-Books*, vol. i., October 25, 1836, October 4, 1840.

Chambers, Robert, his edition of Burns, *English Note-Books*, vol. i., October 3, 1853.

Champlain, Lake, *The Dolliver Romance, etc.*, The Inland Port.

Champs Elysées, the, *French and Italian Journals*, vol. i., January 9, 1858.

"**Chances, The**," by the Duke of Buckingham, quotation from, *American Note-Books*, vol. i., October 24, 1838.

Chandler, J. A., Clerk of Court, *American Note-Books*, vol. i., July 26, 1837.

Change, American love of, *Our Old Home*, Leamington Spa; in an important circumstance without change in the kind of life, *The Blithedale Romance*, chapter xvi.; in friends, *ibid.*; sense of, in familiar objects, *Twice-Told Tales*, vol. i., Wakefield; the final, *Twice-Told Tales*, vol. ii., The Haunted Mind, last paragraph.

Changeling, a supposed, *Our Old Home*, Consular Experiences.

Changes, great, how wrought, *Twice-Told Tales*, vol. ii., Snow Flakes.

Channing, William Ellery, the poet, *American Note-Books*, vol. ii., April 8, 11, 1843, October 29, 1851, *English Note-Books*, vol. ii., April 5, 1856, *Mosses from an Old Manse*, vol. i., The Old Manse, near the middle, vol. ii., Earth's Holocaust, P.'s Correspondence, *The Blithedale Romance*, Preface, *The Scarlet Letter*, The Custom-House, middle.

Chant, Donatello's, summons to the creatures of the woods, *The Marble Faun*, vol. ii., chapter ii.

Chantrey, Sir Francis, works of, *English Note-Books*, vol. ii., June 17, August 31, 1856, Taylor Institute.

Chapel of Monte Beni, description of, *The Marble Faun*, vol. ii., chapter vi.

Chapels in the Roman churches, *The Marble Faun*, vol. ii., chapter xiii.

Character, affected by circumstances, suggestion of, *American Note-Books*, vol. i., October 7, 1837 ; a man's mistakes about his own, *The House of the Seven Gables*, chapter xv. ; a powerful, *American Note-Books*, vol. ii., 1842 ; a singular, *American Note-Books*, vol. i., October 24, 1838.

Characters, hints for, *American Note-Books*, vol. i., July 26, 1837.

Characters, negative, *Mosses from an Old Manse*, vol. ii., The Old Apple-Dealer ; noticeable, *American Note-Books*, vol. i., July 29, August 11, 15, 18, 19, 23, 26, 31, September 1, 3, 4, 5, 1838.

Charity, *American Note-Books*, vol. ii., August 30, 1842 ; posthumous, *Mosses from an Old Manse*, vol. i., The Procession of Life.

Charity-schools, *English Note-Books*, vol. ii., April 12, 1857.

Charlecote Park and Hall, *Our Old Home*, Recollections of a Gifted Woman.

Charlemont, Mass., *American Note-Books*, vol. i., August 31, 1838.

Charles I., of England, *True Stories*, chapter vi. of Biographies (in 16mo ed. only), *Twice-Told Tales*, vol. i., The Gray Champion, vol. ii., Endicott and the Red Cross; at Chester, *English Note-Books*, vol. i., October 1, 1853; face of, *Our Old Home*, Near Oxford; judges of, *Twice-Told Tales*, vol. ii., Howe's Masquerade; printing-press of, *English Note-Books*, vol. ii., April 12, 1857; queen of, *English Note-Books*, vol. ii., August 31, 1856, Merton College; relics of, *English Note-Books*, vol. i., April 1, 1856, Wooton, vol. ii., July 26, 1857; scene of execution of, *English Note-Books*, vol. i., September 10, 1855; statues of, *ibid.*, and October 14, 1855; Vandyke's pictures of, *English Note-Books*, vol. i., March 24, 1856, vol. ii., July 30, 1857.

Charles II., of England, *Twice-Told Tales*, vol. i., The Gray Champion, The Gentle Boy; influence on New England of, *The Dolliver Romance, etc.*, Dr. Bullivant; mistake of, about the stamp on the shilling, *Fanshawe, etc.*, Sir William Phips, fourth paragraph; New England under, *Grandfather's Chair*, part i., chapter ix.; statue of, *English Note-Books*, vol. i., October 14, 1855.

Charles V., target of, *English Note-Books*, vol. ii., July 26, 1857.

Charles IX., of France, incident of his court, *American Note-Books*, vol. i., July 13, 1838.

Charles River, the, view of, *American Note-Books*, vol. ii., October 13, 1841.

Charlestown, Mass., settlement of, *Grandfather's Chair*, part i., chapter ii.; visit to the navy-yard of, *American Note-Books*, vol. i., August 27, 1837.

Charter Street burial ground, old graves in, *American Note-Books*, vol. i., July 4, 1838.

Chastity, a woman's, *English Note-Books*, vol. i., March 16, 1854.

Chatham, statue of the Earl of, *English Note-Books*, vol. ii., July 13, 1856.

Chaucer, untold tales of, *Mosses from an Old Manse*, vol. i., A Select Party.

Cheever, Ezekiel, master of the Boston Latin School, *Grand-*

father's Chair, part ii., chapters iii., iv.; subject for a drawing, *American Note-Books*, vol. ii., September 14, 1841.

Chelsea, Gardens and Hospital of, *Our Old Home*, Up the Thames.

Chertsey, *English Note-Books*, vol. ii., April 8, 1856.

Cherwell River, the, *English Note-Books*, vol. ii., August 31, 1856.

Chester, England, *English Note-Books*, vol. i., October 1, 13, November 5, 1853, August 24, 1854, August 2, 1855, vol. ii., November 30, 1856; Bishop of, *ibid.*, April 19, 1857; constable of, *ibid.*, vol. i., October 13, 1853; Dutton Family, *ibid.*; old tomb near, *ibid.*, November 29, 1853; Ormerod's History of, *ibid.*, October 13, 1853; Randal, Earl of, *ibid.*

Child, incident of a pauper, *English Note-Books*, vol. i., February 28, 1856, *Our Old Home*, Outside Glimpses of English Poverty.

Child unborn, the, *Mosses from an Old Manse*, vol. i., A Select Party.

Childless People, comfort for, *American Note-Books*, vol. i., October 25, 1836.

Children: charity, *English Note-Books*, vol. i., August 20, 1853; enjoyment of, in repetitions of stories, *Wonder-Book*, Tanglewood Porch; fancies of, *Grandfather's Chair*, part i., chapter iii.; impulse of, to go out into the world, *Twice-Told Tales*, vol. i., Little Annie's Ramble; incidents of, *American Note-Books*, vol. i., 1840; in poverty, *Our Old Home*, Outside Glimpses of English Poverty; insight of, *Mosses from an Old Manse*, vol. i., Feathertop; intimacy of, with literary personages, *Our Old Home*, Lichfield and Uttoxeter; love for, *Twice-Told Tales*, vol. i., Little Annie's Ramble; persecutions by, *Twice-Told Tales*, vol. i., The Gentle Boy; representatives of the men and women of the Golden Age, *Tanglewood Tales*, introduction; reverence of a crowd for, *Twice-Told Tales*, vol. i., Little Annie's Ramble; sayings of, *American Note-Books*, vol. ii., October 13, December 19, 1850, October 13, 1851, *English Note-Books*, vol. i., November 14, 1854, June 11, 1855; shyness of, *Our Old Home*, Outside Glimpses of

English Poverty; society of, *Twice-Told Tales*, vol. i., Little Annie's Ramble; sympathy of, *The Scarlet Letter*, chapter xxi.; understanding of, *Wonder-Book*, Preface; unfortunate, *American Note-Books*, vol. i., October 24, 1838; writing for, *True Stories*, preface to Biographical Stories.

Chillingworth, Roger, a character in *The Scarlet Letter*. Having been deeply wronged, he becomes his own avenger, and is transformed almost into a fiend by the passion of revenge. He first appears in chapter iii.

Chillon, Castle of, *French and Italian Journals*, vol. ii., June 12, 14, 1859.

Chimæra, the, story in the *Wonder-Book*.

Chimney-sweeper, advantage of a, *American Note-Books*, vol. i., letter, February 12, 1840.

Chinese junk, the, *English Note-Books*, vol. i., September 1, 1853.

Chipman, Nathanael, *Fanshawe and Other Pieces*, T. G. Fessenden, third paragraph.

Chippings with a Chisel, a sketch, the scene of which is laid in Martha's Vineyard, in vol. ii. of *Twice-Told Tales*. It first appeared in "The Democratic Review."

Chiron, the Centaur, *Tanglewood Tales*, The Golden Fleece.

Chivalric expedition, a, *Fanshawe*, chapter vii.

Chivalry, age of, *English Note-Books*, vol. ii., July 26, 1857.

Christ: bound to a pillar, fresco by Sodoma, see SODOMA; effective picture of, *French and Italian Journals*, vol. ii., June 8, 1858; pictures of, *American Note-Books*, vol. ii., May 7, 1850.

Christ Church, Oxford, *English Note-Books*, vol. ii., August 31, 1856.

Christening of a ship, the, *English Note-Books*, vol. i., August 2, 1855.

Christians' burden, what it was, *American Note-Books*, vol. i., letter, May 29, 1840.

Christina, Queen, of Sweden, sketch of, *True Stories*, chapter ix. of Biographies. (In 16mo ed. only.)

Christmas Banquet, the, a story in *Mosses from an Old Manse*, vol. ii. It is an annual banquet provided by the will of an eccentric man for the ten most miserable people to be found. The story first appeared in " The Democratic Review." For a suggestion of it see the *American Note-Books,* vol. i., October 25, 1836.

Christmas customs in England, *English Note-Books,* vol. i., December 26, 1855.

Christo Duce, motto given by Whitefield, *Fanshawe and Other Pieces,* Sir William Pepperell, second paragraph.

Church, effect of dwelling near a, *Twice-Told Tales,* vol. i., Sunday at Home.

Church, Benjamin, *Grandfather's Chair,* part i., chapter viii.

Church service, in England and America, *English Note-Books,* vol. i., November 5, 1853.

Churches, *Mosses from an Old Manse,* vol. ii., The New Adam and Eve ; in England, and early settlements of America, *The Snow Image, etc.,* Main Street ; in Rome, *The Marble Faun,* vol. i., chapter i., vol. ii., chapter xiii. ; venality of attendants in Italian, *French and Italian Journals,* vol. i., May 30, 1858.

Churches, English : Bebbington, *English Note-Books,* vol. i., August 29, 1853 ; Boston, — St. Botolph's, *Our Old Home,* Pilgrimage to Old Boston ; Chester, — Cathedral, *English Note-Books,* vol. i., October 1, 1853, August 2, 1855, vol. ii., November 30, 1856 ; St. John's, *ibid.,* vol. i., August 24, 1854 ; Coventry, — *English Note-Books,* vol. ii., October 10, 1857, *French and Italian Journals,* vol. ii., February 5, 1860 ; Dundry, — *American Note-Books,* vol. i., October 25, 1836 ; Gloucester, — Cathedral, *English Note-Books,* vol. ii., June 29, 1856 ; Grantham, — *ibid.,* May 28, 1857 ; Hatton, — *Our Old Home,* Leamington Spa ; Isle of Man, — Kirk Madden, *English Note-Books,* August 10, 1854 ; Lichfield, — Cathedral, *Our Old Home,* Lichfield and Uttoxeter ; Lillington, — *ibid.* ; Leamington Spa, *French and Italian Journals,* vol. ii., November 14, 1859 ; Lincoln, — Cathedral, *Our Old Home,* Pilgrimage to Old Boston ; Liverpool, — St. George's, *English Note-Books,* vol. i., September 7, 1853 ; St. Nicholas, *ibid.,* August 9, September 7, 1853, vol. ii., September 9, 1856 ; London, — St. Paul's, *English Note-Books,* vol. i., September 7, 8, 13, 28, October 6, 1855, March 26, 1856, vol. ii., August 2, 1856, November 11, 12, December 8, 1857; St. Giles', *English Note-Books,* vol. i., March 25, 1856; Nottingham, — *ibid.,* vol. ii., May 29, 1857; Omskirk, — *ibid.,* October 26, 1856; Peterborough, — Cathedral, *ibid.,* May 27, 1857; Rock Ferry, — *ibid.,* vol. i., August 8, 1853; Stanton Harcourt, — *Our Old Home,* Near Oxford; Shrewsbury, — the Holy Cross and St. Mary's, *English Note-Books,* vol. i., September 5, 1855; Stratford, — the Holy Trinity, *Our Old Home,* Recollections of a Gifted Woman; Warwick, — St. Mary's, *French and Italian Journals,* vol. ii., February 18, 1860, *Our Old Home,* About Warwick; Whitnash, — *Our Old Home,* Leamington Spa; York — Cathedral, *English Note-Books,* vol. ii., May 10, 1856.

Churches, French: Amiens, — Cathedral, *French and Italian Journals,* vol. i., January 6, 1858; Avignon, — *ibid.,* vol. ii., June 1, 2, 6, 1859; Lyons, — *ibid.,* June 11, 1859; Paris, — Notre Dame, *ibid.,* vol. i., January 11, 12, 1858; the Madeleine, *ibid.,* January 9, 1858; Valence, — *ibid.,* vol. ii., June 11, 1859; Villeneuve, — *ibid.,* June 6, 1859.

Churches, Italian: Arezzo, — Cathedral, *French and Italian Journals,* vol. i., May 30, 1858; Assisi, — *ibid.,* May 28, 1858; Florence, — Cathedral, *ibid.,* vols. i., ii., June 5, 7, 10, September 7, 1858; of the Annunziata, *ibid.,* vol. ii., July 8, September 10, 1858; of the Badia, *ibid.,* July 16, 1858; Or San Michele, June 28, 30, September 3, 1858; San Lorenzo, *ibid.,* June 19, September 7, 17, 1858; San Marco, *ibid.,* July 10, 1858; Santa Croce, *ibid.,* June 28, September 29, 1858; Santa Maria Novella, *ibid.,* July 4, September 7, 1858; Foligno, — *ibid.,* vol. i., May 27, 1858; Genoa, — San Lorenzo, *ibid.,* January 24, 1858; Perugia, — Cathedral, *ibid.,* May 28, 29, 1858; Rome, — Church of the Capuchins, *ibid.,* vol. i., February 17, 1858, vol. ii., May 15, 1859, *The Marble Faun,* vol. i., chapter xx.; Domine, quò Vadis? *French and Italian Journals,* vol. i., March 11, May 9, 1858; the Pantheon, *ibid.,* February 21, May 1, 1858; St. Agnes, *ibid.,* May 1, 1858; St. Andrea, *ibid.,* February 20, 1858; St. Gesù, *ibid.,* March 1, 1858; St. Ignazio, *ibid.,* February 21, 1858; St. John Lateran, *ibid.,*

February 14, 1858; San Luigi dei Franchesi, *ibid.*, February 15, 1858; Santa Maria degl' Angeli, *ibid.*, February 19, 1858; Santa Maria del Popolo, *ibid.*, February 17, 1858; Santa Maria Maggiore, *ibid.*, February 10, 1858; St. Peter's Cathedral, *ibid.*, February 7, 9, 20, 21, March 27, April 10, 25, June 5, vol. ii., October 21, 1858, *The Marble Faun*, vol. i., chapter xii., vol. ii., chapters xiii., xiv., xv.; San Pietro in Vincoli, *French and Italian Journals*, vol. i., April 16, 1858; San Sebastiano, *ibid.*, May 9, 1858; San Stefano, *ibid.*, May 8, 1858; Sistine Chapel, *ibid.*, May 15, 1858; Trinità dei Monti, *ibid.*, February 17, 1858; San Querico, — *ibid.*, vol. ii., October 13, 1858; Siena, — Cathedral, *ibid.*, October 3, 4, 5, 9, 10, 11, 12, 1858.

Churches, Scotch: Kirk Alloway, *Our Old Home*, Some of the Haunts of Burns; Dumfries, — St. Michael's, *ibid.*; Glasgow, — Cathedral, *English Note-Books*, vol. ii., July 1, 1857; St. Mungo's, *ibid.*, May 10, 1856; Linlithgow,— *ibid.*, July 8, 1857; Mauchline, — scene of "The Holy Fair," *Our Old Home*, Some of the Haunts of Burns; Stirling, — *English Note-Books*, vol. ii., July 7, 1857.

Churches, Swiss: Geneva, — Cathedral, *French and Italian Journals*, vol. ii., June 11, 1859; Lausanne, — Cathedral, *ibid.*, June 14, 1859.

Churches, Welsh, *English Note-Books*, vol. i., July 19, 1854.

Churchill, Charles, character of his satire, *Fanshawe and Other Pieces*, T. G. Fessenden, middle of sketch.

Churchill. See MARLBOROUGH.

Cider-making, *American Note-Books*, vol. ii., October 29, November 3, 1851. See VINTAGE.

Cignani, Carlo, cartoons by, *English Note-Books*, vol. i., March 24, 1856.

Cilix, *Tanglewood Tales*, The Dragon's Teeth.

Cilley, Greenleaf, *Fanshawe, etc.*, Jonathan Cilley.

Cilley, Jonathan, *American Note-Books*, vol. i., July 28, August 27, 1837; sketch of, included in the volume with *Fanshawe.*

Cilley, Joseph, *Fanshawe, etc.*, Jonathan Cilley.

Cimabue, pictures by, *French and Italian Journals*, vol. ii., June 17, July 4, 1858.

Circe's Palace, title of a story in *Tanglewood Tales.*

Circulating Library, a, *Twice-Told Tales,* vol. ii., The Seven Vagabonds.

Circumspection, *The Blithedale Romance,* chapter xviii.

Citizen-soldiers, a representative of, *Fanshawe and Other Pieces,* Sir William Pepperell, first paragraph.

City, use of the word in England, *Our Old Home,* Lichfield and Uttoxeter.

City Cries, *Twice-Told Tales,* vol. i., Little Annie's Ramble.

City Hall of Salem, the, *Twice-Told Tales,* vol. ii., The Sister Years.

City of Destruction, the, *Mosses from an Old Manse,* vol. i., The Celestial Railroad.

City Tavern, the, Boston, *American Note-Books,* vol. i., June 22, 1835.

Civic Banquets, an article in *Our Old Home,* describing some public banqueting-halls of England, and dinners given by the Mayors of Liverpool and London.

Civita Castellana, *French and Italian Journals,* vol. i., May 24, 1858.

Civita Vecchia, *French and Italian Journals,* vol. i., January 24, 1858.

Claimants, American, to English soil, *Our Old Home,* Consular Experiences.

Clairvoyance of illness, the, *The Blithedale Romance,* chapter vi., near the end. See MESMERISM.

Claphams, burial place of the, *English Note-Books,* vol. ii., April 11, 1857.

Clare, Lord Chancellor, incident of, *American Note-Books,* vol. i., October 25, 1836.

Clarens, Switzerland, *French and Italian Journals,* vol. ii., June 12, 1859.

Clark, Rev. Mr., character in The Minister's Black Veil, *Twice-Told Tales,* vol. i.

Clarke, Doctor, character in Lady Eleanore's Mantle, *Twice-Told Tales,* vol. ii.

Clarke, Lieutenant-governor, of New York, *English Note-Books,* vol. ii., November 30, 1856.

Clarke, Mr., *English Note-Books,* vol. i., September 7, 1855.

Clarke, Sarah, *English Note-Books,* September 13, 1855; pictures by, *American Note-Books,* vol. i., letter, June 11, 1840.

Class distinctions in America, *The Blithedale Romance,* chapter xx.

Classic Legends, wonderful identity of, *Wonder-Book,* Preface.

Classification of men, a new, *Mosses from an Old Manse,* vol. i., The Procession of Life.

Claude, pictures of, *English Note-Books,* vol. i., March 26, vol. ii., August 2, 1856, December 8, 1857, *French and Italian Journals,* vol. ii., June 8, 1858, *The Marble Faun,* vol. ii., chapter xxiv.

Claudian Aqueduct, the, *French and Italian Journals,* vol. ii., October 23, 1858.

Claverhouse, relic of, *English Note-Books,* vol. ii., May 10, 1856, Abbotsford; reminiscence of, *ibid.,* July 10, 1857.

Clay, Henry, letter from, *The Dolliver Romance and Other Pieces,* A Book of Autographs.

Clement's Inn, London, *English Note-Books,* vol. i., September 15, 1855.

Cleopatra, Story's statue of, *The Marble Faun,* Preface, vol. i., chapter xiv., vol. ii., chapter xvi.

Clergy, the, lack of one safeguard of, *Our Old Home,* Consular Experiences; motives for zeal of, *The Dolliver Romance and Other Pieces,* Dr. Bullivant; respect for, *Our Old Home,* Consular Experiences.

Clergyman, a business-like, *English Note-Books,* vol. i, August 24, 1853; a typical, *American Note-Books,* vol. ii., August 30, 1842; story of an American, *Our Old Home,* Consular Experiences; story of an English, *English Note-Books,* vol. i., November 29, 1853.

Clergymen, fidelity of the friends of, *The Scarlet Letter,* chapter xxiv.; in early New England, *ibid.,* chapter xxii., *Fanshawe and Other Pieces,* Sir William Phips, second paragraph; in war time, *Septimius Felton,* page 67 (12mo); of the English Church, *Our Old Home,* Pilgrimage to Old Boston, near the end.

Clifford, Lord, story of, *French and Italian Journals,* vol. ii., August 3, 1858.

Clifford, Mr., Speaker of the Maine Legislature, *Fanshawe and Other Pieces,* Jonathan Cilley.

Cliffords, home of the, *English Note-Books,* vol. ii., April 10, 1857.

Clifton Villa, *English Note-Books,* vol. ii., June 15, 1856.

Clinch, Miss, *English Note-Books,* vol. i., September 29, 1855.

Clinton, De Witt, *Mosses from an Old Manse,* vol. ii., Sketches from Memory, The Canal Boat.

Clitumnus River, the, *French and Italian Journals,* vol. i., May 26, 1858.

Cloistered walks, *English Note-Books,* vol. i., September 30, 1855.

Cloisters, *French and Italian Journals,* vol. ii., July 4, 1858.

Closes, cathedral. See CATHEDRALS.

Clothes, significance of, *Our Old Home,* A London Suburb.

Cloud-picture, a, *American Note-Books,* vol. ii., October 21, 1851.

Clouds, *Twice-Told Tales,* vol. i., Sights from a Steeple; suggestion of, *American Note-Books,* vol. i., January 4, 1839.

Clover, name given to one of the children to whom the stories of the *Wonder-Book* and *Tanglewood Tales* were told.

Cloyse, Goody, a character in the story Young Goodman Brown, *Mosses from an Old Manse,* vol. i.

Clubs, London: Milton, *English Note-Books,* vol. ii., April 4, 1856; Reform, *ibid.,* April 5, 1856.

Coal, measuring, *American Note-Books,* vol. i., letters February 11 and 12, 1840, May 29, 1840.

Coal-grates, *English Note-Books,* vol. i., September 2, 1853.

Coarseness of the world's judgments, *The Marble Faun,* vol. ii., chapter xi.

Cobbett, William, *Mosses from an Old Manse,* vol. ii., P.'s Correspondence; character of the satire of, *Fanshawe and Other Pieces,* T. G. Fessenden, middle.

Cocktails, an artist in, *The Blithedale Romance,* chapter xxi.

Coffin, the, *Our Old Home*, About Warwick; the rattle of earth upon, *The Blithedale Romance*, chapter xxviii.

Coins, famous, *Mosses from an Old Manse*, vol. ii., A Virtuoso's Collection.

Colburn, Adam, a character in The Shaker Bridal, *Twice-Told Tales*, vol. ii.

Colchis, *Tanglewood Tales*, The Golden Fleece.

Cold Men, quick eyes of, *American Note-Books*, vol. i., December 6, 1837.

Cold Spring, the, North Salem, *American Note-Books*, vol. i., June 18, 1835, October 7, 1837.

Coldstream Guards, monument to the officers of the, *English Note-Books*, vol. ii., August 2, 1856.

Coleman, Ann, punishment of, *The Snow Image, etc.*, Main Street.

Coleridge, Hartley, cottage of, *English Note-Books*, vol. i., July 21, 1855; grave of, July 19, 1855.

Coleridge, S. T.: the albatross in "The Ancient Mariner," *English Note-Books*, vol. ii., October 30, 1857, *Mosses from an Old Manse*, vol. ii., A Virtuoso's Collection; Christabel, *Mosses from an Old Manse*, vol. i., A Select Party, vol. ii., P.'s Correspondence; Pantisocracy of, *The Blithedale Romance*, chapter viii.; plant connected with, *English Note-Books*, vol. ii., April 8, 1856; quotation from, *American Note-Books*, vol. i., October 25, 1835.

Coliseum, the, *French and Italian Journals*, vol. i., February 3, March 23, 1858, *The Marble Faun*, vol. i., chapters i., xvii.

College-life, its happiness, *Fanshawe*, chapter i.

Collegians, *American Note-Books*, vol. i., August 15, 1838; love-making of, *Fanshawe*, chapter i., near the end; marks of the classes of, *ibid.*, chapter i.; opinions of class-mates of, *English Note-Books*, vol. i., August 2, 1855.

Colman, Rev. Dr., *Twice-Told Tales*, vol. i., The Prophetic Pictures, *The Snow Image, etc.*, Old News, part i.

Cologne, foreign, of Ashfield, *American Note-Books*, vol. i., July 27, 1838.

Colonial system, the, a perfect representative of, *Twice-Told Tales*, vol. ii., Old Esther Dudley; vanishing glory of, *ibid.*

Colonna Palace, the, *French and Italian Journals*, vol. i., April 15, 1858.

Colony, first requisites of a, *The Scarlet Letter*, chapter i.; Mrs. Hutchinson's, *Fanshawe, etc.*, Mrs. Hutchinson, last paragraph.

Color, use of in sculpture, *French and Italian Journals*, vol. i., June 7, 1858.

Colton, Commodore, *American Note-Books*, vol. i., August 27, 1837.

Columbaria, *French and Italian Journals*, vol. i., March 3, 1858, *The Marble Faun*, vol. ii., chapter xxi.

Columbaria, Villa, *French and Italian Journals*, vol. ii., September 11, 1858.

Columbus, autograph of the son of, *English Note-Books*, vol. ii., April 8, 1856; the history of in bas-reliefs by Randolph Rogers, *The Marble Faun*, Preface.

Comet of 1858, the, *French and Italian Journals*, vol. ii., September 28, October 4, 9, 1858.

Common, Boston, *American Note-Books*, vol. i., July 4, 1838; letter, April 19, 1840, *English Note-Books*, vol. i., September 8, 1855.

Communion of St. Jerome, the, *French and Italian Journals*, vol. i., April 25, 1858.

Communists of Blithedale, the, *The Blithedale Romance*, chapter viii.; dress of, *ibid.;* objects of, chapter iii.; position of toward society at large, *ibid.;* scheme of, as seen in after years, *ibid.*, chapter xxix.

Comus, a reminder of, *Twice-Told Tales*, vol. i., The Maypole of Merry Mount.

Conant, Roger, first settler of Salem, *The Snow Image, etc.*, Main Street, *Grandfather's Chair*, part i., chapter ii.

Concealment producing the effect of guilt, *Mosses from an Old Manse*, vol. ii., Roger Malvin's Burial.

Concord, Mass., battle of, *Mosses from an Old Manse*, vol. i., The Old Manse, near the beginning; dwellings in, Septimius Felton, pp. 4, 5 (12mo); inhabitants of, *American Note-Books*, vol. ii., August 5, 1842; scenery of, *ibid.*, August 7, 1842.

Concord Bridge, *Mosses from an Old Manse,* vol. i., The Old Manse, near the beginning.

Concord Monument, *Mosses from an Old Manse,* vol. i., The Old Manse, near the beginning

Concord River, *American Note-Books,* vol. ii., August 5, 7, 24, 1842, April 9, 25, 27, 1843, *Mosses from an Old Manse,* vol. i., The Old Manse, Buds and Bird Voices.

Condescension, easier to give than to receive, *The Blithedale Romance,* chapter iv ; effect of, *The House of the Seven Gables,* near the end of chapter viii.

Confectioner's Window, a, *Twice-Told Tales,* vol. i., Little Annie's Ramble.

Confession of sin, *The Scarlet Letter,* chapters x., xi.

Confessional, the, *French and Italian Journals,* vol. ii., October 9, 1858, *The Marble Faun,* vol ii., chapter xiv.

Confessor, a father, reflections of, *American Note-Books,* vol. ii., 1842.

Confusion, emblem of the world's, *Twice-Told Tales,* vol. i., The Toll-Gatherer's Day.

Congress, the Continental, *The Dolliver Romance, etc.,* A Book of Autographs.

Congreve, monument of, *English Note-Books,* vol. i., September 30, 1855; quotation from, *ibid.,* vol. ii., June 29, 1856, Gloucester.

Connaught Rangers, the, *English Note-Books,* vol. i., April 3, 1854.

Connoisseurs, *English Note-Books,* vol. ii., August 20, 1857.

Conscience, at Vanity Fair, *Mosses from an Old Manse,* vol. i., The Celestial Railroad ; incumbrance of an evil, *Mosses from an Old Manse,* vol. ii., The Intelligence Office ; personification of, *Twice-Told Tales,* vol. i., Fancy's Show Box.

Consecration of a dwelling, ceremony of, *The House of the Seven Gables,* chapter i.

Conservatism, in old age, *Mosses from an Old Manse,* vol. ii., P.'s Correspondence ; need of getting back to occasionally, *The Blithedale Romance,* chapter xvi.

Conservators, Palace of the, Rome, *French and Italian Journals,* vol. i., March 1, 1858.

Consolation: for mourners, *Fanshawe*, chapter ix.; of the Roman Church, see CATHOLICISM.

Constables of Chester, ancient privilege of, *English Note-Books*, vol. i., October 13, 1853.

Constantine the Great, birthplace of, *English Note-Books*, vol. ii., May 10, 1856, York; statue of, *French and Italian Journals*, vol. i., February 14, 1858.

Constitution, The, incident of the fight of with the Macedonian, *American Note-Books*, vol. i., August 27, 1837.

Consul, the American, at Paris (Duncan K. McRae), *French and Italian Journals*, vol. i., January 12, 1858.

Consular Experiences, first article in *Our Old Home*, — notes of the author's experience while United States Consul at Liverpool, which office he filled from 1853 till 1857.

Consulate, the American, in Liverpool, *Our Old Home*, beginning.

Consuls, appeals to the charity of, *English Note-Books*, vol. i., May 23, 1855; applications to, *ibid.*, October 8, 1853, August 12, 1855; qualifications necessary to, *Our Old Home*, Consular Experiences; queer claims on, *ibid.*

Contempt, wisdom of, *Mosses from an Old Manse*, vol. ii., A Virtuoso's Collection.

Contests, interest in, *Our Old Home*, Up the Thames.

Contract, letting a, *American Note-Books*, vol. i., August 23, 1838.

Contribution, a church, *The Dolliver Romance and Other Pieces*, The Antique Ring.

Convent-bells in Italy, *The Marble Faun*, vol. ii., chapter iv.

Conventionalism of life, *Mosses from an Old Manse*, vol. i., The Old Manse, after the middle.

Conversation, English idea of good, *English Note-Books*, vol. ii., April 8, 1856; of the miserable, *Mosses from an Old Manse*, vol. ii., The Christmas Banquet.

Conway, Wales, Town and Castle, *English Note-Books*, vol. i., July 19, September 13, 1854.

Cooke, Mr., *Twice-Told Tales*, vol. i., The Prophetic Pictures.

Cookery, French and English, *French and Italian Journals*, vol.

i., January 6, end, January 10, 1858; in the woods, *Mosses from an Old Manse*, vol. i., The Old Manse, after the middle; Italian, *French and Italian Journals*, vol. i., June 7, 1858. Zenobia's, *The Blithedale Romance*, chapter vi., end.

Copinger, Mr., incident of, *American Note-Books*, vol. i., October 25, 1836.

Copley, J. S., *Mosses from an Old Manse*, vol. ii., Drowne's Wooden Image; pictures of, *English Note-Books*, vol. ii., July 28, 1857; portrait of Hancock by, *The Dolliver Romance and Other Pieces*, A Book of Autographs.

Coppet, Switzerland, *French and Italian Journals*, vol. ii., June 12, 1859.

Copp's Hill burial-ground, *Twice-Told Tales*, vol. ii., Lady Eleanore's Mantle.

Copying Pictures, *French and Italian Journals*, vol. ii., June 10, 13, 1858, *The Marble Faun*, vol. i., chapter vi.

Cordial for long life, a, *The Dolliver Romance*, third fragment.

Corinne, a scene in, *The Marble Faun*, vol. i., chapter xvi.

Corn, Indian, beauty of, *American Note-Books*, vol. ii., August 10, 1842.

Cornelius Agrippa, *Mosses from an Old Manse*, vol. i., The Birthmark; magic glass of, *Mosses from an Old Manse*, vol. ii., A Virtuoso's Collection.

Cornhill, Boston, *Twice-Told Tales*, vol. i., The Gray Champion; in 1670, *The Dolliver Romance, etc.*, Dr. Bullivant.

Cornwall, Barry. See PROCTER, B. W.

Coroner, Diary of a, *English Note-Books*, vol. i., March 16, 1854.

Coroner's Court, scenes at a, *English Note-Books*, vol. i., March 16, 1854, vol. ii., December 31, 1856.

Correggio, pictures by, *French and Italian Journals*, vol. ii., June 30, September 21, 1858.

Corsini Palace, *French and Italian Journals*, vol. ii., October 21, 1858.

Corso, the, *French and Italian Journals*, vol. ii., October 17, 1858, *The Marble Faun*, vol. ii., chapter xxiii.

Cosmopolite, a little, *American Note-Books*, vol. i., letter, May 30, 1840.

Costumes, variety of in Rome, *French and Italian Journals*, vol. i., February 19, 1858.

Cotton, introduction of, into the United States, *English Note-Books*, vol. i., May 18, 1855.

Cotton, Rev. John, *Grandfather's Chair*, part i., chapter iv., *Fanshawe, etc.*, Mrs. Hutchinson, third paragraph; light of upon his errors, *ibid.*, fourth paragraph; memorial to, *Our Old Home*, Pilgrimage to Old Boston.

Councils: military, at Boston, subject for drawing, *American Note-Books*, vol. ii., September 14, 1841; of passengers in a street, a, *ibid.*, vol. i, October 25, 1836; of the ancient church, the, *Fanshawe, etc.*, Mrs. Hutchinson, fifth paragraph.

Count of Monte Beni, the. See DONATELLO.

Country-life in Italy, *The Marble Faun*, vol. ii., chapter vii.

Courts, *Mosses from an Old Manse*, vol. ii., The New Adam and Eve; English, *English Note-Books*, vol. i., August 21, 1854.

Coventry, *English Note-Books*, vol. i., July 1, 1855, vol. ii., October 10, 1857, *French and Italian Journals*, February 5, 1860; St. Mary's Hall of, *Our Old Home*, Civic Banquets.

Coverdale, Miles, a character in *The Blithedale Romance*, a poet and the narrator of the story. His personality is kept as much as possible out of sight, except in its quality as a close and sympathetic observer of the three principal characters. He is taken for Hawthorne himself, whom he resembles in this quality of observer and analyst.

Cow, the, *Twice-Told Tales*, vol. i., A Rill from the Town Pump.

Cowden Knowe, the, *English Note-Books*, vol. ii., May 10, 1856, Dryburgh.

Cow Island, *American Note-Books*, vol. ii, October 9, 1841.

Cowley, Abraham, house of, *English Note-Books*, vol. ii., April 8, 1856.

Cowslip, name given to one of the children to whom the stories of the *Wonder-Book* and *Tanglewood Tales*, were told.

Craggs, Secretary, statue of, *English Note-Books*, vol. ii., August 7, 1856.

Cranes, war of with the pygmies, *Tanglewood Tales*, The Pygmies.

Cranfield, Ralph, hero of the story The Threefold Destiny, *Twice-Told Tales*, vol. ii.

Crawford, Ethan, *Mosses from an Old Manse*, vol. ii., Sketches from Memory, Our Evening Party among the Mountains, *Twice-Told Tales*, vol. ii., The Ambitious Guest.

Crawford House, White Mountains, *Mosses from an Old Manse*, vol. ii , Sketches from Memory, Our Evening Party among the Mountains.

Crawford, Thomas, *The Marble Faun*, vol. i., chapter xiv.; studio of, *French and Italian Journals*, vol. i., March 11, 1858.

Creed, the, effect on the heart of, *Twice-Told Tales*, vol. i., Sunday at Home.

Cremation of the dead, *English Note-Books*, vol. i., September 29, 1855.

Crete, Island of, *Tanglewood Tales*, The Minotaur.

Cricket, the game of, *Our Old Home*, A London Suburb.

Cricket, song of the, *American Note-Books*, vol. ii., August 22, 1842, *Mosses from an Old Manse*, vol. i., The Old Manse, after the middle.

Crime, alienating effect of, *The Marble Faun*, vol. i., chapter xiii.; classification of men by, *Mosses from an Old Manse*, vol. i., The Procession of Life; finer perceptions blunted by, *The Marble Faun*, vol. i., chapter xx.; influence of, *American Note-Books*, vol. ii., 1842; insulating power of, *The Marble Faun*, vol. i., chapter xi.

Crimean War, the: effect of, *English Note-Books*, vol. i., January 3, 1855; English feeling regarding, *English Note-Books*, vol. i., February 23, April 3, October 6, November 14, 1854, July 30, 1855; Hawthorne's idea of, *ibid.*, February 21, 1855; Mr Layard on, *ibid.*, April 24, 1855; one result of, *ibid.*, January 3, 1855.

Criminal trials, the appetite for, *American Note-Books*, vol. i., October 25, 1836.

Criminals, number of, reformed by a philanthropist, *The Blithedale Romance*, chapter xxviii.

Crispin, St., chair of, *English Note-Books*, July 8, 1857.

Critic, a typical, *The Snow Image, etc.*, Main Street.

Criticism, *Twice-Told Tales*, Preface; folly of in certain places, *Our Old Home*, Lichfield and Uttoxeter; worldly, on the artist, *Mosses from an Old Manse*, vol. ii., The Artist of the Beautiful.

Critics, American and London newspaper, *Our Old Home*, Recollections of a Gifted Woman; charges of, *The Snow Image*, dedication.

Crittenden, Thomas L., predecessor of Hawthorne at Liverpool, *English Note-Books*, vol. i., August 5, 10, 1853, *Our Old Home*, Consular Experience. (Name not given).

Crombie, Hugh, a character in *Fanshawe*, first mentioned in chapter iv. He is something of a poet and musician and a consummate liar, who after a life of vicious adventure has settled down to one of quiet selfishness as landlord of the inn of the college town, having married the landlady, Widow Hutchins.

Cromwell, Oliver, *True Stories*, chapter vi. of Biographies (only in 16mo ed); depredations of the soldiers of, *English Note-Books*, vol. ii., June 29, 1856, Gloucester, *Our Old Home*, Pilgrimage to Old Boston, Lincoln; incident of the time of, *English Note-Books*, vol. ii., August 21, 1856; mask of, *ibid.*, December 7, 1857; pictures of, *American Note-Books*, vol. i., August 22, 1837, *English Note-Books*, vol. ii., April 10, 1857; treatment of New England by, *Grandfather's Chair*, part i., chapter v.

Crosland, Newton, *English Note-Books*, vol. i., March 25, vol. ii., July 6, 1856, Blackheath.

Cross, the black, in the Coliseum, *The Marble Faun*, vol. i., chapter xvii.

Crosses, wayside, in Italy, *The Marble Faun*, vol. ii., chapter vii.

Crowds, in Europe and America, *French and Italian Journals*, vol. i., January 17, vol. ii., June 28, September 10, 1858.

Crows, *Mosses from an Old Manse*, vol. i., Buds and Bird Voices, *American Note-Books*, vol. i., July 26, 1838, vol. ii., August 22, 1842.

Croxteth, seat of Lord Sefton, *English Note-Books*, vol. i., March 23, 1854.

Crucifixion, tradition about the, *American Note-Books*, vol. ii., September 5, 1852.

Crusaders, resemblance to, of a provincial army, *Fanshawe and Other Pieces*, Sir William Pepperell, first paragraph.

Crypts, *English Note-Books*, vol. ii., June 29, 1856, Gloucester, April 13, July 1, 11, 1857, Durham.

Crystal Hills (White Mountains), the, *Twice-Told Tales*, vol. i., The Great Carbuncle.

Crystal Palace, the, *English Note-Books*, vol. ii., September 27, November 16, 1857, *Our Old Home*, Up the Thames.

Cuckoo, note of the, *English Note-Books*, vol. i., May 31, 1855.

Cuffing, a sound, when deserved, *The Blithedale Romance*, chapter iv.

Cumberland, mountains of, *English Note-Books*, vol. i., July 21, 1855.

Cumnor, Village and Church, *Our Old Home*, Near Oxford.

Cunningham, Allan, *Mosses from an Old Manse*, vol. ii., P.'s Correspondence.

Cupid, weapons of, *American Note-Books*, vol. ii., June 9, 1853.

Cups, famous, *Mosses from an Old Manse*, vol. ii., A Virtuoso's Collection.

Curse : of Adam, the, *The Blithedale Romance*, chapter xxiv. ; of a people, the, *Twice-Told Tales*, vol. ii., Edward Randolph's Portrait.

Curtains, effect of, *Mosses from an Old Manse*, vol. i., The Birthmark.

Curtis, George William (Howadji), *The Blithedale Romance*, Preface.

Curtius, chasm where he plunged, *The Marble Faun*, vol. i., chapter xviii.

Curwen, Captain, sheriff of Essex, *The Snow Image, etc.*, Main Street.

Curwen House, the, Salem, *The Snow Image, etc.*, Main Street. This house is thought to be the original of the "House of the Seven Gables."

Cushing, Caleb, *French and Italian Journals,* vol. ii., March 23, 1859.

Cushman, Charlotte, *English Note-Books,* vol. i., July 19, 1855.

Custom, sway of over the mode of wreaking passion, *The Blithedale Romance,* chapter ix., near the end.

Custom-House of Salem, the, *The Scarlet Letter,* introductory chapter, and preface to the second edition.

Custom-Houses, effect of office in, *The Scarlet Letter,* The Custom-House, near the end; experience in, compared with farm-work, *American Note-Books,* vol. ii., May 4, June 1, August 12, 1841; life in, *ibid.,* vol. i., letter of March 23, 1840.

Cutts, Lord Thomas, of Grondale Abbey, *American Note-Books,* vol. ii., 1842.

Cutts, President, *American Note-Books,* vol. ii., 1842.

Cwlyd River, *English Note-Books,* vol. i., September 13, 1854.

Cyane, the, visit to in Boston Harbor, *American Note-Books,* vol. i., June 16, 1838.

Cymbeline, King, *Our Old Home,* About Warwick.

Cynics, *Twice-Told Tales,* vol. i, The Great Carbuncle; as critics of poetry, *The Snow Image, etc.,* The Great Stone Face; hint for a story of a, *American Note-Books,* vol. i., September 7, 1835.

Cynosure, the, vessel for which Drowne's Wooden Image was made, *Mosses from an Old Manse,* vol. ii.

Cyzicus, *Tanglewood Tales,* The Golden Fleece.

D ——, Mr., a writer for the "London Times," *English Note-Books,* vol. ii., April 4, 1856.

Dabney, Colonel, a character in *The Dolliver Romance,* a sensual and brutal old man, who forces the cordial of life from the apothecary, and dies of an over-draught.

Dabney, Mrs., heroine of The Wedding Knell, in *Twice-Told Tales,* vol. i.

Dacy, Sybil, a character in *Septimius Felton,* an English girl mysteriously connected with Septimius, and the heroine of the romance.

Dædalus, *Tanglewood Tales,* The Minotaur.

Daguerreotypes, *The House of the Seven Gables,* chapter vi.

Dahlia, the, *Septimius Felton,* page 131 (12mo).

Dallas, George M., United States Minister to England, *English Note-Books,* vol i., March 15, vol. ii., July 6, 1856.

Dalton, Village and Abbey, *English Note-Books,* vol. i., July 13, 1855.

Dalton, Dr., statue of, *English Note-Books,* vol. ii., May 24, 1856, Manchester.

Dana, Charles A., *The Blithedale Romance,* Preface.

Dana, Frank, *American Note-Books,* vol. ii., September 28, 1841.

Danaë, *Wonder-Book,* The Gorgon's Head.

Danby, Francis, a picture by, *English Note-Books,* vol. ii., July 28, 1857.

Dance, Donatello's, *The Marble Faun,* vol. i., chapter x.

Dandelion, name given to one of the children to whom the stories of the *Wonder-Book* and *Tanglewood Tales* were told.

Danforth, Robert, a character in the story The Artist of the Beautiful, *Mosses from an Old Manse,* vol. ii. He is a blacksmith, and a man of coarse mental and moral fibre.

Dante, *Mosses from an Old Manse,* vol. i., Rappaccini's Daughter, The Hall of Fantasy; cast and portrait of, *French and Italian Journals,* vol. ii., August 12, 1858; the forest in the Inferno, *Mosses from an Old Manse,* vol i., Fire Worship, *The Blithedale Romance,* chapter xii.; monument of, *French and Italian Journals,* vol. ii., June 28, 1858.

Danvers, Mass., *American Note-Books,* vol. i., October 25, 1836.

D'Anville, Duke, expedition of, *Grandfather's Chair,* part ii., chapter vii.

Darius, casket of, *Mosses from an Old Manse,* vol. ii., A Virtuoso's Collection.

Darnley, apartments of at Holyrood, *English Note-Books,* vol. ii., May 10, 1856; house of, *ibid.,* July 7, 1857.

Dauphin, the, legend of, *English Note-Books,* vol. i., June 30, 1854.

Davee, Mr., Speaker of the Maine Legislature, *Fanshawe and Other Pieces,* Jonathan Cilley.

Davenant, Sir William, the mother of, *English Note-Books,* vol. ii., August 31, 1856.

Davenport, Rev. John, *Grandfather's Chair,* part i., chapter iv.

David, the last Welsh prince, *English Note-Books,* vol. i., September 5, 1855.

David, St., *English Note-Books,* vol. ii., July 11, 1857.

David Swan, A Fantasy. A short sketch in *Twice-Told Tales,* vol. i., illustrating the great number of possibilities that come just within reach without being dreamed of.

Davidson, Margaret, lines from, *The Dolliver Romance and Other Pieces,* A Book of Autographs.

Davis, J. B., *English Note-Books,* vol. ii., April 8, 1856.

Davis, Thomas, *Mosses from an Old Manse,* vol. i., The Old Manse, near the beginning.

Dawson, Richard, death of, *English Note-Books,* vol. i., October 22, 1853.

Deacon, Mr., monument of, *English Note-Books,* vol. ii., May 27, 1857.

Dead, the: appreciation of, *Septimius Felton,* pp. 17, 18 (12mo); control of the world by, *The House of the Seven Gables,* chapter xii., near the end; disposal of, *French and Italian Journals,* vol. i., May 8, 1858; expression of, *Septimius Felton,* p. 39 (12mo); influence of on authors, *The Dolliver Romance, etc.,* Graves and Goblins; possible experience of, *Our Old Home,* Lichfield and Uttoxeter; transformed to flowers, *American Note-Books,* vol. i., October 25, 1836; type of the communion of the, *Twice-Told Tales,* vol. i., The Vision of the Fountain.

Deafness, an effect of, *American Note-Books,* vol. i., September 9, 1838.

Death, *Mosses from an Old Manse,* vol. ii., The New Adam and Eve, *Septimius Felton,* pp. 107, 108 (12mo); affectation in, *The Blithedale Romance,* chapter xxvii., near the end; gives the warmth to life, *Septimius Felton,* p. 214 (12mo); the great chief marshal, *Mosses from an Old Manse,* vol. i., The Procession of Life; instruments of, *ibid.,* vol. ii., A Virtuoso's

Collection; like the waking from a troubled dream, *American Note-Books*, vol. i., October 25, 1836; a lover of the scenes of, *ibid.*, September 7, 1835; may be deceived, *ibid.*, vol. ii., 1842; memorials of, in all forms of life, *Mosses from an Old Manse*, vol. i., Buds and Bird Voices; the river of, *Mosses from an Old Manse*, vol. i., The Celestial Railroad, end; small account taken of, *The House of the Seven Gables*, chapter xxi.; true idea of character given by, *The House of the Seven Gables*, chapter xxi.; unimportance of the time of, *Septimius Felton*, p. 42 (12mo); works cut short by, *Mosses from an Old Manse*, vol. ii., The Artist of the Beautiful.

Deathless Man, legend of a, *Septimius Felton*, p. 111 *et seq.* (12mo).

Deathlessness, conditions of, *Septimius Felton*, pp. 175–177 (12mo); rules for, *ibid.*, p. 126 *et seq.*

De Blandeville, Earl of Chester, *English Note-Books*, vol. i., September 13, 1854.

Dee, the River, view of, *English Note-Books*, vol. i., October 1, 1853; bridge over, *ibid.*, November 5, 1853.

Dee, Dr. John, magic glass of, *English Note-Books*, vol. ii., December 7, 1857, *Septimius Felton*, p. 196 (12mo).

Deerfield River, the, *American Note-Books*, vol. i., August 31, 1838.

Defiance, Mt., *The Snow Image, etc.*, Old Ticonderoga.

Deficiencies, pride in, *The House of the Seven Gables*, chapter v., middle.

De Grey, Archbishop, tomb of, *English Note-Books*, vol. ii., April 13, 1857.

De la More, Sir John, hall built by, *English Note-Books*, vol. i., September 7, 1853.

De la Motte, Mr., photograph by, *English Note-Books*, vol. ii., September 9, 1856.

Delectable Mountains, the, *Mosses from an Old Manse*, vol. i., The Celestial Railroad.

De Lisle, Lords, crest of, *Our Old Home*, About Warwick.

Deloraine, William of, *English Note-Books*, vol. ii., July 11, 1857.

Delphi, *Tanglewood Tales,* The Dragon's Teeth, *Mosses from an Old Manse,* vol. ii., A Virtuoso's Collection.

Deluge, the, *Our Old Home,* Outside Glimpses of English Poverty.

Deluge, the, on a small scale, *American Note-Books,* vol. ii., April 25, 1843.

Delusions . common to all the world, *The Blithedale Romance,* chapter xv.; that hover around truth, *Mosses from an Old Manse,* vol. i., The Old Manse, toward the end.

Demas, *Mosses from an Old Manse,* vol. i., The Celestial Railroad.

Democracy Unveiled, satiric poem, *Fanshawe, etc.,* T. G. Fessenden.

Democrat, faith in the ideal necessary to a, *Mosses from an Old Manse,* vol. i., The Hall of Fantasy.

Demophoön, Prince, *Tanglewood Tales,* The Pomegranate Seeds.

Demosthenes, allusion to, *Twice-Told Tales,* vol. ii., Footprints on the Sea-Shore, near the end.

Denbigh, *English Note-Books,* vol. i., September 20, 1854.

Denis, St., legend of, *French and Italian Journals,* vol. i., January 9, 1858.

Dennie, Joseph, former reputation of, *Fanshawe, etc.,* T. G. Fessenden, third paragraph.

Dennison, Bishop, *English Note-Books,* vol. ii., June 17, 1856.

Dentist and Preacher, a, *American Note-Books,* vol. i., July 29, 1838.

De Quincey, house of, *English Note-Books,* vol. i., July 21, 1855.

Derby, Earls of, *English Note-Books,* vol. i., September 7, 1853; burial place of, *ibid.*, vol. ii., October 26, 1856; family seat of, *ibid.*, March 23, 1854.

Derby family in Salem, the, *The Dolliver Romance, etc.,* Browne's Folly, *The Scarlet Letter,* The Custom-House.

Derwentwater, Lake and Castle, *English Note-Books,* vol. i., July 21, 1855.

Descriptive Literature, *Our Old Home,* Up the Thames.

Despair, of a strong character, *Twice-Told Tales*, vol. ii., The Shaker Bridal.

Despair, Castle of, *Mosses from an Old Manse*, vol. i., The Celestial Railroad.

De Staël, Madame, residence of, *French and Italian Journals*, vol. ii., June 12, 1859.

Destinies, need of mingling of the darker colors in human, *The Blithedale Romance*, chapter x., end; partial knowledge of events that influence our, *Twice-Told Tales*, vol. i., David Swan.

De Vere, Lord, a character in The Great Carbuncle, *Twice-Told Tales*, vol. i., a type of worldly show and vanity.

Devil, the, *Mosses from an Old Manse*, vol. i., Young Goodman Brown; marks of in the face, *The Blithedale Romance*, chapter xviii.

Devil in Manuscript, The, a story in *The Snow Image and Other Twice-Told Tales*, of the fate of manuscript tales in which an unsuccessful author had tried to paint the character of the devil as conceived in the early superstitions of New England. It is, perhaps, autobiographic to some extent, the fate of the manuscripts in the story being the same as those of "Seven Tales of my Native Land," written somewhere about 1830, and never published.

Devonshire, the Duke of, *English Note-Books*, vol. ii., April 5, 1856, April 11, 1857.

Devotion, the parenthetical, of Italians, *The Marble Faun*, vol. ii., chapter vii.

Dewey, Dr. Orville, *Wonder-Book*, Bald-Summit.

Dial, The, (Boston 1840–44, edited by Margaret Fuller and R. W. Emerson), *American Note-Books*, vol. ii., April 8, 9, 1843; article by Thoreau in, *ibid.*, September 1, 1842; one characteristic of its utterances, *The Blithedale Romance*, chapter vii.

Dickens, Charles. *Mosses from an Old Manse*, vol. ii., P.'s Correspondence; aristocratic aspirations of, *English Note-Books*, vol. ii., April 5, 1856; Barnaby Rudge's raven, *Mosses from an Old Manse*, vol. ii., A Virtuoso's Collection; domestic tastes of, *English Note-Books*, vol. ii., July 11, 1856; Little Dorrit, *ibid.*, vol. i., March 22, 1856; places reminding of, *Our Old Home,* Outside Glimpses of English Poverty; temporary residence of, *French and Italian Journals,* vol. i., January 24, 1858; industry of, *English Note-Books,* vol. i., October 22, 1853.

Dickon, familiar of Mother Rigby in Feathertop, *Mosses from an Old Manse,* vol. i.

Dieskau, Baron, *Grandfather's Chair,* part ii., chapter ix.

Differences of character essential in love, *The Marble Faun,* vol. ii., chapter xvi.

Digby, Richard, character in the apologue, The Man of Adamant in *The Snow Image, etc.,* representing religious bigotry.

Dighton, drum major, *Twice-Told Tales,* vol. ii., Howe's Masquerade.

Dignity of small potentates, *Twice-Told Tales,* vol. ii., The Seven Vagabonds.

Dimmesdale, Arthur, one of the chief characters in *The Scarlet Letter*. He is a clergyman of Boston, and is introduced in chapter iii. His story exhibits the workings of concealed sin and remorse on a delicate and sensitive nature.

Dining, manner of, a mark of civilization, *American Note-Books,* vol. ii., May 6, 1850.

Dining out, *American Note-Books,* vol. ii., April 14, 1844.

Dining-service, design for a, *American Note-Books,* vol. ii., August 10, 1842.

Dinners, in England and America, *Our Old Home,* Civic Banquets; a perfect, *ibid.*; with a colonial governor, *Fanshawe, etc.,* Sir William Phips, sixth paragraph; of the Lord Mayors, *Our Old Home,* Civic Banquets.

Diocletian's Baths, *French and Italian Journals,* vol. i., February 19, 1858.

Diorama, a, *American Note-Books,* vol. i., August 13, 1838.

Dirt, *Our Old Home,* Outside Glimpses of English Poverty.

Disappointment: of poets and artists in their finished work, *The Marble Faun,* vol. ii., chapter xvi.; worst form of, *Our Old Home,* Consular Experiences.

Discomforts, keeping above, *American Note-Books*, vol. i., letter February 7, October 4, 1840.

Disease: among the poor, *Our Old Home*, Outside Glimpses of English Poverty; a respecter of rank, *Mosses from an Old Manse*, vol. i., The Procession of Life; classification of men by, *ibid.*; moral, symbolized, *American Note-Books*, June 1, 1842.

Diseased, the: egotists, *Mosses from an Old Manse*, vol. ii., Egotism; love of exhibiting their afflictions, *Mosses from an Old Manse*, vol. ii., Egotism and The Christmas Banquet.

Diseases, imaginary, cures for, *American Note-Books*, vol. ii., June 1, 1842.

Dismal-View, Mr. (name applied to a Brook-farmer), *American Note-Books*, vol. ii., April 16, 1841.

Disraeli, Benjamin, *English Note-Books*, vol. ii., April 8, 1856.

Dissenters, religious and social, a feeling peculiar to, *The Blithedale Romance*, chapter xi.

Distance, effect of on sublime facts, *Our Old Home*, Lichfield and Uttoxeter.

Distrust, *American Note-Books*, August 22, 1837; toward the age, *Mosses from an Old Manse*, vol. ii., P.'s Correspondence.

Disunionists, a suggested place for, *Our Old Home*, Up the Thames.

Divinity, a backsliding doctor of, *Our Old Home*, Consular Experiences.

Divinity and humanity combined in Christ. See SODOMA.

Dixey, a workingman appearing incidentally several times as a critic of Hepzibah's Experiment, in *The House of the Seven Gables*, principally in chapters iii., xix., and xxi.

Doctors: a London, *English Note-Books*, vol. ii., December 20, 1857; a Pennsylvanian, *ibid.*, vol. i., September 16, 17, 1855; the village, a character in Ethan Brand in *The Snow Image and Other Twice-Told Tales.*

Doctor Heidegger's Experiment, a story of the Fountain of Youth in *Twice-Told Tales*, vol. i.

Dodona, the Oak of, *Tanglewood Tales*, The Golden Fleece.

Dodsley, Robert, grave of, *English Note-Books*, vol. ii., July 11. 1857.

Dogs, *American Note-Books,* vol. i., July 29, August 26, 31, 1838; insight of, *Mosses from an Old Manse,* vol. i., Feather-top.

Dolce, Carlo, picture of the Eternal Father by, *French and Italian Journals,* vol. ii., June 17, July 13, 1858.

Dolliver, Doctor, a character in *The Dolliver Romance,* an honest and simple old apothecary who has come into possession of the elixir of life. He is said to be modeled after Seymour Kirkup. See KIRKUP.

Dolliver Romance, The, an unfinished novel on which the author was engaged at his death. It is founded, like *Septimius Felton,* on the idea of an elixir of life. Three fragments are given. The author's plan seems to have been only imperfectly formed, as the fragments give two different accounts of the source from which the old doctor receives the elixir. The story was to have been published as a serial in the "Atlantic Monthly," but only one part was finished for publication.

Dolls, *Twice-Told Tales,* vol. i., Little Annie's Ramble.

Dolly, chambermaid at Harley College, character in *Fanshawe,* appears in chapter vii.

Domenichino, St. Sebastian by, *French and Italian Journals,* vol. i., February 19, 1858.

Domenico of Venice, death of, *French and Italian Journals,* vol. ii., August 19, 1858.

Dominicus Pike. See PIKE.

Donatello, Count of Monte Beni, a character in *The Marble Faun,* introduced in chapter i. His resemblance to the Faun of Praxiteles is typical of the freshness and naturalness of his character. He is, perhaps, intended as a type of the race in its progress from its primitive kindred with the lower creatures in unconscious simplicity, through transgression and suffering, up to its higher phase of conscious moral choice.

Donkey, anecdote of a, *English Note-Books,* vol. ii., October 7, 1856.

Don Quixote, *Mosses from an Old Manse,* vol. i., Monsieur du Miroir, vol. ii., Passages from a Relinquished Work, A Flight in a Fog, *Our Old Home,* Civic Banquets; Rosinante of, *Mosses from an Old Manse,* vol. ii., A Virtuoso's Collection.

Don Rodrigo, the Goth, *Mosses from an Old Manse,* vol. ii., Egotism.

Doomsday, *Mosses from an Old Manse,* vol. i., The Hall of Fantasy, near the end, vol. ii., The New Adam and Eve.

Doon, the River, *Our Old Home,* Some of the Haunts of Burns.

Dorcas Malvin, the wife of Reuben Bourne in Roger Malvin's Burial, *Mosses from an Old Manse,* vol. ii.

Dorchester Heights, *Grandfather's Chair,* part iii., chapter viii.

Doria Family, palace, portraits, and busts of, *French and Italian Journals,* vol. i., March 10, 1858.

Dorothy Pearson, a character in The Gentle Boy, *Twice-Told Tales,* vol. i.

Doubts of clergymen, *Septimius Felton,* p. 12 (12mo).

Douglas, Earl, murder of, *English Note-Books,* vol. ii., May 10, 1856, July 7, 1857 (both under Stirling).

Douglas, Judge Stephen A., *English Note-Books,* vol. i., October 19, 1853.

Douglass, Dr., *Fanshawe, etc.,* Sir William Pepperell, third paragraph.

Dove, a solitary, *American Note-Books,* vol. i., May 16, 1850, *The Blithedale Romance,* chapter xvii., end.

Doves, Hilda's, *The Marble Faun,* vol. i., chapter vi.

Dow, Gerard, *English Note-Books,* vol. ii., August 9, 1857, *The Marble Faun,* vol. ii., chapter xii.

Downes, Commodore, *American Note-Books,* vol. i., August 27, 1837.

Downing, Emanuel and George, *The Snow Image and Other Twice-Told Tales,* Main Street.

Downing Street, origin of its name, *English Note-Books,* vol. ii., August 7, 1856.

Dragons of Scripture, theory regarding, *American Note-Books,* vol. i., September, 1836.

Dragon's Teeth, The, title of a story in *Tanglewood Tales,* also mentioned in The Golden Fleece.

Drapery in statuary, *French and Italian Journals*, vol. i., June 4, 1858.

Drawings, suggestions for, *American Note-Books*, vol. ii., September 14, 1841.

Dreamers, *Twice-Told Tales*, vol. ii., Night Sketches.

Dreams, *The Blithedale Romance*, chapter v., end; at the moment of awaking, *Twice-Told Tales*, vol. ii., The Haunted Mind; from lighter sorrows, *The Snow Image, etc.*, Old Ticonderoga; of a morbid fancy, a, *The Dolliver Romance, etc.*, Journal of a Solitary man, i.; truth in, explanation of, *American Note-Books*, vol. i., October 24, 1838.

Dress, of colonial times, *Grandfather's Chair*, part ii., chapter vi.; of the eighteenth century, *Twice-Told Tales*, vol. i., The Wedding Knell, vol. ii., Lady Eleanore's Mantle; of the time of Louis XIV., *Fanshawe and Other Pieces*, Sir William Phips, third paragraph.

Drinking, Yankee habits of, *The Blithedale Romance*, chapter xxi.; the true purpose of, *ibid.*

Drinks, favorite, of each stage of potatory life, *The Blithedale Romance*, chapter xxi.

Drinkwater, Sir John, anecdote of, *Our Old Home*, Civic Banquets.

Drowne, Deacon, *Twice-Told Tales*, vol. ii., Howe's Masquerade.

Drowne's Wooden Image, a story in *Mosses from an Old Manse*, vol. ii., the scene of which is laid in colonial Boston. It is a story of the power of love to put the quickening touch of genius to work otherwise merely mechanical.

Drowned, fantasy concerning the, *American Note-Books*, vol. i., October 24, 1838.

Drowning, the ugliest mode of death, *The Blithedale Romance*, chapter xxvii.

Drugs, *The Dolliver Romance*, second fragment.

Druids, memorials of the, *Our Old Home*, A London Suburb.

Drusus, the arch of, *French and Italian Journals*, vol. i., March 3, 1858.

Dryburgh Abbey, *English Note-Books*, vol. ii., May 10, 1856.

Dryden, projected epic of, *Mosses from an Old Manse*, vol. i., A Select Party.

Dry-goods Store, a, *Mosses from an Old Manse*, vol. ii., The New Adam and Eve.

Dudley, Earl of Leicester, *Our Old Home*, About Warwick.

Dudley, Esther, heroine of the tale of that name in volume ii. of *Twice-Told Tales*, one of the last of the loyalists of New England.

Dudley, Paul, stone-wall of, *The Blithedale Romance*, chapter xxiv.

Dudley, Thomas, Governor of Massachusetts, *Grandfather's Chair*, part ii., chapter v., *Twice-Told Tales*, vol. ii., Howe's Masquerade.

Duels, *American Note-Books*, vol. i., December 6, 1837, *Fanshawe, etc.*, Jonathan Cilley.

Dufferin, Lord, *French and Italian Journals*, vol. ii., May 16, 17 1860.

Dumbarton Castle, *English Note-Books*, vol. ii., May 10, 1856, July 2, 1857.

Dumfries, *Our Old Home*, Some of the Haunts of Burns.

Dummer, Lieutenant-Governor, *Grandfather's Chair*, part ii., chapter v.

Duncraggan, village of, *English Note-Books*, vol. ii., July 5, 1857.

Dungeon, a, in every heart, *Twice-Told Tales*, vol. ii., The Haunted Mind.

Dunkirk of America, the, *Fanshawe, etc.*, Sir William Pepperell, first paragraph.

Dunlap's History of the Arts of Design, *Twice-Told Tales*, vol. i., The Prophetic Pictures, note.

Dunmail Raise, *English Note-Books*, vol. i., July 21, 1855.

Duns Scotus, works of in MS., *English Note-Books*, vol. ii., August 31, 1856, Merton College.

Dunster, Henry, President of Harvard, *Grandfather's Chair*, part i., chapter v.

Dunton, John, *Fanshawe, etc.*, Sir William Phips, last paragraph; journal of, *The Dolliver Romance, etc.*, Dr. Bullivant.

Dürer, Albert, "Christ disputing with the Doctors" by, *French and Italian Journals,* vol. i., February 20, 1858.

Durham, *English Note-Books,* vol. ii., August 31, 1856, July 11, 1857.

Dutch Painters, the, *The Marble Faun,* vol. ii., chapter xii. See PAINTERS.

Duttons, the ancient privilege of the, *English Note-Books,* vol. i., October 13, 1853.

Duty, what motives may underlie the idea, *The Blithedale Romance,* chapter xx., middle.

Du Val, pictures by, *English Note-Books,* vol. ii., September 6, 1857.

Dwight, John S., *The Blithedale Romance,* Preface.

Dwight, Timothy, *Mosses from an Old Manse,* vol. i., A Select Party; autograph of, *The Dolliver Romance and Other Pieces,* A Book of Autographs.

Dyer, Mary, *Grandfather's Chair,* part i., chapter vii.

Dying, *The Blithedale Romance,* chapter vi.; a plan for, *ibid.,* chapter xv.

Dying Gladiator, the. See GLADIATOR.

Dyspepsia, *Mosses from an Old Manse,* vol. ii., Egotism.

E——, Mr., of Merton College, *English Note-Books,* vol. ii., article, Oxford.

Eagle: the American, *The Scarlet Letter,* The Custom-House; movement of the, *American Note-Books,* vol. i., September, 1836.

Earl, an English, *English Note-Books,* vol. i., April 12, 1855.

Earth, the, destruction of, *Mosses from an Old Manse,* vol. i., The Hall of Fantasy, near the end; the final taste of, *The Dolliver Romance,* first fragment; weariness of, *Mosses from an Old Manse,* vol. i., The Hall of Fantasy, near the end.

Earthly Deeds, value of, *Mosses from an Old Manse,* vol. ii., The Artist of the Beautiful.

Earth's Holocaust, a sketch or parable in *Mosses from an Old Manse,* vol. ii., of a bonfire for consuming all the worn-out, useless, and hurtful trash in the world.

East Boston, *American Note-Books*, vol. i., June 22, 1835.

Eastham, *English Note-Books*, vol. i., April 3, August 10, 1854.

East Wind, the, *American Note Books*, vol. i., letter, June 11, 1840, August 21, 1840.

Eating-house, fancy about an, *American Note-Books*, vol. ii., December 19, 1850.

Eaton Hall, *English Note-Books*, vol. i., August 24, 1854; flower seen at, *Septimius Felton*, p. 132 (12mo).

Ecclesiastes, the Book of, philosophy of, *Septimius Felton*, p. 124 (12mo).

Echo, suggestion for a tale about, *American Note-Books*, vol. i. December 6, 1837.

Echoes, mountain, *Mosses from an Old Manse*, vol. ii., Sketches from Memory, Our Evening Party among the Mountains.

Ecstasy after long depression, *The Dolliver Romance and Other Pieces*, The Antique Ring.

Eden: after the fall, *The Marble Faun*, vol. ii., chapter v.; allusion to the garb of, *The Blithedale Romance*, chapter iii.; the serpent of, *Mosses from an Old Manse*, vol. ii., A Virtuoso's Collection; spring-time in, *ibid.*, vol. i., Buds and Bird Voices.

Edgar, a character in The Maypole of Merry Mount, *Twice-Told Tales*, vol. i.

Edgartown, Martha's Vineyard, *Twice-Told Tales*, vol. ii., Chippings with a Chisel.

Edgehill, battle-ground of, *Our Old Home*, About Warwick.

Edinburgh, Town and Castle, *English Note-Books*, vol. ii., May 10, 1856, July 9, 10, 1857.

Edith, a character in The Maypole of Merry Mount, *Twice Told Tales*, vol. i.

Edith, a character in The White Old Maid, *Twice-Told Tales*, vol. ii.

Editors of newspapers, good fortune of, *The Snow Image and Other Twice-Told Tales*, Old News, part i.

Education in the Puritan provinces, *Fanshawe and Other Pieces*, Sir William Phips, second paragraph.

Edward the Confessor, shrine of, *English Note-Books*, vol. i., October 5, 1855, *Our Old Home*, Up the Thames.

Edward I., of England, *English Note-Books*, vol. i., September 13, 20, 1854.

Edward II., tomb of, *English Note-Books*, vol. i., June 29, 1856, Gloucester.

Edward IV., relics of, *English Note-Books*, vol. ii., October 30, 1857, *Our Old Home*, About Warwick.

Edward Fane's Rosebud, title of a short sketch in *Twice-Told Tales*, vol. ii. For the suggestion of the story see *American Note-Books*, vol. i., September 7, 1835.

Edward Randolph's Portrait, one of the Legends of the Province House in *Twice-Told Tales*, vol. ii.

Effort, the wholesome effect of, *The House of the Seven Gables*, chapter iii.

Egeria, supposed site of the fountain of, *French and Italian Journals*, vol. i., March 3, 1858.

Egg Rock, *Twice-Told Tales*, vol. ii., The Village Uncle.

Eggs, famous, *Mosses from an Old Manse*, vol. ii., A Virtuoso's Collection.

Egotism, charge of, against the author, *The Snow Image*, dedication; of enthusiasts, *The Blithedale Romance*, end of chapter xix.; of the sick, *Mosses from an Old Manse*, vol. ii., Egotism.

Egotism; or, The Bosom Serpent, a story in *Mosses from an Old Manse*, vol. ii. The serpent, which gives the man an unnatural power of discovering the guilty secrets of other men, is expelled by an emotion that takes him for a moment out of himself. The story first appeared in "The Democratic Review." For a suggestion of it see *American Note-Books*, vol. i., October 25, 1836.

Egremont, the boy of, *English Note-Books*, vol. ii., April 11, 1857.

Egyptian Antiquities, *English Note-Books*, vol. i., September 29, 1855, vol. ii., December 7, 1857.

Egyptian darkness, *Mosses from an Old Manse*, vol. ii., A Virtuoso's Collection.

Eildon Hills, the, *English Note-Books*, vol. ii., May 10, 1856, Melrose, Dryburgh.

Eldredge, Mr., purser of the Niagara, *English Note-Books*, vol. ii., June 25, 1857.

Eleanor, Queen, apartments of, *English Note-Books*, vol. i., September 13, 1854.

Election-week in New England, *The Snow-Image, etc.*, Old News, part i., *The Scarlet Letter*, chapters xxi., xxii., xxiii.; a relic of Whitsuntide, *English Note-Books*, vol. i., May 30, 1855, vol. ii., June 7, 1857.

Elector of Saxony, relic of an, *English Note-Books*, vol. ii., July 28, 1857.

Elgin marbles, the, *English Note-Books*, vol. i., Sept. 29, 1855.

Elijah, cave of, *The Snow Image, etc.*, The Man of Adamant.

Elinor, a character in The Prophetic Pictures, *Twice-Told Tales*, vol. i. An indistinct impression conveyed in her face of something strange in occasional expressions of her lover's is caught by the painter, so that the picture is prophetic of a future settled expression of her features.

Eliot, George. See EVANS, MARIAN.

Eliot, Rev. John, *American Note-Books*, vol. ii., April 28, 1841, *Grandfather's Chair*, part i., chapters vii., viii.

Eliot's Pulpit, *The Blithedale Romance*, chapter xiv.

Eliotson, Dr., *English Note-Books*, vol. ii., April 8, 1856.

Elixir of Life, the subject of the novels *Septimius Felton* and *The Dolliver Romance*, is referred to in Dr. Bullivant and A Virtuoso's Collection, in *Mosses from an Old Manse*.

Elizabeth, character in The Minister's Black Veil, *Twice-Told Tales*, vol. i.

Elizabeth, Queen, *The Dolliver Romance, etc.*, The Antique Ring: associations of, with the Temple, *English Note-Books*, vol. ii. November 12, 1857; portraits of, *ibid.*, July 30, 1857; quotation from, *Fanshawe*, chapter i.; relics of, *English Note-Books*, vol. ii., May 29, 1857, *Our Old Home*, Pilgrimage to Old Boston, near the end.

Ellenborough, Lord, *French and Italian Journals*, vol. i., May 23, 1858.

Ellen's Isle, *English Note-Books*, vol. ii., July 5, 1857.

Ellenwood, Mr., hero of the story The Wedding Knell, in

Twice-Told Tales, vol. i. His character has grown morbid and eccentric by the lack of necessity for exertion, of ties of affection, and objects of interest outside of himself.

Ellesmere, Earl of, residence of, *English Note-Books*, vol. i., September 8, 1855.

Elliot, Commodore, *American Note-Books*, vol. i., August 27, 1837.

Elliston, Roderick, hero of the story Egotism, in *Mosses from an Old Manse*, vol. ii. He is the victim of disease and delusion, and illustrates the tendency to egotism of people with chronic disease or an absorbing passion. To him is imputed the authorship of The Christmas Banquet.

Elwes, Gervase, relationship of, to the Hawthornes, *English Note-Books*, vol. i., May 20, 1854. See HELWYSE

Emerson, R. W., *The Scarlet Letter*, middle of introduction, *American Note-Books*, vol. ii., September 28, 1841, August 5, 15, 22, 1842; gift of Miss Martineau to, *English Note-Books*, vol. ii., July 9, 1856; one character of the essays of, *The Blithedale Romance*, chapter vii.; pilgrimages to, *Mosses from an Old Manse*, vol. i., The Old Manse, toward the end; a schoolmate of, *American Note-Books*, vol. ii., May 14, 1850; talks with, *ibid.*, April 8, 11, 1843; walk with, *ibid.*, October 10, 1842; where "Nature" was written, *Mosses from an Old Manse*, vol. i., The Old Manse, near the beginning.

Emerson, Rev. William, *American Note-Books*, vol. ii., August 8, 9, 1842, December 19, 1850.

Emotions, mixture of, *Mosses from an Old Manse*, vol. i., Rappaccini's Daughter, near the middle.

Emperors of Rome, wickedness of, *French and Italian Journals*, vol. ii., June 8, 1858.

Empiricism, *The Dolliver Romance*, third fragment.

Enchanted Castle, the, *English Note-Books*, vol. i., July 21, 1855.

Enchanted Ground, the, of Bunyan, *Mosses from an Old Manse*, vol. i., The Old Manse, after the middle, The Celestial Railroad, near the end.

End of the World, the, *Mosses from an Old Manse*, vol. i., The Hall of Fantasy.

Endicott and the Red Cross, a sketch from New England history in *Twice-Told Tales*, vol. ii.

Endicott, John, Governor of Massachusetts, *Twice-Told Tales*, vol. i., A Rill from the Town Pump, The Maypole of Merry Mount, The Gentle Boy, vol. ii., Howe's Masquerade; *Grandfather's Chair*, part i., chapters ii., iii., v., *Fanshawe, etc.*, Mrs. Hutchinson, fifth paragraph; first appearance of, in Salem, *The Snow Image, etc.*, Main Street; portrait of, *American Note-Books*, vol. i., August 22, 1837; wife of, *The Snow Image, etc.*, Main Street.

Ends that men toil for, *American Note-Books*, vol. i., December 6, 1837.

Enfield, Rev. William, grave of, *English Note-Books*, vol. i., March 13, 1854.

England, agriculture in, *English Note-Books*, vol. i., September 16, 1855; aristocracy of, *ibid.*, January 3, 1855, vol. ii., July 13, 1856; autumn in, *ibid.*, November 10, 1857; beauty of, *ibid.*, vol. i., July 21, 1855; beggars in, *ibid.*, December 10, 1853; by-ways in, *Our Old Home*, Leamington Spa; charitable institutions of, *English Note-Books*, vol. i., July 1, 1855, *Our Old Home*, A London Suburb; charity children in, *English Note-Books*, vol. i., August 20, 1853; Christmas in, *ibid.*, December 26, 1855, vol. ii., December 31, 1856; churches of, *ibid.*, vol. i. July 1, 1855; class distinctions in, *ibid.*, December 13, 1853; climate of, *ibid.*, June 17, 1854, September 24, 1855, vol. ii., August 10, October 26, 1856, *Our Old Home*, Near Oxford; clouds in, *English Note-Books*, vol. ii., July 3, 1857; crowds in, *ibid.*, December 6, 1857, *Our Old Home*, A London Suburb; curious kind of begging in, *English Note-Books*, vol. i., October 19, 1854; decline of the empire of, *ibid.*, September 30, 1855; deer of, *ibid.*, August 24, 1854; destined fall of old institutions of, *Our Old Home*, About Warwick, near the end; differences of, with America, *English Note-Books*, vol. ii., April 4, 1856; distinction between, and the United States, *ibid.*, vol. i., July 16, 1855; domestic architecture of, *Our Old Home*, Pilgrimage to Old Boston; dwellings of, *English Note-Books*, vol i., March 13, 1854, August 12, 1855; east wind in, *ibid.*,

May 3, 1855; emblem of, *Our Old Home,* About Warwick; feminine beauty in, *ibid.*, A London Suburb; fog in, *English Note-Books,* vol. i., November 14, 1853; fruits of, *ibid.*, July 6, 1854, *Our Old Home,* A London Suburb; funeral in, *English Note-Books,* vol. i., August 22, 24, 1853; geniuses of, *ibid.*, vol. ii., July 30, 1857; gentlemen's seats in, *ibid.*, vol. i., February 19, 1855; handsomest man seen in, *ibid.*, April 12, 1855; hedges of, *Our Old Home,* Recollections of a Gifted Woman; holidays in, *English Note-Books,* vol i., August 8, 20, 27, 1853; homes in, *ibid.*, February 28, 1856, vol. ii., June 17, 1856, Salisbury and Stonehenge, *Our Old Home,* Near Oxford, near the end; hotels in, *ibid.*, Lichfield and Uttoxeter; interest of, *English Note-Books,* vol. ii., June 7, 1857; landscape-gardening in, *Our Old Home,* Leamington Spa; landscapes of, *ibid.*, Recollections of a Gifted Woman; lawyers in, *English Note-Books,* vol. i, March 27, 1855; looks of the lower classes in, *ibid.*, August 17, 1855; magistrates of, *ibid.*, vol. ii., March 1, 1857; manners in, *ibid.*, vol. i., February 27, 1854; monuments to heroes of, *ibid.*, September 28, 1855; mode of carrying burdens in, *ibid.*, August 10, 1853; mountains of, *ibid.*, July 16, 1855; nature in, *ibid.*, July 13, 1855; oaks of, *ibid.*, August 24, 1854; old people in, *Our Old Home,* Recollections of a Gifted Woman; old towns of, *English Note-Books,* vol. i., July 1, September 5, 1855; painters of, *ibid.*, vol. ii., July 28, August 9, 1857; poetic descriptions of, *Our Old Home,* Recollections of a Gifted Woman; police of, *English Note-Books,* vol. ii., March 1, 1857; police court in, *ibid.*, vol. i., January 6, February 20, 1854; populace of, *ibid.*, August 8, 1853; preaching in, *Our Old Home,* A London Suburb; procession in, *English Note-Books,* vol ii., April 19, 1857; railway carriages in, *ibid.*, June 29, 1856; rank of judges in, *ibid.*, vol. i, August 15, 1853; religion in, *ibid.*, August 25, 1855; representative men of, *ibid.*, vol. ii., June 7, 1857; scenery of, *ibid.*, vol. i., August 15, 29, 1853, September 16, 1855, vol. ii., June 29, 1856 (Gloucester), June 7, 1857, *Our Old Home,* Pilgrimage to Old Boston; school-girls in, *English Note-Books,* vol. i., August 17, 1855; schools of, *Our Old Home,* About Warwick;

self-made men of, *English Note-Books*, vol. ii, April 8, 1856; skating in, *ibid.*, vol. i., February 19, 1855; spring in, *ibid.*, vol. ii., May 10, 1857; stone as influenced by the climate of, *ibid.*, vol. i., August 29, 1853, *Our Old Home*, Leamington Spa; stone fences in, *English Note-Books*, vol. i., July 13, 1855, *Our Old Home*, Recollections of a Gifted Woman; summer of, *Our Old Home*, A London Suburb; sunshine of, *English Note-Books*, vol. i., July 6, 1854; tamer aspect of nature in, *Our Old Home*, Recollections of a Gifted Woman; tendency of life and education in, *English Note-Books*, vol. ii., August 31, 1856, Christ Church; trees of, *ibid.*, vol. i., August 8, 1853, March 23, July 19, 1854, *Our Old Home*, Recollections of a Gifted Woman; uncleanliness in, *ibid.*, A London Suburb, Recollections of a Gifted Woman; unfavorable to enthusiasms, *ibid.*, Recollections of a Gifted Woman; verdure of, *English Note-Books*, vol i., August 8, 1853; villages in, *Our Old Home*, Leamington Spa; wild flowers of, *English Note-Books*, vol. i., March 13, 1854; wines used in, *ibid.*, August 8, 1853; winter in, *ibid.*, vol. ii., October 27, 1857; women of, *ibid.*, vol. i., December 13, 1853, June 2, November 28, 1855, January 1, 1856, *Our Old Home*, Leamington Spa, Civic Banquets; yeomen of, *English Note-Books*, vol. i., July 13, 1855.

English, the, amusements of, *English Note-Books*, vol. i., September 13, 1854, August 12, 1855; attitude of, toward intruders, *The Marble Faun*, vol. ii., chapter xxiv.; belligerent tendencies of, *Our Old Home*, Outside Glimpses of English Poverty; caution of, *English Note-Books*, vol. i., December 13, 1853; character of, *Our Old Home*, A London Suburb; charge of asperity toward, *ibid.*, dedication; curiosity of, *English Note-Books*, vol. i., June 20, 1854; delight of, in the sight of butcher's meat, *ibid.*, vol. ii., April 11, 1857; dislike of, to beggary, *Our Old Home*, Outside Glimpses of English Poverty; dress of, *ibid.*, Civic Banquets; drinking habits of, *ibid.*; earthliness of, *ibid.*, end of Leamington Spa; eating of, *English Note-Books*, vol. i., September 27, 28, December 26, 1855, March 6, 1856; effect of success on, *ibid.*, October 6, 1854; feeling of, toward Americans, *ibid.*, vol. ii., May 24,

1856, Manchester and Liverpool, *Our Old Home,* Leamington Spa, end; fees to, *English Note-Books,* vol. i., October 14, 1855, *Our Old Home,* Recollections of a Gifted Woman; first and later impressions of, *ibid.*, Civic Banquets; genius of, *ibid.*, A London Suburb; habit of patching new with old, *English Note-Books,* vol. i., October 11, 1855; humaneness of, *Our Old Home,* Consular Experiences; ideas of Americans of, *English Note-Books,* vol. ii., June 29, 1856, Manchester, *Our Old Home,* Near Oxford, Civic Banquets, near the end; ideas of the battle of New Orleans of, *ibid.*, beginning of Consular Experiences; ideas of funerals of, *English Note-Books,* vol. i., August 24, 1853; ideas of weather of, *ibid.*, May 31, 1855; ignorance of public affairs of, *ibid.*, July 16, 1855; immense blunder of, *Our Old Home,* Up the Thames; in Cromwell's time, *English Note-Books,* vol. ii., May 27, 1857; indifference of, to historical associations, *Our Old Home,* Up the Thames; inevitable question for, *ibid.*, Outside Glimpses of English Poverty, end; intolerance of, *English Note-Books,* vol. i., November 14, 1854; kindness of, *ibid,* end of vol. i., article Battle Abbey, *Our Old Home,* Civic Banquets; legal documents of, *English Note-Books,* vol. i., October 19, 1854; loyalty of, *Our Old Home,* Civic Banquets; manners of, *English Note-Books,* vol. ii., July 13, 1856; morality of, *Our Old Home,* A London Suburb, end; naval heroes of, *ibid.*, A London Suburb; opinion of, among Americans in England, *ibid.*, vol. i., September 29, 1855; oratory of, *ibid.*, vol. ii., December 21, 1856, *Our Old Home,* Civic Banquets; panic excitements of, *ibid.*, near the end; physical characters of, *ibid.*, August 27, 1853, vol. ii., May 10, 1856, *Our Old Home,* Civic Banquets; piracy of, in literature, *American Note-Books,* vol. ii., May 6, 1850; pride of, in having a class above them, *English Note-Books,* vol. i., January 6, 1854; pride of, in nautical superiority, *ibid.*, August 15, 1853; real conservatism of, *Our Old Home,* Civic Banquets; regard of, for literary men, *ibid.*, Up the Thames; rejoicings of, *English Note-Books,* vol. i., October 14, 1855; relations of, with Americans, *ibid.*, December 26, 1855; reliableness of, *Our Old Home,* Consular Experiences, near the end; resemblance of, to the Romans, *ibid*, at the beginning; respect of, for aristocratic pretensions, *ibid.*, Outside Glimpses of English Poverty; reverence of, for old associations, *ibid.*, Leamington Spa; sanctity of dinners to, *ibid.*, Civic Banquets; secret of practical success of, *ibid.*, Consular Experiences; simplicity of, *English Note-Books*, vol. ii., August 9, 1857; sports of, *ibid.*, vol. i., May 30, 1855, *Our Old Home*, A London Suburb; unwise treatment of America by, *ibid.*, Consular Experiences; want of forbearance of, toward American faults, *ibid.*, dedication; wholesome coarseness and peculiar vanity of, *French and Italian Journals*, vol. ii., September 21, 1858.

Englishmen, descriptions of two, *French and Italian Journals*, vol. ii., September 21, 1858.

English Note-Books, Passages from the, were edited by Mrs. Hawthorne, and published in two volumes in 1870. They cover the period from 1853 to 1858, the time of the author's residence in England as Consul at Liverpool.

English, Philip, *American Note-Books*, vol. i., August 27, 1837; house of, in Salem, *English Note-Books*, vol. i., July 1, 1855.

English traveler, an, *Mosses from an Old Manse*, vol. ii., Sketches from Memory, The Canal Boat.

Engraving on glass, specimen of ancient, *American Note-Books*, vol. i., October 24, 1838.

Enjoyment: in literary work, *Twice-Told Tales*, Preface; when good religiously, *The Marble Faun*, vol. ii., chapter vii.

Enna, the Vale of, *Tanglewood Tales*, The Pomegranate Seeds.

Enterprise, common experience on the eve of a new, *The House of the Seven Gables*, chapter iii., beginning.

Enthusiasm: blind, *The Blithedale Romance*, chapter xix., near the end; moods of, *Our Old Home*, Lichfield and Uttoxeter.

Enthusiasts, contact of, with vulgar minds, *The Snow Image and Other Twice-Told Tales*, Ethan Brand.

Ephraim, Father, a Shaker elder in the sketch The Shaker Bridal, *Twice-Told Tales*, vol. ii.

Epimetheus, *Wonder-Book*, The Paradise of Children.

Episcopal service, the, *English Note-Books*, vol. ii., April 12, 1857.

Epitaphs: on Elizabeth Hampson, *English Note-Books*, vol. i., December 1, 1853; on Nathanael Mather, *Fanshawe*, chapter x., end, *American Note-Books*, vol. i., July 4, 1838; on John Treeso, *Our Old Home*, Leamington Spa; triteness of, *Twice-Told Tales*, vol. ii., Chippings with a Chisel.

Equestrian Statues, *English Note-Books*, vol. ii., December 27, 1857.

Erie Canal, the, *Mosses from an Old Manse*, vol. ii., Sketches from Memory, The Canal Boat.

Ernest, hero of the story The Great Stone Face in *The Snow Image and Other Twice-Told Tales.* He grows up under the influence of faith in a future man who shall fulfill an old prophecy of one to come resembling the Face, and in his simplicity not suspecting that he is himself its fulfillment.

Espy, Professor, *Mosses from an Old Manse*, vol. i., The Hall of Fantasy.

Essays, subjects for. See SUGGESTIONS.

Essex, the Earl of, the favorite of Elizabeth, introduced into the legend in The Antique Ring, in *The Dolliver Romance and Other Pieces;* ring of, *Mosses from an Old Manse*, vol. ii., A Virtuoso's Collection.

Essex Historical Society, portraits and relics in its possession, *American Note-Books*, vol. i., August 22, 1837.

Eternity, the idea of, *Twice-Told Tales*, vol. ii., Footprints on the Sea-Shore.

Ethan Brand: a Chapter from an Abortive Romance, a story in *The Snow Image and Other Twice-Told Tales.* It is located in Berkshire County, Mass., and may have been suggested in part by the visit to a lime-kiln described in the *American Note-Books*, vol. i., September 7, 1838.

Etherege, Sylph, heroine of a story of that name in *The Snow Image and Other Twice-Told Tales.*

Etruscan Bracelet, Miriam's, *The Marble Faun*, vol. ii., chapter xxv.

Etty, William, pictures of, *English Note-Books*, vol. ii., August 9, 1857.

Europa, *Tanglewood Tales*, The Dragon's Teeth.

Eurylochus, *Tanglewood Tales,* Circe's Palace.

Eurystheus, King, *Tanglewood Tales,* The Pygmies.

Euston Station, entrance hall of, *English Note-Books,* vol. ii. September 9, 1856.

Evangeline, Longfellow's, foundation of, *American Note-Books,* vol. i., October 24, 1838, *Grandfather's Chair,* part ii., chapter viii.

Evangelist, *Mosses from an Old Manse,* vol. i., The Celestial Railroad.

Evans, Marian (George Eliot), *French and Italian Journals,* vol. ii., February 5, 1860.

Eve, statue of, *English Note-Books,* vol. ii., November 16, 1857.

Evelyn family, representative of the, *English Note-Books,* vol. i., April 1, 1856, Wooton.

Evelyn, John, home of, and manuscripts by, *ibid.*

Evening Party among the Mountains, Our, one of the Sketches from Memory in *Mosses from an Old Manse,* vol. ii.

Events, strangeness of common, if foreseen, *American Note-Books,* 1842; that pass away without actual accomplishment, *Twice-Told Tales,* vol. i., David Swan.

Evidence better than that of the senses, *Mosses from an Old Manse,* vol. i., Rappaccini's Daughter, toward the end.

Evil, effect of a knowledge of, on the innocent, *The Marble Faun,* vol. i., chapter xxiii., vol. ii., chapter xi.; men overestimate their capacity for, *Twice-Told Tales,* vol. i., Fancy's Show Box, mixed with good, *The Marble Faun,* vol. ii., chapter xvii.; of circumstances assimilating the, *Mosses from an Old Manse,* vol. i., The Old Manse, near the beginning; perception of, *ibid.,* vol. i., Young Goodman Brown, vol. ii., Egotism; theory of its necessity for developing intellect and character discussed in *The Marble Faun,* vol. ii., chapters, vi. and xxv., and, in fact, suggested as a problem throughout the volume.

Evil Eye, the, *French and Italian Journals,* vol. ii., August 3, 1858.

Evil Passion, a type of, *American Note-Books,* vol. i., October 25, 1836.

Excavations on the Campagna, *French and Italian Journals,* vol. i., May 8, 1858.

Exchange, the, *Mosses from an Old Manse,* vol. ii., The New Adam and Eve.

Excitements, of English and Americans, *Our Old Home,* Civic Banquets, near the end.

Exhibitions, great, a humbug, *English Note-Books,* vol. ii., July 26, 1857; traveling, *The Blithedale Romance,* chapter xxiii.

Exile, *French and Italian Journals,* vol. ii., September 29, 1858, *English Note-Books,* vol. i., January 16, 1856.

Exiles, feeling of, toward America, *English Note-Books,* vol. i., May 30, 1855.

Experience, *American Note-Books,* vol. i., October 25, 1836; of sorrow in its effect on the intellect, *The Marble Faun,* vol. ii., chapter iv.

F——, English comedian, *American Note-Books,* vol. i., May 11, 1838.

Fabriano, Gentile da, "Adoration of the Magi," by, *French and Italian Journals,* vol. ii., June 17, July 13, 1858.

Faces, few good, in the world, *American Note-Books,* vol. i., August 31, 1835; kind of rudeness in the expression of, *The Blithedale Romance,* chapter xi.

Factory villages, *American Note-Books,* vol. i., July 26, 1838.

Faed, Thomas, *English Note-Books,* vol. ii., April 5, 1856.

Faery Land of romance, none in America, *The Blithedale Romance,* Preface.

Failure, the certain consummation of visions worth having, *The Blithedale Romance,* chapter ii.

Fairfield, Daniel, punishment of, *The Snow Image and Other Twice-Told Tales,* Main Street.

Fairs: Brighton, *American Note-Books,* vol. ii., September 27, 1841; a Florentine, *French and Italian Journals,* vol. ii., September 10, 1858.

Faith, *Twice-Told Tales,* vol. ii., Night Sketches, *Septimius Felton,* p. 12 (12mo); in the future, *Twice-Told Tales,* vol. ii., The Sister Years.

Faith, the wife of Young Goodman Brown, in the story of that name, *Mosses from an Old Manse*, vol. i.

Faith Egerton, character in the story The Threefold Destiny, *Twice-Told Tales*, vol. ii.

Falkland, Lord Deputy, portrait of, *English Note-Books*, vol. ii., July 30, 1857.

Falstaff, *English Note-Books*, vol. i., June 21, 1855; battle-field of, *ibid.*, September 5, 1855.

Fame, *American Note-Books*, vol. i., October 25, 1836; dream of, *Fanshawe*, chapter ii.; posthumous, *The Dolliver Romance, etc.*, Ghosts and Goblins, *Twice-Told Tales*, vol. ii., The Ambitious Guest; real character of, *Mosses from an Old Manse*, vol. ii., Passages from a Relinquished Work, The Village Theatre; sure method of degrading, *ibid.*, P.'s Correspondence; to women, *Fanshawe, etc.*, Mrs. Hutchinson, first paragraph.

Families long residence of, in one place, *The Scarlet Letter*, The Custom-House; old, *The House of the Seven Gables*, end of chapter xii.

Family Party, a, *American Note-Books*, vol. ii., May 8, 1850.

Family record, a curious, *American Note-Books*, vol. i., September 9, 1838.

Famous persons, effect of visits to the haunts of, *English Note-Books*, vol. ii., May 10, 1856, Abbotsford.

Famous places, want of emotion in, *Our Old Home*, Recollections of a Gifted Woman.

Fanaticism, religious, *Twice-Told Tales*, vol. i., The Gentle Boy.

Fancy, its office in brightening the characters of history, *Fanshawe, etc.*, Sir William Phips, first paragraph.

Fancy Ball, suggestion for a, *American Note-Books*, vol. i., October 25, 1836.

Fancy's Show Box, — A Morality, title of one of the *Twice-Told Tales* in vol. i. It deals with the question how far the guilt of an action pertains to the intention unaccomplished.

Faneuil Hall, *French and Italian Journals*, vol. ii., July 2, 1858, *Grandfather's Chair*, part iii., chapter ix.

Fanshawe, a novel published anonymously in 1828, at Boston, by Marsh and Capen. The author afterwards tried to get the whole edition out of the way. It was republished in 1879 by Houghton, Osgood & Company. The scene is laid at Bowdoin College, at about the middle of the eighteenth century.

Fanshawe, hero of the novel of that name, first appears in chapter ii. He is a poor student, devoted to study and ambitious of success, indifferent in general to the outside world, but keen in analysis, and bold in action when his affections are aroused, generous and self-denying.

Farley, Frank, a member of the Brook Farm community, mentioned in the *American Note-Books*, vol. ii., April 14, 1841, and by initial, June 6, 10, 1844.

Far Niente, Signor, *The Snow Image, etc.*, Little Daffydowndilly.

Farquhar, allusion to, *Our Old Home*, Lichfield and Uttoxeter; room where he wrote "The Recruiting Officer," *English Note-Books*, vol. i., September 5, 1855.

Fatality, *Twice-Told Tales*, vol. ii , The Haunted Mind, *Mosses from an Old Manse*, vol. i., The Birthmark, end.

Fate, belief in, *French and Italian Journals*, vol. ii., June 10, 1858; thwartings of, *Mosses from an Old Manse*, vol. i., Rappaccini's Daughter, near the middle; tie of a common, *Twice-Told Tales*, vol. ii., The Ambitious Guest.

Fat Men, *American Note-Books*, vol. ii., May 14, 1850, *Mosses from an Old Manse*, vol. ii., P.'s Correspondence.

Faucett, Helen (Mrs. Theodore Martin), *English Note-Books*, end of vol. i.

Faun, the, a statue by Praxiteles, in the sculpture-gallery of the Capitol at Rome. Its resemblance to Donatello, a character in *The Marble Faun*, alluded to in the first chapter, where the statue is described, and repeatedly throughout the book, may be called the key-note of the story; since Donatello's development from a faun-like simplicity into a higher moral and intellectual nature, through the agency of sin and remorse, forms the burden of the book.

Fauns, *Tanglewood Tales*, The Pomegranate Seeds, *French and Italian Journals*, vol. i., April 18, 22, 1858; not in literature, *ibid.*

Fauntleroy, a character in *The Blithedale Romance*, whose early history is given in chapter xxii. See Moodie.

Faust, pen of, *American Note-Books*, vol. ii., December 19, 1850, *Mosses from an Old Manse*, vol. ii., A Virtuoso's Collection; a servant of, *ibid.*, The Intelligence Office.

Fawkes, Guy, lantern of, *English Note-Books*, vol. ii., August 31, 1856, Bodleian Library.

Fay, Lilias, heroine of the tale The Lily's Quest, *Twice-Told Tales*, vol. ii.

Fear, the inspiration of the feeble, *Mosses from an Old Manse*, vol. i., Feathertop.

Feathertop; a Moralized Legend, last article in *Mosses from an Old Manse*, vol. i.

Federalist party, the, great men of, *The Dolliver Romance, etc.*, A Book of Autographs; feelings of, expressed in "Democracy Unveiled," *Fanshawe, etc.*, T. G. Fessenden.

Feeing Servants, custom of, *English Note-Books*, vol. i., July 30, 1855.

Fees exacted for the sight of celebrated pictures, *The Marble Faun*, vol. i., chapter xx.

Fellow Traveler, A, a sketch in Passages from a Relinquished Work, in *Mosses from an Old Manse*, vol. ii. The traveler is a young preacher, Eliakim Abbott, wandering under supposed divine guidance for the practice of his calling.

Felton, Gaspar, *Septimius Felton*, p. 223 (12mo).

Felton, Septimius. See Septimius Felton.

Ferguson, Sir Adam, *English Note-Books*, vol. ii., July 11, 1857.

Ferry-girl, a Scotch, *English Note-Books*, vol. ii., May 10, 1856, Dryburgh.

Fessenden, Rev. Thomas, *Fanshawe, etc.*, T. G. Fessenden.

Fessenden, Thomas Green, biographical sketch of, included in the volume with *Fanshawe*.

Festival in Italy, a, *French and Italian Journals*, vol. i., May 24, 1858.

Feudal times, forms remaining from, *Our Old Home*, About Warwick.

Fezandie, Mr., *French and Italian Journals,* vol. i., January 9, 1858.

Fiction: an intended, *Our Old Home,* dedication; worn-out characters of, *Mosses from an Old Manse,* vol. i., Feather-top.

Fiddler of York, the, *English Note-Books,* vol. ii., April 11, 1857.

Fiddlers, battle of the, *English Note-Books,* vol. i., September 13, 1854.

Field, D. D., and others, expedition to Monument Mountain, *American Note-Books,* vol. ii., August 5, 1850.

Fielding, *Mosses from an Old Manse,* vol. i., The Hall of Fantasy; locality of a scene in "Tom Jones," *English Note-Books,* June 29, 1856; reminder of, *Our Old Home,* Outside Glimpses of English Poverty.

Fields, James T., *Wonder-Book,* Bald-Summit, *American Note-Books,* vol. ii., May 6, 1850.

Fiend, the, in the heart of man, *Mosses from an Old Manse,* vol. i., Young Goodman Brown.

Fifth of November, practice in New England on the, *The Snow Image, etc.,* Old News, part i.

Fig-tree, cursing of the, *English Note-Books,* vol. i., February 28, 1856.

Fire, *Mosses from an Old Manse,* vol. i., Fire Worship; a faithful guardian, *American Note-Books,* vol. ii., June 9, 1853; potency of, *The Snow Image, etc.,* The Devil in Manuscript.

Fireplaces, open, *Mosses from an Old Manse,* vol. i., Fire Worship.

Fires in Boston, *The Snow Image, etc.,* Old News, part ii.

Fireside, the, of Blithedale, chapters iii., iv.

Fireside, truth to the, *Mosses from an Old Manse,* vol. i., Fire Worship.

Fire Worship, an essay on open fires in, *Mosses from an Old Manse,* vol. i., first published in "The Democratic Review."

Firfield, *English Note-Books,* vol. ii., April 8, 1856.

Fishermen, *Twice-Told Tales,* vol. ii., The Village Uncle.

Fishing, a line and rod for, *American Note-Books*, vol. ii., December 19, 1850; in Boston Harbor, *ibid.*, vol. i., July 10, 1838; in Concord River, *ibid.*, vol. ii., August 24, 1842; in the sea, *Twice-Told Tales*, vol. ii., The Village Uncle; near Augusta, Maine, *American Note-Books*, vol. i., July 20, 1837.

Fitzwilliam, Earl, property of, *Our Old Home*, Pilgrimage to Old Boston.

Five Points, the, *American Note-Books*, vol. ii., 1842.

Flaminian Gate, the, *The Marble Faun*, vol. i., chapter xii.

Flaminian Way, the, *French and Italian Journals*, vol. i., May 24, 1858.

Flaxman, horses of, *English Note-Books*, vol. ii., December 7, 1857.

Fleece, the golden. See GOLDEN FLEECE.

Fleeced, feeling at being, *English Note-Books*, vol. i., October 19, 1853.

Fleming family, monuments of the, *English Note-Books*, vol. i., July 19, 1855.

Flight in the Fog, A, title of a part of the Passages from a Relinquished Work, in *Mosses from an Old Manse*, vol. ii. It records the flight of a young man from his native village, to begin the life of a traveling story-teller.

Flirtation, a, *American Note-Books*, vol. i., August 12, 1837.

Flogging on shipboard *English Note-Books*, vol. i., November 16, 1855.

Florence, notes of a visit to, *French and Italian Journals*, May 30 to September 29, 1858; anecdote of, *American Note-Books*, vol. ii., December 19, 1850; Casa del Bello (residence of the author), *French and Italian Journals*, vol. i., June 4, 1858; cast of gate from, *English Note-Books*, vol. ii., November 16, 1857; churches of, see under CHURCHES.

Florentines, familiarity of the, *French and Italian Journals*, vol. ii., June 21, 1858.

Flowers; at funerals, *The Blithedale Romance*, chapter xxviii.; famous, *Mosses from an Old Manse*, vol. ii., A Virtuoso's Collection; wild, *American Note-Books*, vol. ii., May 1, 4, October 27, 1841, April 20, 28, May 16, 23, 1851.

Flower-shrubs, human, *American Note-Books*, vol. ii., April 26, 1843.

Fluid, the universally pervasive, *The Blithedale Romance*, chapter xxiii.

Flume, the, White Mountains, *Twice-Told Tales*, vol. ii., The Ambitious Guest.

Fogs, London, *English Note-Books*, vol. ii., November 12, December 6, 8, 1857.

Foligno, town and churches of, *French and Italian Journals*, vol. i., May 27, 1858.

Folkestone, *French and Italian Journals*, vol. i., January 6, 1858.

Folsom, Mr., *American Note-Books*, vol. ii., May 5, 1850.

Foot-it-to-heaven, Mr., *Mosses from an Old Manse*, vol. i., The Celestial Railroad.

Footprint, a bloody, *American Note-Books*, vol. ii., December 19, 1850. See BLOODY FOOTSTEP, THE.

Footprints on the Sea-Shore, an essay in *Twice-Told Tales*, vol. ii.

Foreign lands, danger of staying too long in, *The Marble Faun*, vol. ii., chapter xxv.

Foresight, effect of, on common events, *American Note-Books*, vol. ii., 1842; no such thing as, *English Note-Books*, vol. ii., September 17, 1857.

Forest, solitude of a, *Mosses from an Old Manse*, vol. i., Young Goodman Brown.

Foresters, Ancient Order of, *English Note-Books*, vol. i., August 17, 1855.

Forgiveness of God, time for, *The Blithedale Romance*, chapter xxviii., near the end.

Formality of the last century, *The Dolliver Romance and Other Pieces*, A Book of Autographs.

Fornarina in the Barberini Palace, Raphael's, *The Marble Faun*, vol. ii., chapter xii.

Forrester, Adam, a character in The Lily's Quest, *Twice-Told Tales*, vol. ii.

Forrester, Sir, the hero of a legend in *Septimius Felton*, p. 111 *et seq.* (12mo).

Forster, Anthony, tomb of, and character of, in "Kenilworth," *Our Old Home*, Near Oxford.

Fort, an old, in Maine, *American Note-Books*, vol. i., August 12, 1837.

Fortitude, holy, *Twice-Told Tales*, vol. ii., The Shaker Bridal.

Fortunatus, cap of, *Mosses from an Old Manse*, vol. ii., A Virtusoo's Collection.

Fortuna Virilis, temple of, *French and Italian Journals*, vol. i., March 18, 1858.

Fortune, fancy about, *American Note-Books*, vol. i., October 25, 1836.

Fortunes, results of knowing all the possibilities of our, *Twice-Told Tales*, vol. i., David Swan.

Fortune-Telling, *Twice-Told Tales*, vol. ii., The Seven Vagabonds.

Forums: the Roman, *French and Italian Journals*, vol. i., April 15, 1858, *The Marble Faun*, vol. i., chapter i.; Pompey's, *ibid.*, chapter xix.; Trajan's, *ibid.*, chapter xvi.

Foster, Goody, *The Snow Image, etc.*, Main Street.

Foster, Silas, a character in *The Blithedale Romance*, introduced in chapter iii. He is a practical farmer, and has the direction of the out-door work of the communists. His extreme literalness offers a contrast to the ideality of the others, and through it the author laughs a little at his own fancies.

Foundry, visit to a, *English Note-Books*, vol. i., March 6, 1856.

Fount of Tears, the, *American Note-Books*, vol. ii., December 19, 1850.

Fountain of Youth, the, *Twice-Told Tales*, vol. i., Dr. Heidegger's Experiment; the true, *ibid.*, vol. ii., Edward Fane's Rosebud.

Fountains: strange life of, *Mosses from an Old Manse*, vol. ii., Egotism; in Rome, *The Marble Faun*, vol. i., chapter xvi.

Fourier: comparison of his principles with those of Blithedale, *The Blithedale Romance*, chapters vii., xxix.; lemonade theory of, *American Note-Books*, vol. ii., August 7, 1851.

Fowler, lover of the Lady Ursula, *American Note-Books*, vol. ii., 1842.

Fox, John, monument of, *English Note-Books,* vol. i., March 25, 1856.

Fox, Rev. Mr., of Newburyport, *American Note-Books,* vol. ii., March, 1843.

Fragments from the Journal of a Solitary Man, title of an article in *The Dolliver Romance and Other Pieces.* These seem to be parts of the same story as Passages from a Relinquished Work, in *Mosses from an Old Manse,* or a study of the same subject.

France: notes of travel in, *French and Italian Journals,* first part of vol. i. and last of vol. ii.; British antipathy to, *English Note-Books,* vol. i., April 1, 1856; influence of, during the American Revolution, *The Snow Image, etc.,* Old News, part iii.; scenery of, *French and Italian Journals,* vol. i., January 15, 1858; soldiers of, in Rome, *ibid.,* February 9, 1858; winter in, *ibid.,* January 6, 1858; women of, *ibid.,* January 10, 17, 1858.

Francia, pictures by, *French and Italian Journals,* vol. i., February 25, 1858.

Francis, Rev. Convers, life of Eliot by, *Grandfather's Chair,* part i., chapter viii.

Francis, St., convent and dwelling of, *French and Italian Journals,* vol. i., May 28, 1858.

Franconia Mountains, the, profile in, *The Snow Image, etc.,* The Great Stone Face.

Franklin, Benjamin, *True Stories,* chapters vii. and viii. of Biographies (in 16mo ed. only); cap of, *Mosses from an Old Manse,* vol. ii., A Virtuoso's Collection; court suit of, *English Note-Books,* vol. i., Good Friday, 1854; *Twice-Told Tales,* vol. ii., The Seven Vagabonds; in France, *The Dolliver Romance, etc.,* A Book of Autographs; interesting character of, *French and Italian Journals,* vol. i., January 10, 1858; manuscript book by, *English Note-Books,* vol. ii., April 8, 1856; reputation of, *The Dolliver Romance, etc.,* A Book of Autographs.

Frederic, Emperor (Barbarossa), legend of, *English Note-Books,* vol. i., June 30, 1854.

French, the, *French and Italian Journals,* vol. i., January 8,

1858 ; forts of, in America, *Grandfather's Chair*, part ii., chapter vii. ; hatred of, by New England colonists, *Fanshawe, etc.*, Sir William Pepperell, last paragraph ; morality of, *French and Italian Journals*, vol. i., January 15, 1858 ; novels of, *Mosses from an Old Manse*, vol. ii., Earth's Holocaust ; of the Revolution, *English Note-Books*, vol. ii., May 27, 1857 ; relics of kings of the, *French and Italian Journals*, vol i., January 8, 10, 1858.

French and Italian Journals, the, edited by Mrs. Hawthorne, were published in two volumes in 1872. They cover the period from January, 1858, to June, 1859, together with a few entries in England and America, coming down to August, 1862.

French language, the : lessons in, *American Note-Books*, vol i., July 11, 1837 ; speaking, *French and Italian Journals*, vol. i., January 6, 1858.

Frenchmen : the little, at Bridgton, *American Note-Books*, vol. i., July 5, 13, 15, 24, 1837 ; two young, *ibid.*, vol. ii., May 7, 1850, *English Note-Books*, vol. i., November 2, 9, 1854.

French War, the old, *Grandfather's Chair*, part ii., chapters viii., ix.

Freneau, Philip, *Mosses from an Old Manse*, vol. i., A Select Party.

Frescoes, *French and Italian Journals*, vol. i., May 27, vol. ii., June 28, July 4, 1858 ; symbolic of Italian Christianity, *The Marble Faun*, vol. ii., chapter viii.

Friend : as a title of address, *The Blithedale Romance*, chapter xi. ; of mankind, a, *American Note-Books*, vol. i., July 26, 1838.

Friends : at Concord, *Mosses from an Old Manse*, The Old Manse, near the end ; for a death-bed, *The Blithedale Romance*, chapter vi.

Friendship, obligations of, *The Marble Faun*, vol. ii., chapter xvii.

Frontier life, a subject for pictures, *Twice-Told Tales*, vol. i., The Prophetic Pictures.

Fruits, of Italy, *The Marble Faun*, vol. ii., chapter v.

Fruit-trees, relations of, with man, *American Note-Books*, vol. ii., August 9, 1842.

Fuller, Margaret, afterwards Countess d'Ossoli, author of "Woman in the Nineteenth Century," a frequent visitor at Brook Farm, *American Note-Books*, vol. i., letter November, 1840, vol. ii., April 13, 14, 16, September 28, 1841, August 22, 1842, April 8, 9, 1843, *English Note-Books*, vol. ii., July 13, 1856, *The Blithedale Romance*, chapter vii. ; a guest at Concord, *Mosses from an Old Manse*, vol. i., The Old Manse, near the end (name not given).

Fun of the Fair, the, *Our Old Home*, A London Suburb.

Funerals: a city, *Twice-Told Tales*, vol. i., Sights from a Steeple ; a country, *American Note-Books*, vol. i., August 26, 1838 ; a French, *French and Italian Journals*, vol. i., January 9, 1858 ; in Liverpool, a, *English Note-Books*, vol. i., August 22, 24, 1853 ; of an American lady, *ibid.*, January 17, 1855 ; Puritan, *The Snow Image, etc.*, Main Street ; rites of, *The Blithedale Romance*, chapter xxviii. ; suggestion for wreaths for, *American Note-Books*, vol. i., October 25, 1836.

Furnaces, *Mosses from an Old Manse*, vol. i., Fire Worship.

Furness Abbey, *English Note-Books*, vol. i., July 13, 1855.

Gaetano, a vetturino, *French and Italian Journals*, vol. i., May 24–30, 1858.

Gage, General, *Twice-Told Tales*, vol. ii., Howe's Masquerade, *Grandfather's Chair*, part iii., chapter vii.

Gait, expressive of character, *Blithedale Romance*, chapter xviii.

Galba, the Emperor, country residence of, *French and Italian Journals*, vol. i., March 25, 1858.

Galileo: relics of, *French and Italian Journals*, vol. ii., September 3, 1858 ; tomb of, *ibid.*, June 28, 1858 ; tower of, *ibid.*, August 2, 1858.

Galliard, story of, *American Note-Books*, vol. ii., 1842.

Gallows, the, *Mosses from an Old Manse*, vol. ii., The New Adam and Eve.

Gardening, pleasure of, *American Note-Books*, vol. ii., August 10, 1842, June 23, 24, September 23, 1843, *Mosses from an Old Manse*, vol. i., The Old Manse, near the middle.

Gardens : English, *English Note-Books*, vol. i., August 8, 1853; Blenheim, *Our Old Home*, Near Oxford; Boboli, *French and Italian Journals*, vol. ii., June 10, 21, September 10, 1858; Dr. Melmoth's, *Fanshawe*, chapter iii.; Medici, *The Marble Faun*, vol. i., chapter xxii.; Pincian, *French and Italian Journals*, vol. i., April 30, May 23, 1858; Tuileries, *ibid.*, January 12, 1858.

Gardiner, Me., *American Note-Books*, vol. i., July 11, 1837.

Gardner, Captain, fate of, *The Snow Image, etc.*, Main Street.

Garfield, Rose, a character in *Septimius Felton*, with whom, in the first part, the hero is in love. But the author changed his plan, and she appears afterward as the half-sister of Septimius. She is a pretty girl, of healthful and symmetrical nature.

Garments : famous, *Mosses from an Old Manse*, vol. ii., A Virtuoso's Collection; picture of the seamless, *American Note-Books*, vol. ii., May 7, 1850.

Garofalo, pictures by, *French and Italian Journals*, vol. i., March 1, 10, 1858.

Garrets, *Mosses from an Old Manse*, vol. i., The Old Manse, at the middle, *Twice-Told Tales*, vol. ii., Peter Goldthwaite's Treasure.

Garrick, David, early home of, *Our Old Home*, Lichfield and Uttoxeter.

Garroting, suggestion of, *English Note-Books*, vol. i., December 7, 1857.

Gas, natural spring of inflammable, subject for sketch, *American Note-Books*, vol. i., December 6, 1837.

Gascoigne, Mr., an old politician in Dr. Heidegger's Experiment, *Twice-Told Tales*, vol. i.

Gascoigne, Walter, a character in the tale The Lily's Quest, *Twice-Told Tales*, vol. ii.

Gaskell, Mrs., life of Charlotte Brontë by, *English Note-Books*, vol. ii., April 19, 1857.

Gateways, city, *French and Italian Journals*, vol. ii., September 7, 10, 1858.

Gathergold, a rich merchant in the story The Great Stone Face, in *The Snow Image and Other Twice-Told Tales*.

Gavett, Captain, *American Note-Books,* vol. i., August 11, 1838.

Gay, John: the bootblacks in "Trivia," *Our Old Home,* A London Suburb; bust of, *English Note-Books,* vol. i., September 26, 1855; prefaces to fables of, *Fanshawe, etc.,* Mrs. Hutchinson, near the beginning.

Generals, American Revolutionary, represented by royalists, *Twice-Told Tales,* vol. ii., Howe's Masquerade.

Genesee Falls, the, *The Dolliver Romance, etc.,* Rochester.

Geneva, *French and Italian Journals,* vol. ii., June 11, 1859.

Geneva, Lake, *French and Italian Journals,* vol. ii., June 12, 14, 1859.

Genius: dissipation of men of, *Mosses from an Old Manse,* vol. ii., The Artist of the Beautiful; experience of men of, *ibid.,* vol i., The Birthmark, after the middle; in Englishmen, *Our Old Home,* A London Suburb; social qualities of men of, *Mosses from an Old Manse,* vol. i., The Hall of Fantasy; space between, and stupidity, *American Note-Books,* vol. i., October 25, 1835; works of, *Mosses from an Old Manse,* vol. i., The Old Manse, near the middle

Geniuses: the faults of, *Our Old Home,* Recollections of a Gifted Woman; the one who is to create an American literature, *Mosses from an Old Manse,* vol. i., A Select Party.

Genoa, *French and Italian Journals,* vol. i., January 24, 1858, vol. ii., May 29, 1859.

Genteel, the word, *Our Old Home,* Outside Glimpses of English Poverty.

Gentility, *The House of the Seven Gables,* chapters iii., v., after the middle.

Gentle Boy, The, one of the *Twice-Told Tales* in vol. i. It is a story of the Quaker persecution in Massachusetts Colony.

Gentlemen, use of the word, *The Dolliver Romance, etc.,* A Book of Autographs.

Gentle Reader, the, the author's faith in, *The Marble Faun,* Preface.

George, Lake, *Twice-Told Tales,* vol. i., The Prophetic Pictures, *Mosses from an Old Manse,* vol. i., Monsieur du Miroir;

during the French War, *The Snow Image, etc.*, Old News, part ii.

George, St., old sculpture of, *English Note-Books*, vol. i., April 3, 1854.

George I., of England, posthumous visit of, *Mosses from an Old Manse*, vol. ii., A Virtuoso's Collection; rejoicings in Boston on the accession of, *Grandfather's Chair*, part ii., chapter iv.

George II., march played at the funeral of, *Twice-Told Tales*, vol. ii., Howe's Masquerade; statue of, *English Note-Books*, vol. ii., April 13, 1857.

George III., *Grandfather's Chair*, part iii., chapter vi.; birthday of, *Twice-Told Tales*, vol. ii., Old Esther Dudley; pictures of, *English Note-Books*, vol. i., March 24, 1856.

George IV., portrait of, *English Note-Books*, vol. ii., August 31, 1856, Ratcliffe Library.

Georgiana, heroine of the story The Birthmark, in *Mosses from an Old Manse*, vol. i. She falls a victim to her devotion to her husband and he to science.

German, studying, *American Note-Books*, vol. ii., April 8, 9, 10, 11, 1843.

German Stories, *Mosses from an Old Manse*, vol. ii., Earth's Holocaust.

German Trait, a, *American Note-Books*. vol. i., July 24, 1837.

Geryon, *Wonder-Book*, The Three Golden Apples.

Ghebers, *Mosses from an Old Manse*, vol. i., Fire Worship.

Ghetto, Jewish quarter in Rome, *The Marble Faun*, vol. ii., chapter xvii.

Ghirlandaio, frescoes by, *French and Italian Journals*, vol. ii., July 4, 1858; illuminations by, *ibid.*, September 17, 1858.

Ghost-child, the, *The Blithedale Romance*, chapter xxii., middle.

Ghosts, *American Note-Books*, vol. ii., September 13, 1852, *English Note-Books*, vol. i., November 29, 1853; at the Manse, *American Note-Books*, vol. ii., March 12, 1843. *Mosses from an Old Manse*, vol. i., The Old Manse, at the middle; frequency of, in New England, *ibid.;* of Rome's great men, their density, *The Marble Faun* ,vol. i., chapter xvii.; of those not known to be dead, *English Note-Books,* vol. i., June 30, 1854; story of, *ibid.,* vol. ii., July 16, 1856.

Gibbons, Grinling, carvings by, *English Note-Books,* vol. i., March 24, 1856.

Gibson, John, statues by, *French and Italian Journals,* vol. i., March 14, April 3, 22, May 9, June 7, 1858, *The Marble Faun,* vol. i., chapter xiv.

Gideon's fleece, allusion to (Judges, chapter vi., verses 39, 40), *Fanshawe, etc.,* Sir William Phips, second paragraph.

Gifford, William, *Mosses from an Old Manse,* vol. ii., P.'s Correspondence, *Fanshawe, etc.,* T. G. Fessenden.

Gil Blas, *Mosses from an Old Manse,* vol. ii., Passages from a Relinquished Work, A Fellow-Traveler.

Giles, Lawyer, a character in the story Ethan Brand, in *The Snow Image, etc.,* probably suggested by Lawyer H., in the *American Note-Books,* vol. i., July 29, 1838.

Gillie's Hill, *English Note-Books,* vol. ii., July 7, 1857.

Gin-shops, *Our Old Home,* Outside Glimpses of English Poverty.

Giotto, monument of, *French and Italian Journals,* vol. ii., June 17, 1858; pictures of, *ibid.*

Girard, Stephen, *Mosses from an Old Manse,* vol. ii., The Christmas Banquet.

Girls: little, *Tanglewood Tales,* The Dragon's Teeth, *The Blithedale Romance,* chapter xxii., middle; nervous, *ibid.,* chapter xi.; play of, *ibid.,* chapter ix.

Gladiator, the dying, statue of, *French and Italian Journals,* vol. i., February 23, 1858, *The Marble Faun,* vol. i., chapters i., ii.

Gladstone, Robertson, anecdote told by, *English Note-Books,* vol. i., November 14, 1855.

Glasgow, City, Cathedral, and University, *English Note-Books,* vol. ii., May 10, 1856, July 1, 1857.

Glass as building material, *English Note-Books,* vol. ii., November 16, 1857.

Glenfinlas, valley of, *English Note-Books,* vol. ii., July 6, 1857.

Gloom, real nature of, *American Note-Books,* vol. ii., August 30, 1842.

Gloucester, Cathedral and Town, *English Note-Books,* vol. ii., June 29, 1856.

Glumdalca, in Fielding's burlesque tragedy of Tom Thumb, allusion to, *Fanshawe,* chapter vii.

Gnomes, subject for a child's story, *American Note-Books,* vol i., December 6, 1837.

"God save the Queen," *Our Old Home,* Civic Banquets.

Godiva, Countess, picture of, *Our Old Home,* Civic Banquets.

Godstowe, nunnery of, *Our Old Home,* Near Oxford.

Godwin, Mr., *English Note-Books,* vol. ii., April 8, 1856.

Goethe, *Mosses from an Old Manse,* vol. i., The Hall of Fantasy.

Goffe, Mary, a character in The Man of Adamant, in *The Snow Image, etc.,* representing religious charity.

Gog and Magog, *English Note-Books,* vol. ii., July 13, 1856.

Gold, the power to make, *Mosses from an Old Manse,* vol. i., The Birthmark, middle.

Golden Age, the, *Tanglewood Tales,* Introduction, *The Marble Faun,* vol. ii., chapter i.

Golden Fleece, The, title of a story in *Tanglewood Tales.*

Golden Touch, The, the story of Midas told in the *Wonder-Book.*

Gold-mine, The, at Brook Farm, *American Note-Books,* vol. ii., April 14, 16, May 4, June 1, 1841.

Goldschmidt, Madame. See LIND, JENNY.

Goldsmith, Oliver: allusion to, *The Blithedale Romance,* chapter ix.; bust of, *English Note-Books,* vol. i., September 26, 1855; tour of, on the continent, *Mosses from an Old Manse,* vol. ii., Passages from a Relinquished Work, At Home.

Gonzoli, frescoes by, *French and Italian Journals,* vol. ii., June 28, 1858.

Good, narrowness of the, *Mosses from an Old Manse,* vol. i., The Procession of Life.

Good Friday, superstition about, *English Note-Books*, vol. i., Good Friday, 1854.

Gookin, Deacon, a character in the story Young Goodman Brown, *Mosses from an Old Manse*, vol. i.

Gookin, Justice, a character in Feathertop, *Mosses from an Old Manse*, vol. i.

Gookin, Polly, a character in Feathertop, *Mosses from an Old Manse*, vol. i.

Gordier, story of, *American Note-Books*, vol. ii., 1842.

Gore's Directory, *English Note-Books*, vol. i., September 7, 1853.

Gorgon's Head, The, first story in the *Wonder-Book*.

Goshen, Shaker settlement, The Shaker Bridal, *Twice-Told Tales*, vol. ii.

Gosport, Isles of Shoals, *American Note-Books*, vol. ii., September 5, 1852; church records of, *ibid.*, September 16, 1852.

Gothic Architecture, *English Note-Books*, vol. i., July 1, 1855, *Our Old Home*, Lichfield and Uttoxeter. See ARCHITECTURE.

Gothic imagination, gloom of, the, *Our Old Home*, Lichfield and Uttoxeter.

Gothic sublimity, test of, *ibid.*, Up the Thames.

Gough, Charles, *English Note-Books*, vol. i., August 12, 1855.

Government, the, how regarded by Americans and by Englishmen, *English Note-Books*, vol. i., November 14, 1854.

Governors, Colonial, pageant of, *American Note-Books*, vol. i., 1840, *Twice-Told Tales*, vol. ii., Howe's Masquerade; under James II., *The Snow Image, etc.*, Major Molineux.

Gowans, Stephen, a supposition of, *American Note-Books*, vol. i., October 25, 1836.

Gower, Anna, wife of Endicott, *The Snow Image, etc.*, Main Street.

Graciousness, power of, lost by disuse, *Fanshawe*, chapter i.

Graduates, college, *American Note-Books*, vol. i., August 15, 1838.

Grafton, Rose, a character in Edward Fane's Rosebud, *Twice-Told Tales*, vol. ii.

Grandeur, latent aptitude for, *Our Old Home*, Civic Banquets.

Grandfather's Chair, the Whole History of, a volume of stories for children. In the 16mo edition several biographical sketches are added, and the whole is included under the name *True Stories from History and Biography.* The chair, given to Lady Arabella Johnson by her father, the Earl of Lincoln, is used to connect stories of famous persons who might have sat in it, and events of interest in the early history of America. The stories were written from about 1840 to 1842, and published in two parts in those years by Miss Peabody, in Boston, and Wiley & Putnam in New York. It is mentioned in the *American Note-Books*, vol. ii., September 27, 1841.

Grandfather's Library, *American Note-Books*, vol. ii., September 22, 27, 1841.

Grantham, Town and Church, *English Note-Books*, vol. ii., May 28, 1857.

Grapes, wild, *American Note-Books*, vol. ii., September 25, 26, 1841.

Grasmere, *English Note-Books*, vol. i., July 19, 21, 1855.

Gratitude of the world, *Twice-Told Tales*, vol. ii., The Sister Years.

Gravediggers, feeling toward, *English Note-Books*, vol. ii., May 27, 1857 ; mirthfulness of, *American Note-Books*, vol. ii., October 18, 1841.

Graves and Goblins, title of an article in the volume *The Dolliver Romance and Other Pieces.*

Graves, Mr., of Kentucky, duel fought by, *Fanshawe and Other Pieces*, Jonathan Cilley.

Gravestones, *Twice-Told Tales*, vol. ii., Chippings with a Chisel.

Gray Champion, The, first story in *Twice-Told Tales*, founded on a tradition regarding one of the judges of Charles I.

Gray, Thomas, idea of heaven of, *The Snow Image, etc.*, The Devil in Manuscript.

Graylock, or Saddleback Mountain, Berkshire County, Mass., *American Note-Books*, vol. i., July 26, August 11, 31, September 1, 5, 9, 1838 ; *The Snow Image, etc.*, Ethan Brand ; *Tanglewood Tales*, Introduction.

Gray's Inn, *English Note-Books*, vol. i., September 8, 1855, vol. ii., December 6, 1857.

Great Britain, the, Australian steamer, *English Note-Books*, vol. i., August 9, 15, 1853.

Great Carbuncle, The. A Mystery of the White Mountains; a story in vol. i. of *Twice-Told Tales*, founded on an Indian tradition. The tradition is alluded to in *Mosses from an Old Manse*, vol. ii., Sketches from Memory, Our Evening Party among the Mountains.

Greatheart, Mr., *Mosses from an Old Manse*, vol. i., The Celestial Railroad.

Great Orme's Head, *English Note-Books*, vol. i., September 13, 1854.

Great Stone Face, The, a story in *The Snow Image and Other Twice-Told Tales*. It is probably suggested by the profile in the Franconia Mountains at the Notch, though the description of the Face does not correspond to that of the famous profile. The suggestion of the story to the author's mind is recorded in the *American Note-Books*, vol. i., under date of January 4, 1839.

Great Tom, bell of Lincoln, *Our Old Home*, Pilgrimage to Old Boston.

Grecian buildings, *English Note-Books*, vol. ii., August 31, 1856, Ratcliffe Library.

Greek tragedies, nature of their themes, *Tanglewood Tales*, Introduction.

Green Mountain scenery, *American Note-Books*, vol. i., August 31, 1838.

Greene, Gardiner, hill on the estate of, *American Note-Books*, vol. i., June 22, 1835.

Greenough, Horatio, *The Marble Faun*, vol. i., chapter xiv.; a sculptor's opinion of, *French and Italian Journals*, vol. i., April 3, 1858.

Greenwich, *English Note-Books*, vol. i., September 10, 1855, vol. ii., July 6, 1856; *Our Old Home*, A London Suburb.

Gregarious mode of life, a, *Twice-Told Tales*, vol. ii., Peter Goldthwaite's Treasure.

Gregorie, Major, residence of, *French and Italian Journals*, vol. ii., September 11, 1858.

Greta, The River, *English Note-Books*, vol. i., July 21, 1855.

Greville family, the, *Our Old Home*, About Warwick.

Grey, Lady Jane, a book of, *English Note-Books*, vol. ii., December 7, 1857.

Griswold, R. W., allusion to the collection of poetry by, *The Blithedale Romance*, chapter xxix.

Grit, mark of true, *American Note-Books*, vol. i., July 27, 1838.

Grondale, Abbey, *American Note-Books*, vol. ii., 1842.

Grosvenor, Mrs., a character in the story Sylph Etherege, in *The Snow Image and Other Twice-Told Tales.*

Grotesque, the, in ancient architecture, *English Note-Books*, vol. ii., November 30, 1856, Chester, April 11, 1857, *Our Old Home*, Pilgrimage to Old Boston (Lincoln, and near the end).

Grub Street, *English Note-Books*, vol. i., March 25, 1856.

Guasconti, Giovanni, a character in the story Rappaccini's Daughter, in *Mosses from an Old Manse*, vol. i. He is in many respects a weak character and unworthy of the love of Beatrice, whose death is embittered by the discovery.

Guercino, pictures by, *French and Italian Journals*, vol. i., March 26, 1858, *The Marble Faun*, vol. ii., chapter xiii.

Guernsey, Island of, incident on, *American Note-Books*, vol. ii., 1842.

Guernsey Lily, the, *English Note-Books*, vol. i., October 22, 1853.

Guicciardini, palace of, *French and Italian Journals*, vol. ii., June 28, 1858.

Guido, *French and Italian Journals*, vol. i., April 16, 1858; Aurora of, *ibid.*, February 20, 1858 ; Beatrice Cenci of, *ibid.*, February 20, 1858, *The Marble Faun*, vol. i., chapter vii., vol. ii., chapter xxiv. ; face of Hope by, *French and Italian Journals*, vol. i., April 16, 1858 ; Judith by, *ibid.*, May 21, 1858 ; Michael by, *ibid.*, February 21, 1858, May 15, 1859, *The Marble Faun*, vol. i., chapters xv., xx.

Guildhall: of London, *English Note-Books*, vol. ii., July 13, 1856, April 13, 1857 ; of York, *ibid.*, April 13, 1857.

Guilt: deceptions of, *Mosses from an Old Manse*, vol. i., The Procession of Life; effect of, on the innocent, *The Marble Faun*, vol. i., chapter xxiii.; first rapture and after effects of, *ibid.*, vol. i., chapters xix., xx.; moral seclusion of, *ibid.*, chapter xix.; of unaccomplished deeds, *Twice-Told Tales*, vol. i., Fancy's Show Box.

Guiltiest, brotherhood of all with the, *Twice-Told Tales*, vol. i., Fancy's Show Box.

Gulls, movement of, *American Note-Books*, vol. ii., April 25, 1843, *Mosses from an Old Manse*, vol. i., Buds and Bird Voices.

Gun, the largest in the world, *English Note-Books*, vol. i., March 6, 1856.

Gustavus Adolphus, *True Stories*, chapter ix. of Biographies. (In 16mo ed. only.)

Gwyn, Nell, dairy of, *English Note-Books*, vol. i , September 13, 1855; portrait of, *ibid.*, vol. ii., May 29, 1857.

Gyges, ring of, *Mosses from an Old Manse*, vol. ii., A Virtuoso's Collection.

H ——, H., of Boston, singular character of, *American Note-Books*, vol. i., October 24, 1838.

H ——, Miss, English literary lady, *English Note-Books*, vol. i., August 24, 1853.

H ——, Mr., shipwright of Boston, *English Note-Books*, vol. i., February 18, 1856.

H ——, Monsieur, French consul at Liverpool, *English Note-Books*, vol. i., August 9, 1853.

Haddo, Lord, *English Note-Books*, vol. i., February 18, 1856.

Haddock, the, marks of St. Peter's fingers on, *Twice-Told Tales*, vol. ii., The Village Uncle.

Hades: climate of, *French and Italian Journals*, vol. ii., September 11, 1858; gate of, *Mosses from an Old Manse*, vol. ii., A Virtuoso's Collection.

Hadrian, tomb of. See CASTLE OF ST. ANGELO.

Hagburn, Robert, a character in *Septimius Felton*, whose frank and careless nature forms a contrast to that of Septimius.

Hair, a story of, *English Note-Books,* vol. i., Good Friday, 1854.

Haley family, the, *American Note-Books,* vol. ii., September 11, 1852.

Hall, Colonel, *American Note-Books,* vol. ii., April 14, 1844.

Hall, Mr. and Mrs. S. C., *English Note-Books,* vol. ii., April 8, July 9, August 7, 21, 31, September 9, 1856.

Hall of Fantasy, The, a sketch in *Mosses from an Old Manse,* vol. i. It is a description of a fantastic gathering of people dominated by the imagination, amid a collection of things having no existence but in fancy.

Halleck, Fitz-Greene, *Mosses from an Old Manse,* vol. ii., P.'s Correspondence.

Hamadryads, the, *Tanglewood Tales,* The Pomegranate Seeds.

Hamilton, Alexander, *The Dolliver Romance and Other Pieces,* A Book of Autographs.

Hamilton, Edward. See VAUGHAN.

Hampson, Elizabeth, epitaph of, *English Note-Books,* vol. i., December 1, 1853.

Hampton Court, *English Note-Books,* vol. i., March 24, vol. ii., September 9, 1856.

Hancock, John, *Twice-Told Tales,* vol. ii., Old Esther Dudley, *Grandfather's Chair,* part iii., chapter vi.; actual and historical characters of, *The Dolliver Romance and Other Pieces,* A Book of Autographs; letter from, *ibid.*

Hannah, a character in The Great Carbuncle, *Twice-Told Tales,* vol. i.

Happiness, *American Note-Books,* vol. ii., August 5, 1842, July 9, 1843, November 3, 1851; a man's, destroyed by himself, *ibid.,* vol. i., July 13, 1838; dying without one's, *The Dolliver Romance, etc.,* Journal of a Solitary Man, i.; in uses of things not originally intended, *English Note-Books,* vol. ii., May 28, 1857; often close at hand, *American Note-Books,* vol. i., August 22, 1837, — the moral of The Threefold Destiny; personal experience of, *ibid.,* vol. ii., March 31, April 7, 1843; search for, *ibid.,* vol. i., January 4, 1839.

Harcourt family, the, home and tombs of. See STANTON HARCOURT.

Hardships, voluntary, *The Blithedale Romance*, chapter iv.
Harley College, the scene of *Fanshawe*, drawn from Bowdoin College, Brunswick, Me. It is described in the first chapter.
Harmonia, Queen, *Tanglewood Tales*, The Dragon's Teeth.
Harness, Rev. Mr., *English Note-Books*, vol. ii., April 8, 1856.
Harold, King, carved face, and place of death of, *English Note-Books*, end of vol. i., Battle Abbey; chapel built by a sister of, *ibid.*, vol. ii., May 10, 1856, Edinburgh Castle.
Harpies, The, *Tanglewood Tales*, The Golden Fleece.
Harris, Dr., anecdote of, *American Note-Books*, vol. ii., 1842.
Harris, Rev. Mr., Master of Leicester's Hospital, *Our Old Home*, About Warwick.
Harris, Thomas L., spiritualistic poet, *English Note-Books*, vol. ii., December 20, 1857.
Harrowby, Earl of, *English Note-Books*, vol. i., September 26, 1854.
Harte, Joel T., busts by, *French and Italian Journals*, vol. i., June 7, 1858.
Hartford, settlement of, *Grandfather's Chair*, part i., chapter iv.
Harvard College: establishment of, *Grandfather's Chair*, part i., chapter v.; library of, *Mosses from an Old Manse*, vol. ii., The New Adam and Eve.
Hastings, town of, *English Note-Books*, end of vol. i.
Hastings, Gervayse, hero of the story The Christmas Banquet, *Mosses from an Old Manse*, vol. ii. He is a man conscious of the lack of reality in his nature, and has a sense that he is thereby miserable, yet from the fact itself is incapable of feeling his misery.
Hatch, Mr., *American Note-Books*, vol. ii., September 5, 1852.
Hathorne. See HAWTHORNE.
Hatred, relation of, to love, *The Scarlet Letter*, chapter xxiv., *Mosses from an Old Manse*, vol. ii., Egotism, *Twice-Told Tales*, vol. ii., Chippings with a Chisel.
Hatton, town and church, *Our Old Home*, Leamington Spa.
Hatton, Sir Christopher, *English Note-Books*, vol. ii., November 12, 1857.
Haunted Mind, The, an essay in *Twice-Told Tales*, vol. ii., a

study of the action of the mind between sleeping and waking.

Havre, *French and Italian Journals,* vol. ii., June 22, 1859.

Hawkshead, *English Note-Books,* vol. i., July 21, 1855.

Hawkwood, Squire, *Twice-Told Tales,* vol. ii., The Threefold Destiny.

Hawthorne, spelling of the name, *The Dolliver Romance, etc.,* Time's Portraiture, note.

Hawthorne family (formerly Hathorne), the, in America, *American Note-Books,* vol. i., August 27, 1837, *The Scarlet Letter,* The Custom-House ; in England, *American Note-Books,* vol. i., October 25, 1836, August 22, 1837, *English Note-Books,* vol. i., October 9, 1854 ; hall of, *ibid.,* December 1, 1853.

Hathorne, Judge John, *American Note-Books,* vol. i., August 27, 1837, July 4, 1838.

Hathorne, Major William, *Grandfather's Chair,* part i., chapter v., *The Snow Image, etc.,* Main Street ; a letter of, *English Note-Books,* vol. ii., July 13, 1856.

Hawthorne, E., *American Note-Books,* vol. i., August 27, 1837.

Hawthorne, Henry Atte, *English Note-Books,* vol. ii., August 10, 1856.

Hawthorne, John, *English Note-Books,* vol. i., January 30, 1854.

Hawthorne, Nathaniel, objectivity of the writings of, *American Note-Books,* vol. ii., March, 1843 ; obscurity of, *Twice-Told Tales,* Preface, *The Snow Image,* dedication ; reserve of, *American Note-Books,* vol. ii., March, 1843 ; subject of sermons and lectures, *ibid. ;* view of his life, *English Note-Books,* vol. i., December 25, 1854.

Hawthorne, Mrs. Sophia, Una, Julian, and **Rose,** wife and children of the author, mentioned often by initial in the Note-Books.

Haydon, B. R., pictures of, *English Note-Books,* vol. i., September 28, 1855, March 25, 1856, vol. ii., July 28, 1857.

Haynes, John, Governor of Massachusetts, *Twice-Told Tales,* vol. ii., Howe's Masquerade.

Hazard, Lieutenant, *American Note-Books,* vol. i., June 16, 1838.

Hazles, The, residence of Sir Thomas Birch, *English Note-Books,* vol. i., March 23, 1854.

Heart, the, *Mosses from an Old Manse,* vol. ii., Earth's Holocaust, end; the great conservative, *English Note-Books,* vol. i., January 6, 1854; journal of, *American Note-Books,* vol. i., August 22, 1837.

Hearths, fighting for, *Mosses from an Old Manse,* vol. i., Fire Worship.

Hearts, exchange of, *Mosses from an Old Manse,* vol. ii., The Intelligence Office.

Heaven, knowledge of, *American Note-Books,* vol. ii., September 27, 1841; peculiar feeling about, *ibid.,* vol. i., October 24, 1838; recognition in, *ibid.,* 1840.

Heber, Reginald, *Mosses from an Old Manse,* vol. ii., P.'s Correspondence.

Hecate, *Tanglewood Tales,* The Pomegranate Seeds.

Hedda, Abbot, memorial of, *English Note-Books,* vol. ii., May 27, 1857.

Hedges, in the Netherlands, *American Note-Books,* vol. i., October 25, 1836.

Heights, the impulse to jump from, *The Marble Faun,* vol. ii., chapter iv.

Helicon, Mt., *Wonder-Book,* The Chimæra.

Hell, what men would make of it, *French and Italian Journals,* vol. i., May 15, 1858.

Helle, *Tanglewood Tales,* The Golden Fleece.

Helps, Arthur, *English Note-Books,* vol. ii., April 8, 1856.

Helvellyn, *English Note-Books,* vol. i., July 21, 1855.

Helwyse, Jervase, a character in Lady Eleanore's Mantle, *Twice-Told Tales,* vol. ii. The name appears in the Hawthorne records as borne by a relative in the latter part of the seventeenth century.

Henry VIII., of England, picture of, *English Note-Books,* vol. i., March 25, 1856.

Henry IV., of France, place of assassination of, *French and*

Italian Journals, vol. i., January 9, 1858; relic of, *English Note-Books*, vol. ii , July 28, 1857.

Henry IV., of Germany, reputed tomb of, *English Note-Books*, vol. ii., November 30, 1856.

Hens, converse of, *American Note-Books*, vol. ii., August 10, 1842; manner of, *ibid.*, July 16, 1850; worth studying, *The House of the Seven Gables*, middle of chapter x.

Herald, The New York, not an exponent of American opinion, *English Note-Books*, vol. ii., May 24, 1856, Manchester.

Hercules, *Wonder-Book*, The Three Golden Apples, *Tanglewood Tales*, The Pygmies.

Heredity, *The House of the Seven Gables*, chapter viii.; illustrated by the two daughters of Fauntleroy, *The Blithedale Romance*, chapter xxii. ; how shown, *The Marble Faun*, vol. ii., chapter i.

Herkimer, George, a sculptor in the story Egotism, in *Mosses from an Old Manse*, vol. ii. He also appears in connection with The Christmas Banquet.

Hermitage, Coverdale's, *The Blithedale Romance*, chapters xii., xxiv.

Hermit's Vow, a, *Twice-Told Tales*, vol. ii., Footprints on the Sea-Shore.

Herodias, the daughter of, Miriam's sketch of, *The Marble Faun*, vol. i., chapter v.

Heroes: faces of, *Our Old Home*, A London Suburb; need a heroic world, *American Note-Books*, vol. ii., May 7, 1850.

Heroism, as distinguished from absurdity, *The Blithedale Romance*, near the end of chapter xix.; one degree of, *ibid.*, near the end ; the truest, *ibid.*, chapter ii.

Hesperides, gardens of the, *Wonder-Book*, The Three Golden Apples, *Tanglewood Tales*, The Pygmies.

Heytebury, Lord, *English Note-Books*, vol. i., September 26, 1855.

Heywood, John, *English Note-Books*, vol. i., September 22, 1854, April 7, 1855.

Heywood, Mrs., dinner party of, *English Note-Books*, vol. ii., July 10, 1856.

Hibbins, Mistress, sister of Governor Bellingham, *The Scarlet Letter*, chapters ii., viii., xii., xx., xxii.

Higgins, Ned, a voracious urchin introduced into *The House of the Seven Gables*, in chapter iii., and appearing several times in the course of the story.

Higgins, Susan, *Twice-Told Tales*, vol. ii., Howe's Masquerade.

Higginson, Rev. Francis, Salem, *Twice-Told Tales*, vol. i., A Rill from the Town Pump, *The House of the Seven Gables*, chapter i., *Grandfather's Chair*, part i., chapter ii.

Highlanders, costume of the, *English Note-Books*, vol. ii., May 10, 1856.

Highlands, The Scottish, *English Note-Books*, vol. ii , May 10, 1856, York, July 2 to 8, 1857.

Hilda, a character in *The Marble Faun*, introduced in chapter i. She is a young New England girl, studying art in Rome, of peculiarly pure and beautiful character, whose moral struggle and discipline come through an accidental knowledge of the sin of others. Her personal appearance is described in vol. i., chapter vii. Her appreciation of the old painters and skill in copying them are made to depend on her perfect whiteness of soul and ignorance of evil. (See vol. i., chapter vi.) Signor Panini's picture of, vol. ii., chapter xi.; tower of, vol. i., chapter vi. The original of Hilda's tower is described in the *French and Italian Journals*, vol. i., May 15, 1858.

Hildreth, Richard, author of History of the United States, *American Note-Books*, vol. ii., May 5, 1850.

Hillard, George S., *American Note-Books*, vol. ii., September 27, 1841, August 15, 1842, *Mosses from an Old Manse*, vol. i., The Old Manse, at the middle, *The Scarlet Letter*, The Custom-House, middle.

Hill Difficulty, *Mosses from an Old Manse*, vol. i., The Celestial Railroad.

Hill scenery and towns of Italy, *The Marble Faun*, vol. ii., chapter viii.

Hills, in summer and autumn, *American Note-Books*, vol. ii., October 18, 1841.

Hinchman, Rev. Mr., *English Note-Books*, vol. ii., June 17, 1856, Stonehenge.

Hints, for a character, *American Note-Books*, vol. ii., December 19, 1850; for stories, sketches, and essays, see SUGGESTIONS.

Hippodamia, Princess, *Wonder-Book*, The Gorgon's Head.

Hippolyta, *Wonder-Book*, The Three Golden Apples.

Hispaniola, wreck off the coast of, *Fanshawe and Other Pieces*, Sir William Phips, second paragraph.

Historic Scenes, *Mosses from an Old Manse*, vol. i., The Old Manse, near the beginning.

History, kind of knowledge given by, *Fanshawe and Other Pieces*, Sir William Phips, first paragraph.

Hodge, Otis, *American Note-Books*, vol. i., July 29, August 23, 1838.

Hogarth, pictures of, *English Note-Books*, vol. ii., July 28, August 9, 1857.

Holbein, masterpiece of, *Our Old Home*, Civic Banquets, *English Note-Books*, vol. i , March 25, 1856.

Holborn, *English Note-Books*, vol. i., September 8, 1855.

Holgrave, a character in *The House of the Seven Gables*. He is a young man of versatile talent and a complete radical, with no reverence for family pretensions, — a type of the American spirit as contrasted with the antiquated claims of the Pyncheons.

Holidays, Yankee intolerance of, *The Blithedale Romance*, chapter xvi.

Holinshed, Raphael, citation from, *American Note-Books*, vol. i., September, 1836.

Holland, Mr., *English Note-Books*, vol. i., October 22, 1853.

Holles, Gervayse portrait of, *English Note-Books*, vol. ii., July 30, 1857. See ELWES and HELWYSE.

Hollingsworth, one of the principal characters in *The Blithedale Romance*, first appearing in chapter iv. He is a philanthropist, aiming at the establishment of an institution for reforming criminals. He has been a blacksmith, and is a man of narrow cultivation, but intense will and earnestness. The growing distortion of his mind and conscience in the pursuit of his aim, out of which arise his relations to Zenobia and Priscilla, brings on the catastrophe of the story, and is one of the chief interests in it. His theory and purpose are described in chapter v., his piety is alluded to at the beginning of chapter vi., his tenderness in the middle of the same chapter, his motives for joining the communists in chapter vii., his oratory in chapter xiv.; his scheme is declared in chapter xv.

Hollow of the Three Hills, The, a short sketch in vol. i. of *Twice-Told Tales*, a witch-story symbolic of the action of remorse.

Holmes, Oliver Wendell, *Wonder-Book*, Bald-Summit.

Holofernes, see JUDITH.

Holy Isle, *English Note-Books*, vol. ii., May 10, 1856, Newcastle.

Holyrood Palace, *English Note-Books*, vol. ii., May 10, 1856, July 8, 9, 1857.

Holywell Street, London, *English Note-Books*, vol. i., September 30, 1855.

Home: changes of, *English Note-Books*, vol. i., September 2, 1853; the instinct for, *The House of the Seven Gables*, chapter ix., toward the end; pleasure in, *American Note-Books*, vol ii., August 7, October 10, November 24, 1842, March 31, 1843; right to a, *English Note-Books*, vol. i., February 19, 1855.

Home, D. D., spiritualistic medium, *French and Italian Journals*, vol. ii., June 9, September 1, 11, 29, 1858.

Homelessness, *English Note-Books*, vol. i., July 30, 1855.

Homer, *Mosses from an Old Manse*, vol. i., The Hall of Fantasy.

Homes, *Our Old Home*, Recollections of a Gifted Woman, end; of great men, *English Note-Books*, vol. ii., July 11, 1857; pleasant, *ibid.*, May 27, 1857.

Home-sickness, *The Blithedale Romance*, chapter xviii.

Honesty, a delightful pastime, *The Blithedale Romance*, chapter xvi., near the end.

Honey, Mrs., lodging house of, *English Note-Books*, vol. ii., August 9, September 10, 1857.

Hocker, Rev. Thomas, *Grandfather's Chair*, part i., chapter iv.

Hooper, Rev. Mr., *Twice-Told Tales*, vol. i., The Minister's Black Veil.

Hoosic Mountain, *American Note-Books*, vol. i., August 31, 1838.

Hope, *Twice-Told Tales*, vol. ii., The Haunted Mind, *Wonder-Book*, The Paradise of Children.

Hopeless Company, a, *American Note-Books*, vol. i., December 6, 1837.

Horatius Cocles, bridge defended by, *French and Italian Journals*, vol. i., March 18, 1858.

Horseshoe crab, the, *Twice-Told Tales*, vol. ii., Footprints on the Sea-Shore.

Horticultural Register, the, newspaper, *Fanshawe and Other Pieces*, T. G. Fessenden.

Hosmer, Harriet, *French and Italian Journals*, vol. i., April 3, May 23, 1858, vol. ii., March 15, 1859, *The Marble Faun*, Preface, vol. i., chapter xiii.

Hospitals, visits to, *English Note-Books*, vol. i., May 20, 1854, November 16, 1855; suggestion for tales of the inmates of, *ibid.*, vol. ii., October 10, 1857.

Hotel-life, for families, *American Note-Books*, vol. i., May 11, 1838; in England, *English Note-Books*, vol. i., July 30, 1855.

Hotels: charges at, *English Note-Books*, vol. ii., June 18, 1856; people at a, *American Note-Books*, vol. i., May 11, 1838; various classes of, subject for an article, *ibid.*, October 16, 1837.

Hotels, American: at Appledore, Laighton's, *American Note-Books*, vol. ii., August 30, September 8, 1852; near Augusta, Maine, Robinson's, *ibid.*, vol. i., July 20, 1837; in Boston, *ibid.*, June 22, 1835, May 11, June 16, 1838; in East Boston, *ibid.*, June 22, 1835; at Nahant, *ibid.*, August 31, 1835; at Worcester, Temperance House, *ibid.*, July 27, 1838.

Hotels, English: at Boston, the Peacock, *Our Old Home*, Pilgrimage to Old Boston; at Chester, the Royal, *English Note-Books*, vol. i., October 1, 1853; at Lake Windermere, Lowwood, *ibid.*, July 16, 1855; at Lichfield, the Black Swan, *Our Old Home*, Lichfield and Uttoxeter; at Lincoln, the Saracen's Head, *ibid.*, Pilgrimage to Old Boston; at Liverpool, American, *English Note-Books*, vol. i., September 14, 1853; at Oxford, Crown Inn, *ibid.*, vol. ii., August 31, 1856; at Woodstock, the Black Bear, *Our Old Home*, Near Oxford.

Hotels, French: at Lyons, Hotel de Provence; at Marseilles, Hotel d'Angleterre; at Paris, Hotel de Louvre, *French and Italian Journals*, vol i., January 15, 1858.

Hotels, Italian: at Florence, Della Fontana, *French and Italian Journals*, vol. i., May 30, 1858, To Florence; at Foligno, *ibid.*, May 27, 1858; at Incisa, *ibid.*, May 30, 1858; at Perugia, *ibid.*, May 28, 1858; at Terni, Tre Colonne, *ibid.*, May 25, 1858.

Hotels, Scotch: at Mauchline, Posie Nansie's Inn, *Our Old Home*, Some of the Haunts of Burns.

Hotels, Swiss: at Lake Geneva, Byron, *French and Italian Journals*, vol. ii., June 12, 14, 1859.

Hotspur, battle-field of, *English Note-Books*, vol. i., September 5, 1855.

Houdon, Jean Antoine, statues of St. Bruno and of Washington by, *French and Italian Journals*, vol. i., February 19, 1858.

Housatonia, the (flower), *Wonder-Book*, The Hill-Side.

House of Commons, visit to the, *English Note-Books*, vol. ii., April 8, 1856.

House of the Seven Gables, The, A Romance. This book was written in Lenox, Mass., in 1850–1 and published in Boston by Ticknor, Reed and Fields in 1851. The scene is laid in Salem, Mass., in an old house, the original of which is supposed to be the house in Salem formerly known as "The Curwen House," or "The Witch House," and drawings from an old painting of it have been used in illustration of the story, although the author is understood to have said that he had no particular house in mind. The Curwen House is alluded to in the article "Main Street," in the volume *The Snow Image.* The story deals with the history of a family, the Pyncheons, on whom rested a hereditary curse in consequence of the wrong-doing of an ancestor. A suggestion of the curse in the story may be found in the one invoked upon an ancestor of the author, alluded to in the *American Note-Books,* vol. i., August 27, 1837. The book is alluded to in the *English Note-Books,* vol. ii., April 4, 1856.

Houses: dwellings of generations, *The Marble Faun,* vol. ii., chapter viii.; not built for homes, *Our Old Home,* Leamington Spa; old, *American Note-Books,* vol. ii , October 8, 1841, *Twice-Told Tales,* vol. ii., Edward Randolph's Portrait, at the end; old English, arrangements of, *American Note-Books,* vol. i., September, 1836, *English Note-Books,* vol. ii., June 11, 1856; old, of New England, *The Snow Image,* Main Street.

Hovenden, Peter, and his daughter Annie, characters in the story The Artist of the Beautiful, *Mosses from an Old Manse,* vol. ii., types of worldly natures, though Annie's is idealized by the imagination of her artist-lover.

Howadji. See CURTIS, GEORGE WILLIAM.

Howe, Sir William, *Twice-Told Tales,* vol. ii., Howe's Masquerade, Old Esther Dudley, *Grandfather's Chair,* part iii., chapters viii., ix.; John Adams on, *The Dolliver Romance, etc.,* A Book of Autographs.

Howe's Masquerade, one of the legends of the Province House in *Twice-Told Tales,* vol. ii. A suggestion of it may be found in the *American Note-Books,* vol. i., 1840.

Howes, Mr., *American Note-Books,* vol. ii., April 14, 1844.

Howitt, William and Mary, *English Note-Books,* April 4, 8, 1856.

Howorth, Miss F., *French and Italian Journals,* vol. ii., June 9, 1858.

Howorth, Mr., a picture-cleaner in *Twice-Told Tales,* vol. ii., Edward Randolph's Portrait.

Huckleberry, name given to one of the children to whom the stories of the *Wonder-Book* and *Tanglewood Tales* were told.

Hudson, Captain, of the Niagara, *English Note-Books,* vol. ii., June 25, 1857.

Hudson's Brook, *American Note-Books,* vol. i., August 11, 1838.

Hudson's Cave, near North Adams, *American Note-Books,* vol. i., July 31, August 15, 23, September 7, 1838.

Hugh, St., shrine of, *Our Old Home*, Pilgrimage to Old Boston. (Lincoln.)

Hull, Captain John, *Grandfather's Chair*, part i., chapter vi.

Human Soul, the, represented with its choice of Innocence or Evil in an allegorical figure in the sculpture-gallery in the Capitol at Rome, *The Marble Faun*, vol. i., chapter i.

Humility of a great man, *Fanshawe and Other Pieces*, Sir William Phips, fourth paragraph.

Humor, New England, *The Snow Image, etc.*, Old News, part i.

Humorists: insane, *The Blithedale Romance*, chapter vii., near the end; sombre, *Mosses from an Old Manse*, vol. ii., The Christmas Banquet.

Humphrey, Duke, dining with, *Mosses from an Old Manse*, vol. i., A Select Party, near the end.

Humphrey, Old, a character in the story Ethan Brand, in *The Snow Image, etc.* He is an old man become insane at the loss of his daughter Esther, who has joined a circus company.

Hunnewell, Captain, a character in Drowne's Wooden Image, *Mosses from an Old Manse*, vol. ii.

Hunt, Holman, pictures of, *English Note-Books*, vol. ii., July 28, 1857.

Hunt, Leigh: interview with, *Our Old Home*, Up the Thames; quotation from, *American Note-Books*, vol. ii., June 1, 1842.

Hunter, description of a colonial, *Fanshawe and Other Pieces*, Sir William Phips, fourth paragraph.

Husbands of celebrated women, *Fanshawe and Other Pieces*, Mrs. Hutchinson, sixth paragraph.

Huskisson, statue of, *English Note-Books*, vol. i., September 14, 1853.

Hutchins, the widow. See CROMBIE.

Hutchinson, Mrs. Anne, *The Snow Image, etc.*, Main Street, *Grandfather's Chair*, part i., chapter iv., and sketch of, included in the volume with *Fanshawe;* husband of, sixth paragraph of sketch; tradition concerning, *The Scarlet Letter*, chapter i.

Hutchinson Mob, The, account of, *Grandfather's Chair*, part iii., chapter iii.

Hutchinson, Thomas, Governor of Massachusetts, *Twice-Told Tales*, vol. ii., Howe's Masquerade, Edward Randolph's Portrait, *Grandfather's Chair*, part ii., chapter x., part iii., chapter iii.

Hyde Park, *English Note-Books*, vol. i., September 8, 1855.

Hydra, the, *Wonder-Book*, The Three Golden Apples.

Idea, gift of a new, *The Snow Image, etc.*, Main Street; people of one, *The Blithedale Romance*, chapter vii., near the end, chapter ix., near the beginning, chapter xix., near the end.

Ideal Man, the, *Mosses from an Old Manse*, vol. i., A Select Party.

Ideals, artists', *Mosses from an Old Manse*, vol. i., A Select Party; contact of, with the practical, *Mosses from an Old Manse*, vol. ii., The Artist of the Beautiful; necessity of outward form to, *ibid.*

Ideas of people, height of, *American Note-Books*, vol. i., October 25, 1836.

Identity between the gay and the sorrowful things of life, *The Marble Faun*, vol i., chapter xxv.

Idiot, predictions of an, *English Note-Books*, vol. i., October 22, 1853.

Idleness, longing for, *American Note-Books*, vol. ii., April 25 and June 23, 1843; New England opinion of, *Mosses from an Old Manse*, vol. ii., Passages from a Relinquished Work, At Home.

Ilbrahim, subject of the tale The Gentle Boy, *Twice-Told Tales*, vol. i.

Illness, like death, *The Blithedale Romance*, chapter viii.

Illusions, recognized by themselves, *Mosses from an Old Manse*, vol. i., Feathertop, near the end; the shadows of truths, *Twice-Told Tales*, vol. i., Sunday at Home.

Image, an, more attractive than the original, *Mosses from an Old Manse*, vol. i., The Birthmark, near the middle.

Imagination: dreams of a young man's, *Mosses from an Old Manse*, vol. i., A Select Party; in mercantile pursuits, *Twice-Told Tales*, vol. ii., Peter Goldthwaite's Treasure; lack of, in enthusiasts, *English Note-Books*, vol. i., July 6, 1855; the world of, *Mosses from an Old Manse*, vol. i., The Hall of Fantasy.

Imitators, comparison of, *American Note-Books*, vol. ii., February 22, 1851.

Immortal, the, consciousness of, *American Note-Books*, vol. i., letter April 7, 1840.

Immortality, arguments for, applicable to brutes, *American Note-Books*, vol. ii., December 19, 1850; earthly, *Mosses from an Old Manse*, vol. ii., A Virtuoso's Collection; the instinct of, *Septimius Felton*, p. 15 (12mo); mortals tempered to, *Tanglewood Tales*, The Pomegranate Seeds; need of, *English Note-Books*, vol. i., January 20, 1855; the question of, *Our Old Home*, Outside Glimpses of English Poverty.

Imogen, Shakspeare's, *Our Old Home*, About Warwick.

Impatience, trifling with one's own, *Twice-Told Tales*, vol. ii., The Threefold Destiny.

Imperfection of all Nature's productions, *Mosses from an Old Manse*, vol. i., The Birthmark, near the beginning.

Impertinence, what it depends on, *American Note-Books*, vol. i., July 27, 1838.

Importance of every individual, *American Note-Books*, vol. i., October 25, 1836.

Impressions, first, *American Note-Books*, vol. ii., May 7, 1850.

Impulse to avoid an engrossing subject, *The Marble Faun*, vol. ii., chapter xxii.

Incense, *The Marble Faun*, vol. ii., chapter xiv.

Incidents, striking, *Twice-Told Tales*, vol. i, Wakefield.

Incisa, *French and Italian Journals*, vol. i., May 30, 1858.

Incomprehensibility of the world, *The House of the Seven Gables*, chapter xii., middle.

Independence, proclamation of, *The Snow Image and Other Twice-Told Tales*, A Bell's Biography.

Independence, Mt., *The Snow Image, etc.*, Old Ticonderoga.

Indians, American, *Twice-Told Tales*, vol. ii., The Seven Vagabonds, Endicott and the Red Cross; at college, *Fanshawe*, chapter i.; coming down the Saco, *Mosses from an Old Manse*, vol. ii., Sketches from Memory, The Notch of the White Mountains; converted to the Roman Church, *The Snow Image, etc.*, A Bell's Biography; Eliot's theory of, *Grandfather's Chair*, part i., chapter vii.; legends of, *Mosses from an Old Manse*, vol. ii., Sketches from Memory, Our Evening Party among the Mountains; massacre by, *American Note-Books*, vol. ii., 1842; pow-wows of, *Mosses from an Old Manse*, vol. i, Young Goodman Brown; prophecy of, *The Snow Image, etc.*, The Great Stone Face; relations of with the colonies, *Grandfather's Chair*, part i., chapter vii.; relics of, *Mosses from an Old Manse*, vol. i, The Old Manse, near the beginning; site of a village of, *ibid.*; warfare of, *ibid.*, vol. ii., Roger Malvin's Burial; without monuments, *American Note-Books*, vol. i., December 6, 1837.

Individuality: assuming another's, *The Blithedale Romance*, chapter x., near the beginning; authors' revelations of, *Mosses from an Old Manse*, vol. i., The Old Manse, near the end; maintaining one's own, *The Blithedale Romance*, chapter xi.; marked, unfavorable to community, *ibid.*, chapter viii.

Indulgences, *French and Italian Journals*, vol. i., March 23, 1858.

Infidel ideas, kind of persons assailed by, *Septimius Felton*, p. 211 (12mo).

Influence of high connections in a republic, *The House of the Seven Gables*, chapter i.

Ingersol, Miss, wine-glass belonging to, *American Note-Books*, vol. i., October 24, 1838.

Inglefield, John, a blacksmith, his son, a missionary, and his daughters, Prudence and Mary, characters in the story John Inglefield's Thanksgiving, in *The Snow Image, etc.*

Ingram, Herbert, *English Note-Books*, vol. ii., April 4, 1856.

Inland Port, the, first of the Sketches from Memory, in the volume *The Dolliver Romance and Other Pieces*. It is a sketch of Burlington, Vt.

Innocence, safety of, *The Marble Faun*, vol. ii., chapters xvii., xx.

Innovation, the Titan of, *Mosses from an Old Manse*, vol. ii., Earth's Holocaust.

Inns, old English, *English Note-Books*, vol. ii., April 13, 1857.

Inns of Court, the, *English Note-Books*, vol. i., September 8, 15, 1855, vol. ii., November 12, December 6, 1857.

Inoculation, introduction of, into New England, *Grandfather's Chair*, part ii., chapter v.

Insane, the : an American lady, *English Note-Books*, vol. i., September 12, 1853 ; a young man, *ibid.*, September 12, 14, October 8, 1853.

Insanity, description of a case of, *American Note-Books*, vol. i., July 9, 1837 ; instance of, *ibid.*, vol. ii., June 1, 1842 ; subject for sketches, *ibid.*, vol. i., December 6, 1837.

Inscription on a house in Chester, *English Note-Books*, vol. i., October 1, 1853.

Insects, famous, *Mosses from an Old Manse*, vol. ii., A Virtuoso's Collection ; in spring, *ibid.*, vol. i., Buds and Bird Voices.

Insincerity, effect of, *American Note-Books*, vol. i., December 6, 1837.

Inspector, the Salem Custom-House, *The Scarlet Letter*, The Custom-House.

Inspector of Nuisances, Liverpool, *English Note-Books*, vol. ii , December 15, 1856.

Inspector, The Weekly, political journal, *Fanshawe and Other Pieces*, T. G. Fessenden.

Institute of Fine Arts, Siena, *French and Italian Journals*, vol. ii., October 5, 1858.

Insurrection of 1820, relics of the, *English Note-Books*, vol. ii , July 7, 1857, near the end.

Intellect, the : activity of, *The Blithedale Romance*, near the end of chapter viii. ; classification of men by, *Mosses from an Old Manse*, vol. i., The Procession of Life ; decay of the works of, *ibid.*, The Old Manse, middle ; exclusive cultivation of, *The Snow Image, etc.*, Ethan Brand.

Intelligence Office, The, a sketch in *Mosses from an Old Manse*, vol. ii. It imagines a bureau for recording all human wants, with the lesson, that the wishes are the true index of the character, and the record of them the real account of the Recording Angel. The sketch appeared originally in "The Democratic Review."

Intelligencer, The, newspaper, *Fanshawe and Other Pieces*, T. G. Fessenden toward the end.

Interpreter's House, the, *Mosses from an Old Manse*, vol. i., The Celestial Railroad.

Intrusion, instinctive sense of, *The Blithedale Romance*, chapter xxv.

Inventions, *Fanshawe and Other Pieces*, T. G. Fessenden, fourth and fifth paragraphs; effects of new, *Mosses from an Old Manse*, vol. i, Fire Worship.

Inventors, fantasies of, *Mosses from an Old Manse*, vol. i., The Hall of Fantasy.

Inverannan, *English Note-Books*, vol. ii., July 2, 1857.

Inversnaid, *English Note-Books*, vol. ii., May 10, 1856, July 3, 4, 1857.

Iobates, King, *Wonder-Book*, The Chimæra.

Iolchos, *Tanglewood Tales*, The Golden Fleece.

Ipswich, drive to, *American Note-Books*, vol. i., September 7, 1835.

Ireland family, the, *English Note-Books*, vol. i., September 5, 1855.

Irish, the: emigrant, *The Dolliver Romance, etc.*, The Inland Port; a family of, *English Note-Books*, vol. i., October 19, 1853; shanties of, *American Note-Books*, vol. i., July 9, 15, 1837; officers of, *English Note-Books*, vol. i., April 1, 1856.

Irregularity in old buildings, *Twice-Told Tales*, vol. ii., Edward Randolph's Portrait.

Irving, Washington, signature of, *The Dolliver Romance, etc.*, A Book of Autographs.

Isis, The River, *English Note-Books*, vol. ii., June 11, 1856.

Islands, ownership of, *American Note-Books*, vol. i., August 12, 27, 1837.

Isles of Shoals, visit to the, *American Note-Books*, vol. ii., August 30 to September 16, 1852.

Italians, the: Browning's opinion of, *French and Italian Journals*, vol. ii., June 8, 1858; courtesy of, *The Marble Faun*, vol. ii.

chapters x., xxiii.; curiosity of, *French and Italian Journals*, vol. ii., October 15, 1858; dress of, *ibid.*, October 7, 1858; loquacity of, *ibid.*, vol. i., May 30, 1858, Incisa, *The Marble Faun*, vol. ii., chapter xix.; meanness of, *French and Italian Journals*, vol. i., May 23, 1858; out-door life of, *ibid.*, June 4, 1858; physical strength of, *ibid.*, vol. ii, October 7, 1858; reliability of, *The Marble Faun*, vol. ii., chapter xix; religion and morals of, *French and Italian Journals*, vol. ii., June 16, 1858; superstition of, *ibid.*, August 3, 1858; toleration of *ibid.*, October 10, 1858.

Italy, notes of travel in, *French and Italian Journals*, latter part of vol. i., first of vol. ii.; beggars in, *ibid.*, vol. i., May 25, 27, 29, 30 (to Florence), vol. ii., June 15, October 9, 15, 23, 1858; country scenes in, *ibid.*, vol. i, May 24, 26, 28, 30 (Incisa), vol. ii., October 11, 12, 15, 1858, *The Marble Faun*, vol. ii., chapter vii.; crowds in, *French and Italian Journals*, vol. ii, September 10, 1858; effect of the climate of, on ruins, *The Marble Faun*, vol. i., chapters xviii., xxiv.; filthiness of, *French and Italian Journals*, vol. ii., October 15, 1858; fruits of, *ibid.*, June 15, September 21, 1858; hill scenery and towns of, *The Marble Faun*, vol. ii., chapter viii.; in February, *ibid.*, vol. ii., chapter xxi.; mosquitoes in, *French and Italian Journals*, vol. ii., September 21, 1858; nights of, *ibid.*, September 28, 1858; painters of, see PAINTERS; public officials in, *French and Italian Journals*, vol. ii., October 2, 15, 1858; romance of the history of, *ibid.*, vol. i., June 5, 1858; shrines in, *ibid.*, May 30, 1858 (Incisa); spring in, *ibid.*, vol. ii., March 23, 1859; summer in, *ibid.*, June 15, 1858; the two curses of, *ibid.*, vol. i., May 25, 1858; village scenes in, *ibid.*, May 30, 1858 (Incisa); wayside crosses in, *The Marble Faun*, vol. i., chapter xviii.; women of, *French and Italian Journals*, vol i., May 30, 1858.

J ——, Captain, American shipmaster, *English Note-Books*, vol. i., May 22, 1855.

J ——, Mr., daughters of, *English Note-Books*, vol. i., January 9, 17, 1855.

J——, W., an Irish-American merchant, *English Note-Books*, vol. i., February 19, 1855.

Jackson, Andrew, birth of, and quarrel with the Bentons, *English Note-Books*, vol. i., February 19, 1855; bust of, *Our Old Home*, Consular Experiences, beginning; characteristics of, *French and Italian Journals*, vol. ii., July 8, 1858; note from, *The Dolliver Romance, etc.*, A Book of Autographs.

Jackson, Cyril, statue of, *English Note-Books*, vol. ii., August 31, 1856 (Christ Church).

Jacobs, George, *The Snow Image, etc.*, Main Street.

Jacques, Doctor, *American Note-Books*, vol. i., June 16, 1838.

Jael, Miriam's sketch of, *The Marble Faun*, vol. i., chapter v.

James, St., apparition of, *English Note-Books*, vol. ii., July 8, 1857.

James I., of England, *Twice-Told Tales*, vol. ii., Endicott and the Red Cross; feast given to, *Our Old Home*, About Warwick; relic of, *English Note-Books*, vol. ii., April 13, 1857; statue of, *ibid.*, May 10, 1856 (Stirling); visit of, to Sir Oliver Cromwell, *True Stories*, chapter vi. of Biographies. (Only in 16mo ed.)

James II., of England, New England under, *Grandfather's Chair*, part i., chapter ix., *The Dolliver Romance, etc.*, Dr. Bullivant, *Twice-Told Tales*, vol. i., The Gray Champion.

James III., of Scotland, story of, *English Note-Books*, vol. ii., July 8, 1857.

James Barnes, the (ship), breakfast on, *English Note-Books*, vol. i., October 5, 1854.

James, G. P. R., *Wonder-Book*, Bald-Summit, *Our Old Home*, Up the Thames.

James, Sir J. K., translation of Tasso by, *French and Italian Journals*, vol. ii., May 29, 1859.

Jameson, Mrs. Anna, *French and Italian Journals*, vol. i., May 8, 9, 1858.

Janus Quadrifrons, arch of, *French and Italian Journals*, vol. i., March 18, 1858.

Japan, as a theme for a book, *English Note-Books*, vol. i., December 25, 1854.

Jason, *Tanglewood Tales*, The Golden Fleece.

Jefferson, Thomas: autograph of, *The Dolliver Romance, etc.*, A Book of Autographs; satirized, *Fanshawe, etc.*, T. G. Fessenden, near the middle.

Jenkins, Mr., of Amherst, *American Note-Books*, vol. i., August 31, 1838.

Jephson, Doctor, *Our Old Home*, Leamington Spa.

Jerdan, William, autobiography of, *English Note-Books*, vol. ii., July 10, 30, 1856.

Jerrold, Douglas, *English Note-Books*, vol. ii., April 5, 1856.

Jerusalem, earth of, in the Capuchin Cemetery at Rome, *The Marble Faun*, vol. i., chapter xxi.

Jest, turning to earnest, *American Note-Books*, vol. i., September 7, 1835.

Jesuits, the. See CATHOLICISM.

Jesus: and St. Catharine, picture of, *French and Italian Journals*, vol. i., May 8, 1858; miraculous footprints of, *ibid.*, May 9, 1858; nature of, *English Note-Books*, vol. i., February 8, 1856. See CHRIST.

Jew of Nuremberg, the, a traveling showman in the story Ethan Brand, in *The Snow Image, etc.*

Jew, the wandering. See WANDERING JEW.

Jewels, crown, of England, *Mosses from an Old Manse*, vol. ii., Earth's Holocaust.

Jewess, description of a beautiful, *English Note-Books*, vol. ii., April 8, 1856, *Our Old Home*, Civic Banquets.

Jewess's House, the, Lincoln, *Our Old Home*, Pilgrimage to Old Boston.

Jewsbury, Miss, *English Note-Books*, vol. ii., July 9, 1856.

Job: a dissertation on the book of, *Mosses from an Old Manse*, vol. i., The Old Manse, at the middle; a festival suited to, *ibid.*, vol. ii., The Christmas Banquet; patience of, *The Blithedale Romance*, chapter vi.; tears of, *French and Italian Journals*, vol. ii., July 4, 1858.

Joe, a little boy, son of Bartram, the lime-burner, in the story Ethan Brand, in *The Snow Image, etc.*

John, King, tomb of, *English Note-Books*, vol. i., October 14, 1855.

John XXII., tomb of, *French and Italian Journals,* vol. ii., June 2, 1859.

John the Baptist, curious picture of, *French and Italian Journals*, vol. i., May 28, 1858. See HERODIAS.

John of Gaunt, building by, *English Note-Books,* vol. ii., September 13, 1857.

John Inglefield's Thanksgiving, a story in *The Snow Image and Other Twice-Told Tales.* It was first published in "The Democratic Review" in 1843.

Johnson, Lady Arabella, *The Snow Image, etc.,* Main Street, *Grandfather's Chair*, part i., chapter ii.

Johnson, Isaac, *Grandfather's Chair,* part i., chapter ii.; grave of, *The Scarlet Letter*, chapters i., ix.

Johnson, Michael, *Our Old Home*, Lichfield and Uttoxeter, *True Stories*, chapter iv. of Biographies. (Only in 16mo ed.)

Johnson, Samuel, a sketch of, in the *True Stories*, chapters iv. and v. of Biographies (only in the 16mo ed.); anecdote of, *English Note-Books*, vol. ii., July 2, 1857; birthplace of, *Our Old Home*, Lichfield and Uttoxeter; cat of, *Mosses from an Old Manse*, vol. ii., A Virtuoso's Collection; morality of, *Our Old Home*, Lichfield and Uttoxeter; penance of, *American Note-Books*, vol i., October 24, 1838, *English Note-Books*, vol. ii., August 2, 1857, *Our Old Home*, Lichfield and Uttoxeter; personality of, *Our Old Home*, Lichfield and Uttoxeter; Rasselas, allusion to, *Fanshawe*, chapter i.; relics of, *English Note-Books*, vol. i., January 20, 1855; residence of, *ibid.*, March 22, 1856; staircase of, *ibid.*, March 26, 1856; statues and portrait of, *ibid.*, September 13, 1855, *Our Old Home*, Lichfield and Uttoxeter.

Jokes, newspaper, *The Blithedale Romance*, chapter xxiii.

Joliffe, Colonel, character in Howe's Masquerade, *Twice-Told Tales*, vol. ii.

Joliffe, Miss, granddaughter of the preceding, *ibid.*

Jonathan's Courtship, *Fanshawe, etc.,* T. G. Fessenden.

Jones, Inigo, a building designed by, *English Note-Books,* vol. i., March 25, 1856.

Jones, Mr., sculptor, *English Note-Books*, vol. ii., April 8, 1856, at the end.

Jones, Paul, *English Note-Books,* vol. i., Good Friday, 1854.
Jonson, Ben: "The Alchemist," *English Note-Books,* vol. i., July 27, 1855; tomb of, *Our Old Home,* Up the Thames.
Josiah, hero of the story The Canterbury Pilgrims, in *The Snow Image and Other Twice-Told Tales.*
Joust, a modern, *English Note-Books,* vol. ii., May 28, 1857.
Joy: identity of, with sorrow, *French and Italian Journals,* vol. ii., June 28, 1858; neglected opportunities for, *Mosses from an Old Manse,* vol. i., A Select Party.
Judges, English, *English Note-Books,* vol. i., August 21, 1854; rank of, *ibid.,* August 15, 1853, *Our Old Home,* Civic Banquets.
Judgment, of a man on himself, *The Blithedale Romance,* chapter xviii.
Judgment Day, the, *The Scarlet Letter,* chapter x.; Michael Angelo's painting of, *French and Italian Journals,* vol. i., May 15, 1858.
Judgment Seat, the only one a woman dreads, *The Blithedale Romance,* chapter xxv.
Judith, Miriam's sketch of, *The Marble Faun,* vol. i., chapter v.
Jugurtha, dungeon of, *French and Italian Journals,* vol. i., February 23, 1858.
Julius III. See POPE.
Juniper, the, *American Note-Books,* vol. i., June 15, 1835.
Juno, the, statue in Rome, *The Marble Faun,* vol. i., chapter i.

K——, General, *English Note-Books,* vol. i., April 1, 1856.
Kean, the elder, *Mosses from an Old Manse,* vol. ii., P.'s Correspondence.
Kean, Charles, *English Note-Books,* vol. i., March 27, 1856.
Keats, John, criticism on, and imaginary epic by, *Mosses from an Old Manse,* vol. ii., P.'s Correspondence.
Kemble, John, *Mosses from an Old Manse,* vol. ii., P.'s Correspondence; statue of, *Our Old Home,* Up the Thames.
Kemble, Roger, anecdote of Shakspeare told by, *English Note-Books,* vol. i., January 9, 1855.
Kendal, Barons of, *English Note-Books,* vol. i., July 13, 1855.

Kendal, Rev. Samuel, of New Salem, *Fanshawe and Other Pieces*, T. G. Fessenden.

Kenilworth, Village and Castle, *English Note-Books*, vol. ii., September 13, 1857.

Kennebec River, the, *American Note-Books*, vol. i., July 5, 13, 15, 20, 1837.

Kennedy, John P., *French and Italian Journals*, vol. i., February 23, 1858.

Kensington, *English Note-Books*, vol. i., September 24, 1855, *Our Old Home*, A London Suburb.

Kenyon, an American sculptor in Rome, character in *The Marble Faun*, introduced in chapter i. The statues attributed to him in the book are described from works of Paul Akers and William W. Story, but the author disclaims having drawn the character from any actual personage. He is represented as a good artist, with a warm heart, subtle insight, and delicate sympathies, thoughtful, and "a devout man in his way."

Keswick, *English Note-Books*, vol. i., July 21, 1855.

Keziah, a character in *Septimius Felton*, aunt of the hero, a witch-like old woman.

Kidd, Captain, ghost of one of his men, *American Note-Books*, vol. ii., September 5, 10, 13, 1852.

Killigrew, Colonel, an old debauchee in Dr. Heidegger's Experiment, *Twice-Told Tales*, vol. i.

King Philip's War, *The Snow Image, etc.*, Main Street; veterans of, *Twice-Told Tales*, vol. i., The Gray Champion.

King, Rufus, *Fanshawe, etc.*, T. G. Fessenden, fourth paragraph.

King Street, Boston, *The Snow Image, etc.*, Old News, part iii., *Twice-Told Tales*, vol. i., The Gray Champion, *Grandfather's Chair*, part iii., chapters iv., v.

King, Wm. R., bust of, *French and Italian Journals*, vol. i., June 4, 1858.

King's Chapel, Boston: burial-ground of, *Grandfather's Chair*, part i., chapter ii., *Twice-Told Tales*, vol. ii., Lady Eleanore's Mantle, *The Scarlet Letter*, chapters i., ix.; clergyman of *Twice-Told Tales*, vol. i., The Gray Champion; the original, *American Note-Books*, vol. i., September 7, 1835.

Kings, *English Note-Books*, vol. ii., September 9, 1856; intrusion of, *English Note-Books*, vol. ii., August 31, 1856, Ratcliffe Library; obligations of, *Tanglewood Tales*, The Pomegranate Seeds.

Kirby, William, citation from, *American Note-Books*, vol. i., September, 1836.

Kirkstall Abbey, *English Note-Books*, vol. ii., April 11, 1857.

Kirkstone, Pass of, *English Note-Books*, vol. i., July 21, 1855.

Kirkup, Seymour, an Englishman living in Florence (1858), an antiquarian, spiritualist, and reputed necromancer, *The Marble Faun*, vol. ii., chapter iii., *French and Italian Journals*, vol. ii., August 12, 1858, said to be the original of Grandsir Dolliver, of *The Dolliver Romance*, in some regards.

"**Kissing in the Ring**," game of, *Our Old Home*, A London Suburb.

Kitchen work, *The Blithedale Romance*, chapter iii.

Kittery, Maine, *American Note-Books*, vol. ii., 1842; mighty man of, *Fanshawe, etc.*, Sir William Pepperell, beginning.

Knavery, pleasure in detecting, *Twice-Told Tales*, vol. ii., The Seven Vagabonds.

Kneller, Sir Godfrey, pictures by, *English Note-Books*, vol. i., March 24, 1856; quotation from, *Our Old Home*, Up the Thames.

Knowles, Commodore, *Grandfather's Chair*, part ii., chapter vii.

Knowsley Park, *English Note-Books*, vol. i., March 23, 1854.

Knox, Henry, *Grandfather's Chair*, part iii., chapter v.; family and home of, *American Note-Books*, vol. i., August 12, 1837, vol. ii., 1842; letter from, *The Dolliver Romance, etc.*, A Book of Autographs.

Knox, John: house of, *English Note-Books*, vol. ii., May 10, 1856 (Edinburgh), July 9, 1857; portrait of, *ibid.*, July 1, 1857; pulpit of, *ibid.*, July 7, 1857.

Kossuth, Louis, allusion to, *The Blithedale Romance*, chapter xxix.

Labor, manual: effect of, on the mind, *American Note-Books*, vol. ii., June 1, August 12, 22, 1841; incompatibility of, with mental, *The Blithedale Romance*, chapter viii., near the end; with poetry, *ibid.*

Labyrinth of Crete, the, *Tanglewood Tales*, The Minotaur.

Lacy, Roger, *English Note-Books*, vol. i., October 13, 1853.

Ladies' Monitor, The, title of a volume of poetry, *Fanshawe, etc.*, T. G. Fessenden, toward the end.

Ladislaus, King of Naples, incident concerning, *American Note-Books*, vol. ii., December 19, 1850.

Ladurlad, in the "Curse of Kehama," allusions to, *American Note-Books*, vol. i., July 10, 1838, *Mosses from an Old Manse*, vol. i., Monsieur du Miroir.

Lady, characteristics of a, *The House of the Seven Gables*, chapter v., after the middle.

Lady Eleanore's Mantle, one of the Legends of the Province House, in *Twice-Told Tales*, vol. ii.

Lady-like, the word, *Our Old Home*, Outside Glimpses of English Poverty.

Laestrygonia, *Tanglewood Tales*, Circe's Palace.

Lafayette: autograph of, *The Dolliver Romance, etc.*, A Book of Autographs; visit of, to America, *The Snow Image, etc.*, A Bell's Biography.

Laighton, Mr., Appledore, *American Note-Books*, vol. ii., August 30, September 10, 1852.

Lakes, the, visit to, *English Note-Books*, vol. i., July 13 to 20, 1855.

Lambeth Palace, *English Note-Books*, vol. i., March 24, 1856, *Our Old Home*, Up the Thames.

Lamps: one connected with a story, *American Note-Books*, vol. i., September 7, 1835; famous, *Mosses from an Old Manse*, vol. ii., A Virtuoso's Collection.

Lancashire, scenery of, *Our Old Home*, Pilgrimage to Old Boston.

Lancaster, *English Note-Books*, vol. i., July 30, 1855.

Landlady, an English, *English Note-Books*, vol. i., September 14, 1853.

Landmarks, historical, *English Note-Books*, vol. ii., July 10, 1857.

Landscape, Italian, *French and Italian Journals,* vol. ii., August 2, 1858, *The Marble Faun,* vol. ii., chapter iii.

Lane, Miss Harriet, niece of President Buchanan, *English Note-Books,* vol. i., January 9, September 26, October 5, 1855. (Name in blank.)

Langdon, Mr., inventor, *Fanshawe, etc.,* T. G. Fessenden, fourth paragraph.

Langford, Captain, character in Lady Eleanore's Mantle, *Twice-Told Tales,* vol. ii.

Langton, Ellen, the heroine of *Fanshawe,* a pleasant character, made interesting by her beauty and the circumstances of her story.

Langton, Mr., a character in *Fanshawe,* first appearing in chapter vii., and having little to do, directly, with the story. He is but faintly outlined as reserved, grave, and somewhat severe.

Language, human, inadequacy of, *American Note-Books,* vol. ii., July 14, 1850.

Lansdowne, the Marquis of, *English Note-Books,* vol. ii., July 13, 1856.

Laocoön, the, *French and Italian Journals,* vol. i., March 10, 23, 1858, *The Marble Faun,* vol. i., chapter xv., vol. ii., chapter xviii.; copy of, *French and Italian Journals,* vol. ii., June 8, 1858.

Lapland, a day's labor in, *American Note-Books,* vol. ii., 1842.

Larkhill, visit to, *English Note-Books,* vol. i., February 19, 1855.

Last Supper, the, table at which was eaten, *French and Italian Journals,* vol. i., February 14, 1858.

Latimer, place of martyrdom of, *English Note-Books,* vol. ii., August 31, 1856.

Laud, Archbishop, *Twice-Told Tales,* vol. i., The Gentle Boy, vol. ii., Endicott and the Red Cross.

Laughter, mistimed, *The Snow Image, etc.,* Ethan Brand.

Launch of a ship, the, *English Note-Books,* vol. i., August 2, 1855.

Laurens, Henry, letter from, *The Dolliver Romance, etc.*, A Book of Autographs.

Laurentian Library, the, *French and Italian Journals,* vol. ii., September 17, 1858.

Lauriat, Mr., *Twice-Told Tales,* vol. ii., The Sister Years.

Lausanne, *French and Italian Journals,* vol. ii., June 14, 1859.

Law, the, qualities for success in, *Fanshawe, etc.*, T. G. Fessenden, third paragraph.

Law, Dr., statue of Dr. Johnson erected by, *Our Old Home,* Lichfield and Uttoxeter.

Lawrence, Sir Thomas, pictures of, *English Note-Books,* vol. i., March 23, 1854, vol. ii., July 28, 1857.

Lawson, Deacon, a character in A Bell's Biography, in *The Snow Image and Other Twice-Told Tales.*

Law students, literary, *The Dolliver Romance, etc.*, The Antique Ring.

Lawyer, a, original of a character in Ethan Brand, *American Note-Books,* vol. i., July 29, 1838.

Layard, A. H., *English Note-Books,* vol. i., April 24, 1855 ; collection of, *ibid.*, vol. ii., December 7, 1857.

Lazarus, picture of, *English Note-Books,* vol. i., September 28, 1855.

Leach, Mr., *American Note-Books,* vol. i., August 31, 1838.

Lead-mine, tradition of a, *American Note-Books,* vol. i., July 8, 1837.

Leam, the River, *Our Old Home,* Leamington Spa.

Leamington, *English Note-Books,* vol. ii., June 11, 21, 1856, September 10, 1857.

Leamington Spa, an article in *Our Old Home,* describing that place and some others in its neighborhood, Lillington, Whitnash, and Hatton.

Learning, *American Note-Books,* vol. ii., 1842; results of, *Mosses from an Old Manse,* vol. ii., The New Adam and Eve.

Lectures, *American Note-Books,* vol. i , letter November, 1840, *The Blithedale Romance,* chapter xxiii.

Lee, Ann, mission of, *Twice-Told Tales,* vol. ii., The Shaker Bridal.

Legends: classic, *Wonder-Book*, Preface; of the Bloody Footprint, *English Note-Books*, vol. i., August 25, 1855, *Septimius Felton*, pp. 111 *et seq.* (12mo. ed.) and last page; of the catacombs, *The Marble Faun*, vol. i., chapter iii.; of the Monte Beni family, *ibid.*, vol. ii., chapters ii., iii.; theme for a, *English Note-Books*, vol. i., October 13, 1853; Zenobia's, *The Blithedale Romance*, chapter xiii.

Legends of the Province House, four sketches in *Twice-Told Tales*, vol. ii., located in the old residence of the royal Governors of Massachusetts. They were first published in "The Democratic Review."

Leghorn, *French and Italian Journals*, vol. i., January 24, 1858, vol. ii., May 29, 1859.

Legislation, the ideal, *Mosses from an Old Manse*, vol. ii., The New Adam and Eve.

Leicester, Earls of: burial of one, *English Note-Books*, vol. i., October 22, 1853; tombs of, *Our Old Home*, About Warwick.

Leicester's Hospital, *Our Old Home*, About Warwick.

Leighs of Wilmslow, the, *English Note-Books*, vol. i., December 1, 1853.

Lely, Sir Peter, pictures of, *English Note-Books*, vol. i., March 24, 1856, vol. ii., May 29, July 30, 1857.

Lemonade, of the millennium, *The Blithedale Romance*, chapter vii.

Lenox, Mass., the home of Hawthorne in 1850–51: scenery of, *American Note-Books*, vol. ii., August 24, October 16, 1850, February 12, October 27, 1851; literary residents of, *Wonder-Book*, last chapter.

Leo, the dog, *American Note-Books*, vol. ii., May 27, 31, June 6, 1844.

Leonardo da Vinci, pictures by, *French and Italian Journals*, vol. i., March 10, 1858.

Lepidus, bust of, *French and Italian Journals*, vol. i., March 23, 1858.

Le Plaisir, Monsieur, *The Snow Image, etc.*, Little Daffydowndilly.

Le Sage, author of "Gil Blas," limping devil of, *Twice-Told Tales*, vol. i., Sights from a Steeple.

Lestrange, Sir Nicholas, *Our Old Home*, About Warwick.

Lethe, the River, *Tanglewood Tales*, The Pomegranate Seeds, *Mosses from an Old Manse*, vol. ii., A Virtuoso's Collection.

Letters from Hawthorne, extracts from, *American Note-Books*, end of vol. i.

Leverett, Sir John, Governor of Massachusetts, *Twice-Told Tales*, vol. ii., Howe's Masquerade; portrait of, *American Note-Books*, vol. i., August 22, 1837.

Lewthwaite, Barbara, *English Note-Books*, vol. i., July 19, 1855.

Lexington, Battle of, *Grandfather's Chair*, part iii., chapter vii., *Twice-Told Tales*, vol. i., The Gray Champion, *Septimius Felton*, pp. 18 *et seq.* (12mo).

Lexington Road, the, *Septimius Felton*, p. 4 (12mo).

Leycester, Sir Peter, *English Note-Books*, vol. i., October 13, 1853.

Liberius, Pope, church founded by, *French and Italian Journals*, vol. i., February 10, 1858.

Liberty: of the Pilgrims, *The Snow Image, etc.*, Main Street; sufferers for, *Our Old Home*, Consular Experiences, beginning.

Liberty Tree, the, *Grandfather's Chair*, part iii., chapter ii.; picture of, *American Note-Books*, vol. ii., September 14, 16, 1841.

Libraries: Athenæum, Boston, *American Note-Books*, vol. ii., May 5, 1850; Bodleian, *English Note-Books*, vol. ii., August 31, 1856; British Museum, *ibid.*, vol. i., September 29, 1855, vol. ii., December 7, 1857; Harvard, *Mosses from an Old Manse*, vol. i., The New Adam and Eve; Laurentian, *French and Italian Journals*, vol. ii., September 17, 1858; Ratcliffe, *English Note-Books*, vol. ii., August 31, 1856

Lichfield: meaning of the name, *Our Old Home*, Lichfield and Uttoxeter; cathedral of, *ibid.*

Lichfield and Uttoxeter, an article in *Our Old Home*, describing the early home of Johnson, Addison, and Garrick, and the penance of Dr. Johnson. The feeling of the people of

Uttoxeter about the article is spoken of in the *English Note-Books*, vol. ii., August 2, 1857.

Life: at the Old Manse, *American Note-Books*, vol. ii., August 13, 1842; in installments, fantasy regarding, *ibid.*, vol. i., October 25, 1835; love of, *Mosses from an Old Manse*, vol. ii., The Artist of the Beautiful; power of living but one mode of, *The Blithedale Romance*, chapter xix.; power of prolonging, *Mosses from an Old Manse*, vol. i., The Birthmark, near the middle; shortness of, *Septimius Felton*, pp. 13, 14 (12mo); worth living? *ibid.*, pp. 7 to 9, 13 (12mo).

Light that sometimes breaks in on a minority, *Fanshawe, etc.*, Mrs. Hutchinson, fourth paragraph.

Lighthouse, a, *American Note-Books*, vol. ii., September 9, 1852.

Liliputian man-of-war, a, *American Note-Books*, vol. ii., June 1, 1842.

Lillington, Village and Church, *Our Old Home*, Leamington Spa.

Lilly, citation from, *American Note-Books*, vol. i., January 4, 1839.

Lily's Quest, The, An Apologue, in *Twice-Told Tales*, vol. ii.

Lime-burner, occupation of, *The Snow Image, etc.*, Ethan Brand.

Lime-kilns, description of, *American Note-Books*, vol. i., September 7, 1838, *The Snow Image, etc.*, Ethan Brand.

Lincoln, *Our Old Home*, Pilgrimage to Old Boston.

Lincoln, Earl of, *Grandfather's Chair*, part i., chapter ii.

Lincoln, Francis, Captain of Castle William, *Twice-Told Tales*, vol. ii., Edward Randolph's Portrait.

Lincoln, General, *Grandfather's Chair*, part iii., chapter x.; a typical New Englander, *The Dolliver Romance, etc.*, A Book of Autographs.

Lincoln's Inn, *English Note-Books*, vol. ii., December 6, 1857.

Lind, Jenny, *English Note-Books*, vol. ii., July 9, 1856.

Lindsey, Mr., a character in *The Snow Image*, type of the common-sense, materialistic part of society.

Lindsey, Mrs., a character in *The Snow Image*, a contrast to the matter-of-fact nature of her husband.

Linlithgow, Church, Palace, and Town of, *English Note-Books*, vol. ii., July 8, 1857.

Linnell, John, picture by, *English Note-Books*, vol. ii., August 14, 1857.

Lionized, feeling at being, *English Note-Books*, vol. ii., April 8, July 9, 1856.

Lippi, Fra Filippo, picture by, *French and Italian Journals*, vol. ii., July 16, 1858.

Lisabetta, a character in Rappaccini's Daughter, *Mosses from an Old Manse*, vol. i.

Lisbon, departure for, *English Note-Books*, vol. i., October 6, 11, 1855.

Listeners, good, *Twice-Told Tales*, vol. ii., Edward Randolph's Portrait.

Litchfield, Conn., *American Note-Books*, vol. i., September 9, 1838.

Literary fame, narrowness of, *The Scarlet Letter*, The Custom-House, middle.

Literary interest, visits to places of, *Our Old Home*, Lichfield and Uttoxeter.

Literary Ladies, their choice of names, *The Blithedale Romance*, chapter v.

Literary Men: association of, in the other world, *American Note-Books*, vol. ii., June 1, 1842; position of, in England, *English Note-Books*, vol. ii., April 5, 1856, *Our Old Home*, Up the Thames.

Literary work: affected by farm labor, *American Note-Books*, vol. ii., June 1, 1841; by outside pressure, *ibid.*, August 22, 1841; freedom necessary for, *ibid.*, September 25, 1841; in summer, *ibid.*, July 28, 1843; prospects of living by, *ibid.*, August 22, 1841; seclusion necessary for, *ibid.*, September 22, 1841; time given to, *ibid.*, March 31, 1843.

Literature: destruction of, *Mosses from an Old Manse*, vol. ii., Earth's Holocaust; juvenile, *True Stories*, preface to biographies; in New England in 1760, *The Snow Image, etc.*, Old News, part ii.; interest in those connected with, *English Note-Books*, vol. ii., July 11, 1857, Durham; number of the really great in, *Our Old Home*, Up the Thames; of London book-stalls, *English Note-Books*, vol. i., September 30, 1855; reverence for, *Mosses from an Old Manse*, vol. i., The Old Manse, near the middle.

Litterateur, a young English, *Our Old Home*, Consular Experiences, near the end.

Little Annie's Ramble, sketch in *Twice-Told Tales*, vol. i., of a walk with a child through the streets of a town.

Little Byforth, village of, *English Note-Books*, vol. ii., May 2, 8, 1857.

Little Daffydowndilly, an allegorical story of the ubiquity of labor in the world, in *The Snow Image and Other Twice-Told Tales.*

Liverpool: American Chamber of Commerce at, *English Note-Books*, vol. i., August 5, 1853; an American claimant of, *Our Old Home*, Consular Experiences; as a place to get away from, *ibid.*, at the end; cemetery of, *English Note-Books*, vol. i., August 24, September 14, 1853; consulate at, *ibid.*, August 4, 1853; dinner with the mayor of, *ibid.*, August 15, 1853; ferries of, *ibid.*, September 7, 1853; history of, *ibid.*; nautical business of, *ibid.*, September 1, 1853; old buildings of, *ibid.*, August 9, September 7, 1853; St. George's Hall in, *ibid.*, March 27, 1855; street scenes and trade in, *ibid.*, October 20, November 5, 14, December 1, 2, 13, 1853; town hall of, *ibid.*, August 15, 1853; view of, *ibid.*, September 1, 1853.

Living, rules for, *Septimius Felton*, pp. 126 *et seq.* (12mo).

Llandudno, *English Note-Books*, vol. i., September 13, 1854.

Lloyd, Mayor, *English Note-Books*, vol. i., September 26, 1854.

Loch Katrine, *English Note-Books*, vol. ii., July 5, 1857.

Loch Lomond, *English Note-Books*, vol. ii., May 10, 1856, July 2, 4, 1857.

Lockhart, J. G., *English Note-Books*, vol. i., October 3, 1853.

Lodgings, living in, *English Note-Books*, vol. i., June 21, 1855, vol. ii., September 13, 1856.

Lodore, the fall of, *English Note-Books*, vol. i., July 21, 1855.

London, *English Note-Books*, vol. i., September 7 to 15, 24 to October 6, 1855, March 22 to 27, April 4 to 8, vol. ii., July 6 to 16,

July 29 to August 7, 1856, November 10, 1857, to January 3, 1858, *Our Old Home*, Up the Thames, *French and Italian Journals*, vol. ii., May 16, 17, 1860; an American's delight in, *Our Old Home*, A London Suburb; at night, *English Note-Books*, vol. i., September 25, 1855; Billingsgate market, *ibid.*, vol. ii., November 15, 1857; boys of Christ's Hospital, *ibid.*, November 11, 1857; British Museum, *ibid.*, November 11, December 7, 1857; charm of old names of, *ibid.*, November 10, 1857; Crystal Palace, *ibid.*, November 16, 1857; described to children, *The Snow Image, etc.*, Main Street; distant view of, *Our Old Home*, A London Suburb; Inns of Court, *English Note-Books*, vol. i., September 15, 1855, vol. ii., November 12, December 6, 1857; Marlborough House, *ibid.*, December 8, 1857; old buildings and wall of, *ibid.*, vol. i., March 25, 1856; out of season, *ibid.*, vol. ii., August 7, 1856; predicted downfall of, *Our Old Home*, Up the Thames; Smithfield, *English Note-Books*, vol. ii., November 15, 1857; Somerset House, *ibid.*, November 12, 1857; streets of, *ibid.*, December 6, 20, 1857; the Temple, *ibid.*, November 12, 1857; theatre in, *ibid.*, vol. i., September 27, 1855; Tower Hill, *ibid.*, vol. ii., November 15, 1857.

London Suburb, A, an article in *Our Old Home*, describing Blackheath, Greenwich, and Greenwich Hospital and Fair.

Longfellow, H. W., *American Note-Books*, vol. ii., March 31, 1843, *Wonder-Book*, Bald-Summit, *The Scarlet Letter*, The Custom-House, middle, *Mosses from an Old Manse*, vol. ii., P.'s Correspondence; home of, *Grandfather's Chair*, part iii., chapter ix., *The Dolliver Romance, etc.*, A Book of Autographs; poem of "Evangeline," see EVANGELINE; quotation from, *Our Old Home*, Leamington Spa; wife of, *American Note-Books*, vol. ii., May 27, 1844.

Longsword, Earl of Salisbury, statue of, *English Note-Books*, vol. ii., June 17, 1856.

Long Wharf, Boston, in summer, *American Note-Books*, vol. i., letter August 27, 1839.

Lonsdale, Earl, statue of, *English Note-Books*, vol. ii., June 28, 1857.

Looking-glass, suggestion about a, *American Note-Books*, vol. i., December 6, 1837.

Lorenzo, the Magnificent. See MEDICI.

Lot's wife, *Mosses from an Old Manse,* vol. i., The Celestial Railroad, vol. ii., A Virtuoso's Collection.

Loudon, Earl of, *American Note-Books,* vol. ii., September 14, 1841.

Lough, sculptor of Southey's tomb, *English Note-Books,* vol. i., July 21, 1855.

Louis XIV., gift of, to the Jesuits, *The Snow Image, etc.,* A Bell's Biography; relic of, *Our Old Home,* Pilgrimage to Old Boston.

Louis Napoleon, *English Note-Books,* vol. i., September 17, 1855.

Louisburg, siege of, *Fanshawe, etc.,* Sir William Pepperell, *Grandfather's Chair,* part ii., chapter vii.; effects of, *The Snow Image, etc.,* Old News, part ii., *Fanshawe, etc.,* Sir William Pepperell, third paragraph; Voltaire's opinion of, *ibid.,* last paragraph.

Louvre, the, *French and Italian Journals,* vol. i., January 8, 10, 1858.

Love: affected by selfishness, *Mosses from an Old Manse,* vol ii., Roger Malvin's Burial; after death, *The Dolliver Romance, etc.,* Ghosts and Goblins; attracts a peculiar to an ordinary nature, *Fanshawe,* chapter ix.; charm that lies just outside of, *The Marble Faun,* vol. ii., chapter xvi.; class whose principle is, *Mosses from an Old Manse,* vol. i., The Procession of Life; differences of character in, *The Marble Faun,* vol. ii., chapter xvi.; first happiness of, *The Blithedale Romance,* chapter ix., near the close; hint for a sketch of, *American Note-Books,* vol. i., September 7, 1835; idea that it is a woman's only resource, *The Blithedale Romance,* chapter xxviii.; the one principle of, *ibid.,* chapter xxv., end; peculiar kind of pique in, *The Marble Faun,* chapter xviii.; regard of, for experience, *The Snow Image, etc.,* The Canterbury Pilgrims; rife at Blithedale, *The Blithedale Romance,* chapter ix., near the beginning; treason to, *Mosses from an Old Manse,* vol. i., The Birthmark, near the end; unites a man to his race, *Fanshawe,* chapter ii., end; when ended, *The Blithedale Romance,* chapter xvi., near the end.

Lovell's Fight, *Mosses from an Old Manse,* vol. ii., Roger Malvin's Burial, *Fanshawe, etc.,* Sir William Pepperell, fourth paragraph.

Lover, Samuel, *English Note-Books,* vol. ii., July 9, 1856.

Lover's Leap. *English Note-Books,* vol. ii., July 2, 1857.

Lovers, estrangements of, *Septimius Felton,* p. 78 (12mo); ghosts of guilty, *The Dolliver Romance, etc.,* Ghosts and Goblins.

Loving-cup, ceremony of the, *Our Old Home,* Civic Banquets.

Lowell, factory girls from, *Mosses from an Old Manse,* vol. i., The Procession of Life.

Lowell, J. R., *English Note-Books,* vol. i., September 14, 1855, *Mosses from an Old Manse,* vol. i., The Old Manse, near the beginning; admiration for Keats of, *ibid.,* P.'s Correspondence.

Loyalty, *Our Old Home,* Civic Banquets; in New England, *The Snow Image, etc.,* Old News, parts i. and iii.

Lucas, statue of Dr. Johnson by, *Our Old Home,* Lichfield and Uttoxeter.

Luce, Captain, of the Arctic, *English Note-Books,* vol. i., October 16, 1854.

Luck, reckoning upon, *Twice-Told Tales,* vol. ii., Peter Goldthwaite's Treasure.

Lucy family, seat of the, *Our Old Home,* Recollections of a Gifted Woman.

Ludlow, Walter, a character in The Prophetic Pictures, *Twice-Told Tales,* vol. i. The painter finds in his face incipient insanity, and by bringing it out in his portrait makes the picture prophetic.

Ludovisi, Villa, *French and Italian Journals,* vol. i., March 26, 1858.

Luini, Bernardo. See BERNARDO.

Lunatic, letter of a, *Mosses from an Old Manse,* vol. ii., P.'s Correspondence.

Lunatic Asylum, Liverpool, governor of the, *English Note-Books,* vol. i., September 14, 1853.

Luther: asserted origin of, *The Scarlet Letter,* chapter vi.; inkstand of, *Mosses from an Old Manse*, vol. ii., A Virtuoso's Collection.

Lyceum halls, exhibitions in, *The Blithedale Romance*, chapter xxiii.

Lynceus, *Tanglewood Tales*, The Golden Fleece.

Lyndes, tomb of the, *American Note-Books*, vol. i., July 4, 1838.

Lyons, *French and Italian Journals*, vol. i., January 15, 1858, vol. ii., June 11, 1859.

Lysippus, statue by, *Mosses from an Old Manse*, vol. ii., A Virtuoso's Collection.

M ——, Mr., correspondent of the New York "Courier and Enquirer," *English Note-Books*, vol. i., September 13, 1855.

M ——, Mr., correspondent of the London "Times" at Scutari, *English Note-Books*, vol. ii., April 4, 1856.

Mab, Queen, chariot of, *Mosses from an Old Manse*, vol. ii., A Virtuoso's Collection.

Macaulay, T. B., *English Note-Books*, vol. ii., July 13, 1856; suggestion for the New Zealander of, *Our Old Home*, Up the Thames.

Macchiavelli, tomb and house of, *French and Italian Journals*, vol. ii., June 28, 1858.

Macdonald, James and John, burglary by, *English Note-Books*, vol. ii., March 1, 1857.

Macedonian, The. See Constitution.

MacFarlanes, site of a castle of the, *English Note-Books*, vol. ii., May 10, 1856.

Macgregor, Mr., landlord at Glasgow, *English Note-Books*, vol. ii., May 10, 1856.

Mackay, Dr. Charles, *English Note-Books*, vol. ii., April 4, 5, 6, 8, July 9, 1856. (Name in blank.)

MacRae, Duncan K. See Consul.

Madeleine, church of the, *French and Italian Journals*, vol. i., January 9, 1858.

Madhouse, sounds of a, *Twice-Told Tales*, vol. i., The Hollow of the Three Hills.

Madness, an easy explanation, *Mosses from an Old Manse*, vol. ii., The Artist of the Beautiful.

Madonnas, *English Note-Books*, vol. ii., August 2, 20, 1857, *Twice-Told Tales*, vol. i., The Prophetic Pictures; early, *French and Italian Journals*, vol. ii., October 5, 1858. See MICHAEL ANGELO, MURILLO, RAPHAEL, and SODOMA.

Madrid, chimneys of, *Twice-Told Tales*, vol. i., Sights from a Steeple.

Magdalen, Titian's, of the Pitti Palace, *The Marble Faun*, vol. ii., chapter iii.

Magic, fabled volumes of, *Fanshawe*, chapter ii.

Magic-lantern reversed, *American Note-Books*, vol. i., October 25, 1836

Magistrates, zeal for godliness of, *The Dolliver Romance, etc.*, Dr. Bullivant.

Magnetism, animal, *American Note-Books*, vol. ii., September 27, 1841. The subject is often alluded to in *The Blithedale Romance*, indirectly in the use of its technical terms, and directly in the experience of Priscilla. See MESMERISM.

Maine, first settlers of, their motives and government, rulers and clergy, *Fanshawe, etc.*, Sir William Phips, second paragraph; disputed territory of, *American Note-Books*, vol. i., July 13, 1837.

Main Street, an article in *The Snow Image, etc.*, describing imaginary scenes in the history of a street in Salem from its beginning as a path through the primitive forest.

Mainwaring family, crest of the, *English Note-Books*, vol. i., October 22, 1853.

Major Molineux, a story of colonial times in *The Snow Image and Other Twice-Told Tales*.

Malaria, in Rome, *The Marble Faun*, vol. i., chapter viii., vol. ii., chapter xi.

Malay Pirates, *Our Old Home*, Consular Experiences.

Malmesbury, statue of the Earl of, *English Note-Books*, vol. ii., June 17, 1856.

Malpas, extract from the parish register of, *English Note-Books*, vol. i., October 22, 1853.

Mamertine Prison, the, *French and Italian Journals*, vol. i., February 23, 1858.

Man demon. See MEMMIUS.

Man, Isle of, *English Note-Books,* vol. i., August 10, 1854.

Man of Adamant, The, An Apologue, in *The Snow Image and Other Twice-Told Tales,* is a story of religious bigotry and its effects on the heart; the author's opinion of, *American Note-Books,* vol. ii., September 16, 1841.

Manchester, *English Note-Books,* vol. ii., May 24, July 22 to September 9, 1857; cathedral of, *ibid.*, April 13, 1857; people of, *ibid.*, September 6, 1857.

Mankind, *American Note-Books,* vol. ii., June 1, 1842.

Manners, most unpleasant kind of, *American Note-Books,* vol. ii., September 9, 1852.

Manse, The Old, title of the first article in *Mosses from an Old Manse.* The house was the old parsonage of Concord, Mass., and was the home of the Hawthorne family from 1842 to 1846. Autographs of occupants of, *American Note-Books,* vol ii., December 19, 1850; full description of, *ibid.*, August 8, 1842; ghosts at, *ibid.*, March 12, 1843; visitors to, *ibid.*, August 5, 1842.

Mansfield, Lord, tomb of, *Our Old Home,* Up the Thames.

Manual Labor School, Thompson's Island, *American Note-Books,* vol. i., August 27, 1837.

Manuscripts, collections of, *English Note-Books,* vol. ii., April 8, 1856, *The Dolliver Romance, etc.*, A Book of Autographs.

Marble Faun, The; or, The Romance of Monte Beni, a novel, the scenes of which are laid in Italy, was sketched there, and rewritten in Redcar, Yorkshire, in 1859. It was published in two volumes in Boston in 1860, by Ticknor and Fields, and simultaneously in London by Smith and Elder, under the title **Transformation.** The original of the tower and castle of Monte Beni was probably the Villa Montauto, where the author spent some time in the summer of 1858, and described in the *French and Italian Journals,* vol. ii., August 3, 1858. The original of Hilda's Tower is described in the same book, under date of May 15, 1858. The first sketch is referred to under date of July 27, 1858. The principal characters in the book are Kenyon and Hilda, American students of art in Rome, Donatello, an Italian count, and Miriam, an Italian artist.

Marblehead, a captain from, *English Note-Books*, vol. ii., May 21, 24, 1856, Liverpool.

Marbles, beauty of, *French and Italian Journals*, vol. i., April 18, 1858, *The Marble Faun*, vol. ii., chapter vi.

Marcellus, theatre of, Rome, *French and Italian Journals*, vol. i., February 23, 1858.

Market-day in Perugia, *The Marble Faun*, vol. ii., chapter ix.

Marlborough, the Duke of: palace and Triumphal Pillar of, *Our Old Home*, Near Oxford; manners of a descendant of, *ibid.*; tomb of, *ibid.*

Marlborough House, *English Note-Books*, vol. ii., August 2, 1856, December 8, 1857.

Marmion, Norham Castle, *English Note-Books*, vol. ii., July 11, 1857.

Marriage: abolition of, *Mosses from an Old Manse*, vol. ii., Earth's Holocaust; anniversary of the author's, *American Note-Books*, vol. ii., July 9, 1843; disappointments of, *The Snow Image, etc.*, The Canterbury Pilgrims; effect of, on women's manners, *The Blithedale Romance*, chapter vi., near the end; for money, *Fanshawe*, middle of chapter iv.; free, *English Note-Books*, vol. ii., April 13, 1857; in Italy, *The Marble Faun*, vol. ii., chapter xxii.; a perfectly harmonious, *Mosses from an Old Manse*, vol. i., A Select Party; prompted as often by despair as hope, *The Blithedale Romance*, chapter xxii.; Zenobia's, *ibid.*, near the end.

Marriages, two, *Our Old Home*, Outside Glimpses of English Poverty, end.

Marseilles, *French and Italian Journals*, vol. i., January 15, 17, 1858, vol. ii., May 29, June 1, 1859.

Marsh, George, a martyr, *English Note-Books*, vol. i., April 7, August 25, 1855.

Marshal of Maine, the, *American Note-Books*, vol. i., July 8, 1837.

Marston, Westland, *English Note-Books*, vol. ii., April 8, 1856.

Mars Ultor, Temple of, *The Marble Faun*, vol. i., chapter xvi.

Martha Pierson, a character in The Shaker Bridal, *Twice-Told Tales*, vol. ii.

Martha's Vineyard, visit to, *Twice-Told Tales*, vol. ii., Chippings with a Chisel.

Martin, Theodore, *English Note-Books*, end of vol. i.

Martineau, Harriet, *English Note-Books*, vol. i., August 26, 1854, July 13, 19, 1855.

Martineau, James, *English Note-Books*, vol. ii., May 24, 1856.

Martyr's Chamber, the, *English Note-Books*, vol. i., August 8, 1853.

Martyrs, Quaker, in Massachusetts, *Twice-Told Tales*, vol. i., The Gentle Boy.

Mary, Queen, of England: incident of the accession of, *American Note-Books*, vol. i., October 25, 1836; of the reign of, *English Note-Books*, vol. i., August 25, 1855.

Mary, Queen, wife of William III., portrait of, *English Note-Books*, vol. ii., July 1, 1857.

Mary, Queen of Scots, *Twice-Told Tales*, vol. ii., Endicott and the Red Cross, *English Note-Books*, vol. ii., July 2, 1857; at Stirling Castle, *ibid.*, May 10, 1856; at Holyrood Palace, *ibid.*; birthplace of, *ibid.*, July 8, 1857; counterpane embroidered by, *Our Old-Home*, Pilgrimage to Old Boston, near the end; first tomb of, *English Note-Books*, vol. ii., May 27, 1857; imprisonment of, in Carlisle, *ibid.*, June 28, 1857; portraits of, *ibid.*, May 10, 1856 (Edinburgh Castle and Abbotsford), July 9, 1857; relics of, *ibid.*, April 10, December 7, 1857; statue of, *ibid.*, vol. i., October 5, 1855.

Marygold, daughter of Midas, *Wonder-Book*, The Golden Touch.

Mason, John Y., Minister to France, *French and Italian Journals*, vol. i., January 11, 1858.

Masquerades, *Twice-Told Tales*, vol. i., The Maypole of Merry Mount, *American Note-Books*, vol. ii., September 28, 1841, *The Blithedale Romance*, chapter xxiv., *Twice-Told Tales*, vol. ii., Howe's Masquerade.

Massachusetts, early governors of, *Grandfather's Chair*, part i., chapter ix.

Massacre, the Boston, *The Snow Image, etc.*, Old News, part iii., *Twice-Told Tales*, vol. ii., Edward Randolph's Portrait.

Massey family, the, of Salem, *The Snow Image, etc.*, Main Street.

Match, a good, *American Note-Books*, vol. i., October 17, 1835.

Materialism: force of, over delicate natures, *The Snow Image*, title story; of spiritualism, *The Blithedale Romance*, chapter xxiii., *American Note-Books*, vol. ii., September 27, 1841.

Mather, Cotton, *Twice-Told Tales*, vol. i., The Gray Champion, The Prophetic Pictures, *Grandfather's Chair*, part ii., chapters ii., iv., v.; book by, *American Note-Books*, vol. ii., December 19, 1850; connection of, with the witchcraft delusion, *The Snow Image, etc.*, Main Street, *The House of the Seven Gables*, chapter xiii.; credibility of, *Twice-Told Tales*, vol. ii., Edward Randolph's Portrait; settlement spoken of by, *American Note-Books*, vol. ii., August 30, 1852; subject for a drawing, *ibid.*, September 14, 1841.

Mather, Increase, a book of, *The Dolliver Romance, etc.*, Dr. Bullivant, *Fanshawe, etc.*, Sir William Phips, third paragraph.

Mather, Nathanael, epitaph of, *Fanshawe*, chapter x., end, *American Note-Books*, vol. i., July 4, 1838.

Mathew, Father Theobald, temperance lecturer, *Mosses from an Old Manse*, vol. ii., Earth's Holocaust.

Matlock, town and cavern, *English Note-Books*, vol. ii., June 7, 1857.

Matrimonial bliss, the basis of, *Mosses from an Old Manse*, vol. i., Mrs. Bullfrog.

Matthew, a character in The Great Carbuncle, *Twice-Told Tales*, vol. i. He and his wife Hannah are seeking the wonderful stone from motives of affection.

Matthews, Charles, *Mosses from an Old Manse*, vol. ii., P.'s Correspondence.

Maturin, Charles R., quotation from, *Fanshawe*, head of chapter viii.

Mauchline, *Our Old Home*, Some of the Haunts of Burns.

Maule, Matthew, the first of the Maule family mentioned in *The House of the Seven Gables*. The account of his fate is in chapter i., and the characteristics of his descendants near the end of the same chapter. A grandson of the same name figures in the romance of chapter xiii.

Maule, Thomas, son of Matthew, the carpenter of the Pyncheon House, chapters i. and xxi.

Maule's Well, *The House of the Seven Gables,* chapters i. and vi.

May-day: at Brook Farm, *American Note-Books,* May 1, 1841; at Blithedale, *The Blithedale Romance,* chapter viii.

Mayflower, The, *English Note-Books,* vol. i., September 22, 1854.

Mayor of Liverpool, dinner of the, *English Note-Books,* vol. ii., December 21, 1856.

Mayor of London: office of, *Our Old Home,* Civic Banquets; dinners given by, *English Note-Books,* vol. i., February 19, 1855, *Our Old Home,* Civic Banquets; estimation of, in America, *ibid.*

Maypole of Merry Mount, The, a sketch in *Twice-Told Tales,* vol. ii., in which an incident in New England history is treated with an allegoric intimation of the relations of mirth and seriousness in life. It was first published in "The Boston Token," in 1835.

McClellan, General, mistake of, *Our Old Home,* Consular Experiences.

McKay, Donald, ship built by, *English Note-Books,* vol. i., October 5, 1854.

McNeill, Rev. Dr., *English Note-Books,* vol. i., February 19, 1855.

Meals, solitary, *American Note-Books,* vol. ii., April 10, 1843.

Medbourne, Mr., a ruined merchant in Dr. Heidegger's Experiment, *Twice-Told Tales,* vol. i.

Medea, *Tanglewood Tales,* The Minotaur, Circe's Palace, The Golden Fleece.

Medici, Cosmo de': collection made by, *French and Italian Journals,* vol. ii., June 11, 1858; statue of, *ibid.,* June 5, 1858.

Medici, Lorenzo de': death-night of, *French and Italian Jour-*

nals, vol. ii., September 29, 1858; statue of, *ibid.*, June 19, 27, September 17, 1858.

Medici family, the: busts of, *French and Italian Journals*, vol. ii., June 8, 1858; home of, *ibid.*, June 28, 1858; pictures of, *ibid.*, July 2, 1858; tombs of, *ibid.*, June 19, 1858.

Medici Gardens, the, *The Marble Faun*, vol. i., chapter xxii.

Medicine, experiments in, *Septimius Felton*, p. 152 (12mo).

Mediterranean, the, *French and Italian Journals*, vol. i., January 15, 24, 1858.

Medium, a spiritualistic, *The Blithedale Romance*, chapter xxiii.

Medusa, *Wonder-Book*, The Gorgon's Head.

Meeting-houses of early New England, *The Snow Image and Other Twice-Told Tales*, Main Street.

Meldrum, Sir John, *English Note-Books*, vol. i., September 7, 1853.

Meleager, *English Note-Books*, vol. i., April 12, 1855.

Melmoth, Dr., a character in *Fanshawe*, introduced in the first chapter. He is president of Harley College, is a book-worm, simple and guileless, ignorant of the world, and under strict domestic discipline. His gullibility is displayed in the scene at the inn, chapter v.; his simplicity and old-fashioned bookishness in the expedition detailed in chapter vii.

Melmoth, Mrs., a character in *Fanshawe*, the shrewish wife of Dr. Melmoth, first appearing in chapter i.

Melrose, Village and Abbey, *English Note-Books*, vol. ii., May 10, 1856, July 11, 1857.

Melville, Herman, *Wonder-Book*, Bald-Summit, *English Note-Books*, vol. i., December 25, 1854, vol. ii., November 30, 1856; "Israel Potter" of, *Our Old Home*, Consular Experiences.

Memmius, *The Marble Faun*, vol. i., chapter iv.

Memory: personification of, *Twice-Told Tales*, vol. i, Fancy's Show Box; seeming, *Our Old Home*, Near Oxford.

Men: ashamed of the best in them, *The Blithedale Romance*, chapter vi.; egotism of, *ibid.*, chapter xiv.; feeling of, toward the sick, *ibid.*, chapter vi.; incompleteness of, on the emotional side, *ibid.*

Menagerie, a, *Twice-Told Tales*, vol i., Little Annie's Ramble

Menai Strait, *English Note-Books,* vol. i., July 19, 1854.
Mephistopheles, the, of picture-galleries, *The Marble Faun,* vol. ii., chapter xii.
Mercenary Soldiers, first in America, *Twice-Told Tales,* vol. i., The Gray Champion.
Merchant, a ruined, a character in the story The Canterbury Pilgrims, in *The Snow Image and Other Twice-Told Tales.*
Mercia, legend of two princes of, *Our Old Home,* Lichfield and Uttoxeter.
Mercury (Quicksilver), *Wonder-Book,* The Gorgon's Head, The Paradise of Children, The Miraculous Pitcher; statues of, *French and Italian Journals,* vol. i., January 15, vol. ii., July 4, 16, 1858.
Merlin, *The Dolliver Romance, etc.,* The Antique Ring.
Mermaid, The, name for Susan in The Village Uncle, *Twice-Told Tales,* vol. ii.
Merriment of the melancholy, *The Marble Faun,* vol. i., chapter ix.
Merry England, meaning of the word, *American Note-Books,* vol. i., October 25, 1836.
Mersey River, the, *English Note-Books,* vol. i., August 9, September 1, 1853, vol. ii., August 21, 1856.
Merton College, Oxford, *English Note-Books,* vol. ii., August 31, 1856.
Mesmerism, *American Note-Books,* vol. ii., September 27, 1841, 1842, *The House of the Seven Gables,* chapters xiii., xiv., *The Blithedale Romance,* chapters i., xiii., xxii., xxiii.
Messalina, features of, *French and Italian Journals,* vol. ii., June 8, 1858.
Metanira, Queen, *Tanglewood Tales,* The Pomegranate Seeds.
Metella, Cecilia, tomb of, *French and Italian Journals,* vol. ii., March 11, 1859. See Appian Way.
Meteors, going to waste, *Mosses from an Old Manse,* vol. i., A Select Party.
Methodists, the: a drover belonging to, *American Note-Books,* vol. i., August 19, 1838; in England, *Our Old Home,* A London Suburb.

Michael, the archangel: Guido's picture of, *The Marble Faun*, vol. i., chapters xv., xx.; mosaic copy of the above, *ibid.*, vol. ii., chapter xiii; statue of, on the Castle of St. Angelo, *French and Italian Journals*, vol. i., March 25, 1858.

Michael Angelo, *The Marble Faun*, vol. i., chapter xii.; architecture of, *French and Italian Journals*, vol. i., April 25, 1858; best work of (Lorenzo), *ibid.*, vol. ii., June 19, 27, September 17, 1858; drawings of, *English Note-Books*, vol. ii, August 31, 1856, Taylor Institute; the "Fates," by, *French and Italian Journals*, vol. ii., June 10, 21, 1858; head of Brutus by, *The Marble Faun*, vol. ii., chapter xvi.; home of, *French and Italian Journals*, vol. ii., July 2, 1858; the "Last Judgment," *ibid.*, vol. i., May 15, 1858; Madonna of, *ibid.*, vol. ii., June 30, 1858; monument of, *ibid.*, June 28, 1858; St. Matthew by, *ibid*, July 13, 1858; statue by, *English Note-Books*, vol. ii., November 16, 1857.

Mickle, William Julius, scene of his ballad "Cumnor Hall," *Our Old Home*, Near Oxford.

Midas, King, *Wonder-Book*, The Golden Touch.

Migration, a possible effect of, *American Note-Books*, vol. i., September 7, 1835.

Milford, scene of The Minister's Black Veil, *Twice-Told Tales*, vol. i.

Military Glory, satire on, *Twice-Told Tales*, vol. ii., Snow Flakes.

Military science and poetry, *The Snow Image and Other Twice-Told Tales*, Old Ticonderoga.

Milking, *American Note-Books*, vol. ii., April 13, 14, 16, 1841.

Milkweed, name given to one of the children to whom the stories of the *Wonder-Book* and *Tanglewood Tales* were told.

Millais, picture by, *English Note-Books*, vol. ii., May 24, 1856, Manchester.

Miller, General James, *The Scarlet Letter*, The Custom-House.

Miller, William, founder of the Millerites, *Mosses from an Old Manse*, vol. i., The Hall of Fantasy, near the end, vol. ii., The New Adam and Eve, The Christmas Banquet.

Mills, Clark, statues by, *French and Italian Journals*, vol. i., June 4, 1858.

Milnes, Monckton, Lord Houghton, *English Note-Books*, vol. i., September 22, 29, 1854; breakfast party given by, *ibid.*, vol. ii., July 13, 1856; resemblance of, to Longfellow, *ibid.*, April 19, 1857; wife of, *ibid.*, July 10, 1856.

Milton, John, *Mosses from an Old Manse*, vol. i., The Hall of Fantasy; allusion to "L'Allegro," *American Note-Books*, vol. ii., August 10, 1842; busts of, *Our Old Home*, Up the Thames, *The Marble Faun*, vol. i., Preface, chapter xiii.; "dim, religious light," *ibid.*, vol. ii., chapter viii., *French and Italian Journals*, vol. i., June 5, 1858; grave of, *English Note-Books*, vol. i., March 25, 1856; in Rome, *French and Italian Journals*, vol. i., February 20, 1858; Lycidas, *English Note-Books* vol. ii., December 31, 1856, May 10, 1857; statue of "Il Penseroso," *French and Italian Journals*, vol. ii., June 13, 1858; suggestion of a line of, *Our Old Home*, Outside Glimpses of English Poverty; taste of, for the pleasures of the table, *ibid.*, Civic Banquets; works of, *Mosses from an Old Manse*, vol. ii., Earth's Holocaust.

Mineral Spring, Salem, view from the, *American Note-Books*, vol. i., October 7, 1837.

Minerva, *Wonder-Book*, The Gorgon's Head; temple of, in Rome, *The Marble Faun*, vol. i., chapter xvi.

Minister's Black Veil, The, A Parable, *Twice-Told Tales*, vol. i. This story was first published in "The Boston Token and Atlantic Souvenir," in 1835. Having isolated himself from his fellows outwardly by the mysterious confession expressed in the veil, Mr. Hooper, the minister of the story, is brought closer to them in a subtle insight and sympathy, the source of his great professional power. For conversation suggested by the story, see *American Note-Books*, vol. i., July 15, 1837.

Ministers, foreign, *French and Italian Journals*, vol. i., January 11, 1858.

Ministers, Puritan, portraits of, *Mosses from an Old Manse*, vol. ii., The Old Manse, near the beginning.

Minos, King, *Tanglewood Tales*, The Minotaur.

Minotaur, The, title of the first story in *Tanglewood Tales*.

Minster Pool, the, *Our Old Home*, Lichfield and Uttoxeter.

Miracles, spirit in which they must be wrought, *The Snow Image*, title story.

Miraculous Pitcher, The, story in the *Wonder-Book*.

Miriam, a character in *The Marble Faun*, introduced in chapter i. She is a girl of great beauty and considerable skill as an artist. Her nationality and origin are involved in mystery throughout most of the story, the consequence of her being under the shadow of a crime. The analysis made of the portrait of Beatrice Cenci and the peculiar use of it in the story suggest some analogy in her life to that of Miriam, whose relationship to the murdered monk has been the subject of much conjecture.

Miriam, heroine of the story The Canterbury Pilgrims, in *The Snow Image and Other Twice-Told Tales*.

Mirror, in the old Province House, *Twice-Told Tales*, vol. ii., Old Esther Dudley.

Mirth, sometimes held to a stricter accountability than sorrow, *The Blithedale Romance*, chapter ix., middle.

Miser: ghost of a, *The Dolliver Romance, etc.*, Graves and Goblins; value of the soul of a, *Mosses from an Old Manse*, vol. i., The Celestial Railroad.

Miserable, banquet for the most, *Mosses from an Old Manse*, vol. ii., The Christmas Banquet.

Misery: of long familiarity with distasteful objects, *The Blithedale Romance*, chapter xxii., near the end; the only remedy for the world's, *Our Old Home*, Outside Glimpses of English Poverty, near the end.

Misfortune: alienating effect of, *The Marble Faun*, vol. i., chapters xi., xiii.; impulse given by, *American Note-Books*, vol. ii., September 11, 1852; a means of elevation, *ibid.*, December 19, 1850.

Missionary, a city, suggestion for, *American Note-Books*, vol. i., October 25, 1836.

Mistakes: a generous, *The Blithedale Romance*, chapter iii.;

great, never set wholly right, *The House of the Seven Gables*, chapter xxi., near the beginning; of sagacious men, *ibid.*, chapter xvi., near the beginning; the sense of, *Septimius Felton*, pp. 49, 58 (12mo).

Mitchell, Maria, *French and Italian Journals*, vol. i., January 9, 15, 24, 1858.

Mitford, Mary Russell, *English Note-Books*, vol. ii., April 8, 1856.

Mitre Tavern, the, *English Note-Books*, vol. i., October 3, 1855.

Model, Miriam's. See ANTONIO.

Mohun, Lady, anecdote of, *American Note-Books*, vol. ii., 1842.

Molineux, Major. See MAJOR MOLINEUX.

Monadnoc, Mt., *American Note-Books*, vol. i., August 31, 1838.

Money: coinage of, in Massachusetts colony, *Grandfather's Chair*, part i., chapter vi.; the craving for, *Our Old Home*, Outside Glimpses of English Poverty, near the end.

Monks: choice of sites by, *English Note-Books*, vol. ii., April 11, 1857, *Our Old Home*, About Warwick; Kenyon's opinion of, *The Marble Faun*, vol. ii., chapter iv.; looks of, *French and Italian Journals*, vol. i., February 17, 1858; reason for the existence of, *English Note-Books*, vol. i., September 9, 1855.

Monotony: growing, of life, *Our Old Home*, Up the Thames; need of, *French and Italian Journals*, vol. ii., June 13, 1858.

Mons Meg, an old cannon, *English Note-Books*, vol. ii., May 10, 1856, Edinburgh, July 9, 10, 1857.

Monsieur du Miroir, an essay in *Mosses from an Old Manse*, vol. i., the nature of which is indicated by the name; the author's opinion of the story, *American Note-Books*, vol. ii., September 16, 1841.

Monster, a, *The Blithedale Romance*, chapter xxv.

Montagu, Lady Mary Wortley, *Our Old Home*, Lichfield and Uttoxeter.

Montauto, Villa and Count of, *French and Italian Journals*, vol. ii., August 2, 1858. The original of Donatello's Castle in *The Marble Faun*.

Montcalm, General, *Grandfather's Chair*, part ii., chapter ix.

Monte Beni, *French and Italian Journals*, vol. ii., August 2, 1858.

Monte Beni, Count of. See DONATELLO.

Monte Beni family, the: their pedigree and characteristics, physical and moral, *The Marble Faun,* vol. ii., chapter i.; legends of the family, vol. ii., chapters ii. and iii.

Montefiascone, *The Marble Faun,* vol. ii., chapter xviii.

Montreaux, Switzerland, the *curé* of, *American Note-Books,* vol. ii., 1842.

Montrose, Duke of, relic of, *English Note-Books,* vol. ii., May 10, 1856, Abbotsford.

Monument Mountain, Berkshire County, Mass., *American Note-Books,* vol. ii., August 5, 19, October 13, 1850, February 12, March 11, May 23, 1851, *Wonder-Book,* Bald-Summit, Tanglewood Porch, *Tanglewood Tales,* Introduction.

Monuments: desire for, *Twice-Told Tales,* vol. ii., The Ambitious Guest; device for a, *American Note-Books,* vol. i., 1840; London, *English Note-Books,* vol. i., September 7, 10, 1855; of battle, *Twice-Told Tales,* vol. ii., Snow Flakes; uselessness of, *English Note-Books,* vol. ii., November 12, 1857.

Moodie, Old, a character in *The Blithedale Romance,* who appears in chapter i. The mystery as to his identity forms an important link in the plot of the book. His early history and characteristics are given in chapter xxii., his looks and manner described in chapters x. and xxi. He is said to be drawn from the old man mentioned in the *American Note-Books,* May 7, 1850, as seen at Parker's in Court-House Square, Boston.

Moods, what are to be trusted, *Septimius Felton,* p. 12 (12mo).

Moody, Betty. See BETTY MOODY.

Moody, Rev. Joseph, of York, Maine, note to The Minister's Black Veil, *Twice-Told Tales,* vol. i.

Moon, a child's idea of the, *English Note-Books,* vol. i., November 14, 1854.

Moonlight, *American Note-Books,* vol. i., October 24, 1838; collected, *Mosses from an Old Manse,* vol. i., A Select Party; favorable to fancy, *The Scarlet Letter,* The Custom-House, near the end; in Rome, *The Marble Faun,* vol. i., chapter xvi.

Moon, Man in the, *Mosses from an Old Manse,* vol. i., A Select Party.

Moore, Bramley, dinner with, *English Note-Books,* vol. i., February 27, 1854.

Moore, Robert, a young blacksmith in the story John Inglefield's Thanksgiving, in *The Snow Image, etc.*

Moore, Sir John, statue of, *English Note-Books,* vol. ii., July 1, 1857.

Moore, Thomas, *Mosses from an Old Manse,* vol. ii., Earth's Holocaust; and Byron, *ibid.,* P.'s Correspondence; note in diary of, *English Note Books,* vol. i., October 22, 1853.

Morality, machine for manufacturing, *Mosses from an Old Manse,* vol. i., The Celestial Railroad.

Morbid natures: type of, *Mosses from an Old Manse,* vol. ii., Egotism; treatment of, *The House of the Seven Gables,* chapter ix., end.

Morbidness, mistaken charge of, against Hawthorne, *English Note-Books,* Preface.

More, Sir Thomas, relic of, *English Note-Books,* vol. ii., July 26, 1857.

Morgan, Lady, *English Note-Books,* vol. ii., July 9, 1856.

Morleys, graves of the, *English Note-Books,* vol. ii., April 11, 1857.

Morning light, rectifying power of, *Mosses from an Old Manse,* vol. ii., Rappaccini's Daughter.

Morning walk, a, *American Note-Books,* vol. i., August 26, 1838.

Morris-dance, *Twice-Told Tales,* vol. i., The Maypole of Merry Mount.

Mortality, first greeting with, *Twice-Told Tales,* vol. ii., Edward Fane's Rosebud.

Mortar used in mediæval buildings of Rome, *The Marble Faun,* vol. i., chapter xii.

Morton of Merry Mount, *The Snow Image, etc.,* Main Street.

Mosaic-work, *French and Italian Journals,* vol. i., April 25, vol. ii., September 21, 1858, *The Marble Faun,* vol. ii., chapter xiii.

Moses: horned statue of, *French and Italian Journals,* vol. i., April 16, 1858; statue of, at a fountain, *ibid.,* February 19, 1858.

Moss Giel, farm of Burns, *Our Old Home*, Some of the Haunts of Burns.

Mosses from an Old Manse, a collection of tales and sketches in two volumes, first published at New York in 1846. The stories had previously appeared in periodicals, most of them in "The Democratic Review," published first at Washington, afterwards at New York, from 1838 to 1851.

Mother Goose's Melodies, *Mosses from an Old Manse*, vol. ii., Earth's Holocaust.

Mothers: imaginations of, *The Snow Image*, title story; incident of a, *American Note-Books*, vol. i., October 24, 1838.

Motley, John Lothrop, *French and Italian Journals*, vol. ii., March 9, 1859.

Mounds, *American Note-Books*, vol. i., August 31, 1838.

Mountains: names of, *Mosses from an Old Manse*, vol. ii., Sketches from Memory, The Notch of the White Mountains; of England and America, *English Note-Books*, vol. i., July 21, 1855; living amid, *Tanglewood Tales*, Introduction; of Scotland, *English Note-Books*, vol. ii., May 10, 1856.

Mount Auburn Cemetery, *Mosses from an Old Manse*, vol. ii., The New Adam and Eve.

Mourning, class that love the house of, *Fanshawe*, chapter ix.

Mr. Higginbotham's Catastrophe, a short, humorous story in *Twice-Told Tales*, vol. ii. It was one of the stories to be told by the wandering story-teller in Passages from a Relinquished Work, *Mosses from an Old Manse*, vol. ii. See The Village Theatre in that article.

Mugione, village of, *French and Italian Journals*, vol. i., May 29, 1858.

Müller, Mr., pictures of, *French and Italian Journals*, vol. i., April 27, 1858.

Murderer, ghost of a, *The Dolliver Romance and Other Pieces*, Graves and Goblins.

Murillo, *French and Italian Journals*, vol. i., April 25, 1858, *English Note-Books*, vol. i., March 26, 1856; "Good Shepherd" of, *ibid.*, vol. ii., August 16, 1857; Madonnas by, *French and Italian Journals*, vol. ii., June 13, 1858; St. John by, *English Note-Books*, vol. ii., November 12, December 8, 27, 1857.

Muro Torto, fragment of the old Roman wall, *The Marble Faun*, vol. i., chapter xii.

Murray, Colonel, tomb of, *English Note-Books*, vol. i., August 10, 1854.

Murray, John: book given to Rogers by, *English Note-Books*, vol. ii., May 24, 1856, Manchester; publishing house of, *ibid.*, vol. i., September 14, 1855.

Murray, the Regent, death of, *English Note-Books*, vol. ii., July 8, 1857.

Museums: imaginary, *American Note-Books*, vol. ii., June 1, 1842; article about a (suggestion, perhaps, of A Virtuoso's Collection), *ibid.*, vol. i., October 25, 1836; the British, *English Note-Books*, vol. i., September 24, 1855, March 27, 1856, vol. ii., December 7, 1857; the New England, *Twice-Told Tales*, vol. ii., Edward Randolph's Portrait; the Salem, *The Snow Image, etc.*, Main Street.

Musgrave, Mrs., *English Note-Books*, vol. ii, July 10, 1856.

Mushrooms, *American Note-Books*, vol. ii., October 8, 1841.

Music, *Twice-Told Tales*, vol. i., Sunday at Home.

Musical instruments, famous, *Mosses from an Old Manse*, vol. ii., A Virtuoso's Collection.

Musicians: should not be in sight, *English Note-Books*, vol. ii., April 12, 1857; vagabond, *ibid.*, vol. i., June 20, 1854, June 11, July 27, October 3, 1855.

Musketaquid, the (row-boat), *American Note-Books*, vol. ii., September 2, 1842.

Mussulmans, reverence of, for manuscript, *Mosses from an Old Manse*, vol. i., The Old Manse, near the middle.

My Home Return, part ii. of the Journal of a Solitary Man, in *The Dolliver Romance and Other Pieces.*

Mystery, love of small, *Twice-Told Tales*, vol. i., Wakefield.

Mysticism, the, of the age, *The Blithedale Romance*, chapter xxiii.

N ——, C., *American Note-Books*, vol. ii., April 8, 1843.

Nahant, *American Note-Books*, vol. i., August 31, 1835, *Twice-Told Tales*, vol. ii., The Village Uncle.

Naiad, a, *Twice-Told Tales*, vol. i., The Vision of the Fountain.

Naiads, the, *Tanglewood Tales*, The Pomegranate Seeds.

Names: choice of a, for Blithedale, *The Blithedale Romance*, chapter v.; for butchers and a schoolmistress, *American Note-Books*, vol. ii., June 1, 1842; in the sand, *Twice-Told Tales*, vol. ii., Footprints on the Sea Shore; magic of a, *Mosses from an Old Manse*, vol. ii., Passages from a Relinquished Work, The Village Theatre.

Nantucket, secluded life of, *Twice-Told Tales*, vol. ii., Chippings with a Chisel.

Napoleon I.: fantasy concerning, *Mosses from an Old Manse*, vol. ii., P.'s Correspondence; power of, compared with Louis Napoleon's, *French and Italian Journals*, vol. i., January 9, 1858; veteran of, *English Note-Books*, vol. i., February 27, 1854.

Napoleon III., *French and Italian Journals*, vol. ii., September 29, 1858; attempted assassination of, *ibid.*, vol. i., January 15, 1858; improvement of Paris by, *ibid.*, January 8, 1858; power of, compared with Napoleon I.'s, *ibid.*, January 9, 1858.

Narni, town and castle, *French and Italian Journals*, vol. i., May 25, 1858.

Nar River, or Nera, *French and Italian Journals*, vol. i., May 25, 1858.

Nash, Beau, *French and Italian Journals*, vol. ii., April 23, 1860.

National Gallery, the London, *English Note-Books*, vol. i., March 26, 1856.

Naturalists, antique, *Mosses from an Old Manse*, vol. i., The Birthmark.

Naturalized citizens of America, *English Note-Books*, vol. i., November 2, 1854.

Nature: bounty of, *American Note Books*, vol. ii., August 27, 1842, *Mosses from an Old Manse*, vol. i., The Old Manse, near the middle; fineness of workmanship of, *American Note-Books,* vol. i., October 7, 1837; mysterious ways of, *ibid.*, vol. ii., June 23, 1843; profit of intercourse with, *Mosses from an Old Manse,* vol. i., The Old Manse, after the middle; propriety in the forms of, *ibid.*, Buds and Bird Voices; readiness to convert the human body to her lower purposes, *The Blithedale Romance,* chapter xxviii., end; secrets of, *Mosses from an Old Manse,* vol. i., The Birthmark; sympathy of, *The Scarlet Letter,* chapter xviii.; treachery of, *American Note-Books,* vol. ii., June 2, 1843; uncleanliness of, *Mosses from an Old Manse,* vol. i., Buds and Bird Voices.

Nature: common defect of a delicate, *Mosses from an Old Manse,* vol. ii., The Intelligence Office; glances at our own, *Twice-Told Tales,* vol. ii., Footprints on the Sea Shore.

Naumkeag, first name of Salem, *The Snow Image, etc.,* Main Street.

Naval men, manners of, *English Note-Books,* vol. ii., June 25, 1857.

Naylor, Mr., pictures belonging to, *English Note-Books,* vol. i., September 26, 1854.

Neal, John, *Mosses from an Old Manse,* vol. ii., P.'s Correspondence.

Near Oxford, an article in *Our Old Home,* describing Oxford, Blenheim, Cumnor, Stanton Harcourt, and Nuneham Courtney.

Needham Road, walk on the, *American Note-Books,* vol. ii., October 7, 1841.

Needle-work, *The Marble Faun,* vol. i., chapter v.

Negroes: advertisement of, *American Note-Books,* vol. i., October 25, 1836; at Brook Farm, *ibid.*, vol. ii., April 16, 1841; characters among, *ibid.*, vol. i., August 15, September 9, 1838; favorite picture of heaven of, *Twice-Told Tales,* vol. i., Sunday at Home; melodies of, *English Note-Books,* vol. i., April 1, 1855.

Nelson, Horatio: character and genius of, *Our Old Home,* A London Suburb; English appreciation of, *ibid.*; monument to, *English Note-Books,* vol. ii., July 13, 1856; relics of, *Our*

Old Home, A London Suburb; Southey's life of, *ibid.;* unlikeness of, to his countrymen, *English Note-Books,* vol. ii., July 30, 1857.

Nelson Monument, the, *English Note-Books,* vol. i., September 10, 1855.

Nero, face and character of, *French and Italian Journals,* vol. ii., June 8, 1858.

Netley Abbey, *English Note-Books,* vol. ii., July 6, 1856.

New Adam and Eve, The, a sketch in *Mosses from an Old Manse,* vol. ii. It imagines a newly-created pair coming into the world just after all human beings should have been swept away from it, and their ideas of the works of man remaining. A suggestion of the story is given in the *American Note-Books,* vol. i., October 25, 1836. It first appeared in "The Democratic Review."

Newby Bridge, *English Note-Books,* vol. i., July 13, 27, 1855.

Newcastle, New Hampshire, *American Note-Books,* vol. ii., May 5, 1850.

Newcastle, the Duke of, *English Note-Books,* vol. ii., August 14, 1857, *Our Old Home,* Up the Thames.

Newcastle-upon-Tyne, *English Note-Books,* vol. ii., May 10, 1856.

New College, Oxford, *English Note-Books,* vol. ii., August 31, 1856.

New England, arts, fasts, feasts, funerals, governors, laws, literature, luxuries, manners, slaves, society, and witchcraft of, in 1759–60, *The Snow Image, etc.,* Old News, parts i. and ii.; early government of, *Grandfather's Chair,* part i., chapter v.; early settlers of, *ibid.,* part i., chapter ii.; humor of, *The Snow Image, etc.,* Old News, part i.; picturesqueness of, *ibid.;* summer in, *American Note-Books,* vol. ii., June 2, 1843; type of the hereditary spirit of, *Twice-Told Tales,* vol. i., The Gray Champion; under James II., *ibid.;* villages of, *The Marble Faun,* vol. i., chapter xii., vol. ii., chapter xii., at the close; winter in, *American Note-Books,* vol. ii., March 31, 1843, *Twice-Told Tales,* vol. ii., Snow Flakes.

New Englanders, adventurousness of, *Fanshawe, etc.,* Sir

William Pepperell, first paragraph; hatred of the French by, in early times, *ibid.;* not revengeful, *The Dolliver Romance, etc.*, Dr. Bullivant.

New England Farmer, The, an agricultural newspaper published in Boston, *Fanshawe, etc.*, T. G. Fessenden.

New England Magazine, the, *The Snow Image, etc.*, Old News, part ii.

New Hampshire, first settlers of, their motives and government, rulers and clergy, *Fanshawe, etc.*, Sir William Phips, second paragraph.

New Haven, settlement of, *Grandfather's Chair*, part i., chapter iv.

New Orleans, the battle of: incidents of, *English Note-Books*, vol. ii., December 15, 1856; English ideas of, *Our Old Home*, Consular Experiences, beginning.

Newspaper: name for a, *American Note-Books*, vol. ii., 1842; of the eighteenth century, a, *Fanshawe*, chapter vi.; vividness of a, *Mosses from an Old Manse*, vol. i., The Old Manse, near the middle.

Newstead Abbey, *English Note-Books*, vol. ii., May 29, 1857; mentioned in "Don Juan," *ibid.*

Newton, Sir Isaac: school-days of, *English Note-Books*, vol. ii., May 28, 1857; sketch of, *True Stories*, chapter iii. of Biographies (only in 16mo ed.); statue of, *English Note Books*, vol. ii., May 10, 1856, Dryburgh.

New Year's Day, customs of, *English Note-Books*, vol. i., January 1, 1856.

New Zealander, story of a, *English Note-Books*, vol. i., August 12, 1855.

Niagara Falls, *Twice-Told Tales*, vol. i., The Prophetic Pictures, vol. ii., The Haunted Mind, *The Dolliver Romance, etc.*, Journal of a Solitary Man, i.; cause of first disappointment in, how to look at, and visitors to, *The Dolliver Romance, etc.*, My Visit to Niagara.

Niagara, Fort, siege of, *The Snow Image, etc.*, Old News, part ii.

Niagara, My Visit to, title of an article in the volume *The Dolliver Romance.*

Nicholas, Czar: character of, *English Note-Books*, vol. i., September 26, 1855; attempted assassination of, *ibid.*

Nicholson, Mr., English scientist, *Fanshawe, etc.*, T. G. Fessenden, fourth paragraph.

Nightingale, Florence, gift to, *English Note-Books*, vol. i., March 25, 1856.

Nightingale, Mrs., *English Note-Books*, vol. ii., July 13, 1856.

Nightmare, *Wonder-Book*, The Gorgon's Head.

Night-ride, a, *American Note-Books*, vol. i., July 27, 1838.

Night-scene, a, in Boston Harbor, *American Note-Books*, vol. i., July 10, 1838.

Night Scene, A, one of the Sketches from Memory in the volume *The Dolliver Romance*, describing a fire on the shore of Lake Erie.

Night Sketches beneath an Umbrella, an essay in *Twice-Told Tales*, vol. ii.

Niobe, tears of, *Mosses from an Old Manse* vol. ii., A Virtuoso's Collection.

Nixon, a half-idiot, predictions of, *English Note-Books*, vol. i., October 22, 1853.

Noblemen: burdens of, and republicans as friends to, *English Note-Books*, vol. ii., April 19, 1857; lives of, *Our Old Home*, Near Oxford.

Nobody, *Mosses from an Old Manse*, vol. i., A Select Party.

Nomadic habits natural to mankind, *The Marble Faun*, vol. ii., chapter vii.

Nonsense, should be mingled with wisdom, *The Blithedale Romance*, chapter xv.

Normanby, Marquis of, *Grandfather's Chair*, part ii., chapter ii.

Norris Green, *English Note-Books*, vol. i., February 28, 1856.

Norris, Mr., minister of Salem, *The Snow Image, etc.*, Main Street.

North Branch of Concord River, scenery of, *American Note-Books*, vol. ii., September 18, 1842.

North Cork Regiment, officers of the, *English Note-Books*, vol. i., April 1, 1856.

Northfields, a walk in, *American Note-Books,* vol. i., October 27, 1837.

Northumberland House. *English Note-Books,* vol. i., September 10, 1855.

North Wind, two sons of the, *Tanglewood Tales,* The Golden Fleece.

Norton, Cyril, a character in *Septimius Felton,* a young English soldier appearing in the early part of the book.

Norton, George, mayor of Liverpool, *English Note-Books,* vol. i., September 7, 1853.

Norton, Lady Caroline, *French and Italian Journals,* vol. ii., May 16, 17, 1860.

Norton, Mr., of Martha's Vineyard, *Twice-Told Tales,* vol. ii., Chippings with a Chisel.

Notch, mountain, near North Adams, *American Note-Books,* vol. i., August 22, 1838.

Notch of the White Mountains, The, one of the Sketches from Memory, in *Mosses from an Old Manse,* vol. ii.

Notoriety, craving for, *Mosses from an Old Manse,* vol. ii., Egotism.

Nottingham, *English Note-Books,* vol. ii., May 28, 29, 1857.

Novels: as distinguished from romances, *The House of the Seven Gables,* Preface; moral purposes of, *ibid.*

Novelty, loss of power to deal with, *The House of the Seven Gables,* chapter xi., beginning.

Noyes, Rev. Mr., *The Snow Image, etc.,* Main Street.

Nude figures: in painting, *The Marble Faun,* vol. ii., chapter xii.; in statuary, *ibid.,* vol. i., chapter xiv.

Nuneham Courtney, residence of the Harcourts, *Our Old Home,* Near Oxford, near the end.

Nuns; looks of, *French and Italian Journals,* vol. i., February 17, 1858.

Oakford family, the, *English Note-Books,* vol. i., September 27, 29, 1855.

Oak Hall, *The Snow Image, etc.,* Main Street.

"**Oakum**," a captain's wife, *English Note-Books,* vol. ii., May 24, 1856, Liverpool.

Obelisk in Rome, *The Marble Faun*, vol. i., chapter xii.

Oberon, a name over which Hawthorne published some of his contributions to periodicals It is used in the story The Devil in Manuscript, in *The Snow Image, etc.*, as the name of a literary law-student, and of the solitary man in *The Dolliver Romance, etc.*, Journal of a Solitary Man.

Obscurity of the author, *Twice-Told Tales,* Preface, *The Snow Image, etc.,* dedication.

Observer: the, at the play of destiny, *The Blithedale Romance,* chapter xi., end; training for an, *Twice-Told Tales,* vol. i., The Toll-Gatherer's Day.

O'Conor, Charles, bit of enthusiasm of, *Our Old Home,* About Warwick (printed Conner).

Odors: of decay, *English Note-Books*, vol. ii., April 11, 1857; of old cities, *ibid.*, May 10, 1856, Edinburgh; peculiarities of, *Mosses from an Old Manse,* vol. i., Rappaccini's Daughter, after the middle.

Offense, the, most troublesome to a woman, *The Blithedale Romance,* chapter v.

Office: appointment to, in America, *Our Old Home,* Consular Experiences; loss of, *The Scarlet Letter,* The Custom-House, near the end; prospect of, *American Note-Books,* vol. ii., March 31, 1843.

Offices, political, *American Note-Books,* vol. i., letter, March 15, 1840.

Ogden, Mr., of Chicago, *English Note-Books,* vol. i., August 10, 1853.

Oil-painting, story of the secret of, *French and Italian Journals,* vol. ii., August 19, 1858.

Old Age: in plants and people, *American Note-Books,* vol. ii., April 26, 1843, *Mosses from an Old Manse,* vol. i., Buds and Bird Voices; Scripture description of, *The Dolliver Romance,* first fragment.

Old Apple-Dealer, The, a study of an individual of colorless and negative character in *Mosses from an Old Manse,* vol. ii.

Old Esther Dudley, one of the Legends of the Province House, in *Twice-Told Tales*, vol. ii.

Oldest Inhabitant, the, *Mosses from an Old Manse*, vol. i., A Select Party.

Old-Fashioned School, The, sketch in *Grandfather's Chair*, part ii., chapter iii.

Old French War, The, part ii. of Old News, in *The Snow Image, etc.*, a glance at American life about 1760.

Old Harry, the, *Mosses from an Old Manse*, vol. i., A Select Party.

Old Maidens, asylum for, *English Note-Books*, vol. ii., April 12, 1857.

Old Man of the Sea, the, *Wonder-Book*, The Three Golden Apples.

Old men, moral susceptibility of, *Our Old Home*, A London Suburb.

Old News, an article in *The Snow Image and Other Twice-Told Tales*. It is in three parts, referring to files of Boston newspapers; the first of about 1740, the second 1760, the third 1780.

Old People, in England and America, *Our Old Home*, Pilgrimage to Old Boston, near the end.

Old Province House, the, the former dwelling of the royal governors of Massachusetts, on Washington Street, nearly opposite Milk Street. It stood back from the street, and a brick building was placed in front of it. It is described in Howe's Masquerade, *Twice-Told Tales*, vol. ii.

Old South Church, Boston, *Twice-Told Tales*, vol. ii., Howe's Masquerade, Edward Randolph's Portrait.

Old Ticonderoga, A Picture of the Past, a description of the old fort, with a picture of its history, in *The Snow Image and Other Twice-Told Tales*.

Old Tory, The, part iii. of Old News, in *The Snow Image, etc.*, is the picture of a loyalist during the Revolutionary War.

Old Trafford, Manchester, *English Note-Books*, vol. ii., July 22, 1857.

Old Woman's Tale, An, a sketch in the volume *The Dolliver Romance, etc.*, the scene of which is a Connecticut village.

Oliver, Andrew, Lieutenant Governor of Massachusetts, *American Note-Books*, vol. ii., September 14, 1841; hanging in effigy of, *Grandfather's Chair*, part iii., chapters ii., iii.

Oliver, Peter, *Grandfather's Chair*, part iii., chapter ix.

Olivers, portraits of the, *American Note-Books*, vol. i., August 22, 1837.

Omens, in New England, *The Scarlet Letter*, chapter xii.

Omskirk, Village and Church, *English Note-Books*, vol. ii., October 26, 1856.

On-Dit, Monsieur, *Mosses from an Old Manse*, vol. i., A Select Party.

Onondaga, salt springs of, *The Dolliver Romance and Other Pieces*, A Book of Autographs.

Opium-dreams, *American Note-Books*, vol. ii., September 27, 1841.

Opium-eater, an, *American Note-Books*, vol. i., September 9, 1838.

Opportunity, statue of, *Mosses from an Old Manse*, vol. ii., A Virtuoso's Collection.

Orange, at Brook Farm, *American Note-Books*, vol. ii., September 28, 1841.

Orange, Prince of, William III., *Twice-Told Tales*, vol. i., The Gray Champion.

Orator, the making of an, *English Note-Books*, vol. ii., April 4, 1856.

Oratory, *French and Italian Journals*, vol. ii., July 8, 1858; Donatello's, *The Marble Faun*, vol. ii., chapter iii.

Orchards, *American Note-Books*, vol. ii., August 9, 1842; relation of, to mankind, *Mosses from an Old Manse*, vol. i., The Old Manse, near the middle.

Ore, enchanted, *American Note-Books*, vol. i., Augut 31, 1838.

Orgagna, pictures by, *French and Italian Journals*, vol. ii., July 4, 1858.

Organ-grinder's show, moral of an, *The House of the Seven Gables*, chapter xi.

Organs, facts concerning, *American Note-Books*, vol. i., October 25, 1836.

Originality: false, *Mosses from an Old Manse*, vol. i., The Old Manse, toward the end; kinds of, *American Note-Books*, vol. ii., September 2, 1842.

Originals, dullness of, *American Note-Books*, vol. ii., September 2, 1842.

Ornamental People, in old age, *Mosses from an Old Manse*, vol. i., Buds and Bird Voices.

Orontes, a pet spider, *Septimius Felton*, pp. 155, 161-2 (12mo).

Orphans, fate of, *Mosses from an Old Manse*, vol. ii., Passages from a Relinquished Work, At Home.

Orpheus, *Tanglewood Tales*, The Golden Fleece.

Orrin S——, *American Note-Books*, vol. i., August 11, 19, 26, September 3, 4, 1838.

O'Sullivan, *English Note-Books*, vol. i., September 13, 1854.

O'Sullivan, publisher, *American Note-Books*, vol. ii., March 1, 6, 1843.

Otaheite, handiwork of the queen of, *Our Old Home*, Pilgrimage to Old Boston, near the end

Otricoli, *French and Italian Journals*, vol. i., May 25, 1858.

Otterpool, visit to, *English Note-Books*, vol. i., February 19, 1855.

Our Lady's Chapel of the Forest, *The Snow Image, etc.*, A Bell's Biography.

Our Old Home: A Series of English Sketches. This volume was published in 1863, most of the articles having previously appeared in "The Atlantic Monthly." The experiences from which it was written are recorded in the *English Note-Books*.

Outcast of the Universe, the, *Twice-Told Tales*, vol. i., Wakefield.

Outside Glimpses of English Poverty, an article in *Our Old Home*, describing some of the poorer streets in a large English city.

Overbury, Sir Thomas, allusion to the murder of, *The Scarlet Letter*, chapters ix., xx.

Owls, *American Note-Books*, vol. i., June 22, 1835; use of the wings of an, *ibid.*, September 10, 1852.

Owl's Head, near Thomaston, Maine, *American Note-Books*, vol. i., August 12, 1837.

Ox, an, a true toper, *Twice-Told Tales*, vol. i., A Rill from the Town Pump.

Oxford, *English Note-Books*, vol. ii., June 11, August 31, 1856, *Our Old Home*, end of Near Oxford.

Oxford Barges, *Our Old Home*, Near Oxford, near the end.

Oxford plant, the, *English Note-Books*, vol. ii., August 31, 1856.

Oxfordshire, *Our Old Home*, Near Oxford.

P——, American painter, *French and Italian Journals*, vol. i., June 27, 1858.

P——, Dr., residence of, in Boston, *American Note-Books*, vol. i., July 4, 1838.

P——, Rev. E., incident in the family of, *American Note-Books*, vol. i., October 24, 1838.

P—— O., Mormonite, *English Note-Books*, vol. ii., December 31, 1856.

Paddington, *English Note-Books*, vol. ii., July 16, 1856.

Padua, scene of the story Rappaccini's Daughter, *Mosses from an Old Manse*, vol. i.

Pain, relation of, to pleasure, *The Dolliver Romance*, first scene, near the beginning.

Painted Windows, *English Note-Books*, vol. ii., May 10, 1856, York, April 13, November 12, December 6, 1857, *French and Italian Journals*, vol. i., February 14, May 30, June 5, 1858, vol. ii., June 28, 1858, *The Marble Faun*, vol. ii., chapter viii. emblematic of the Christian faith, *ibid.*

Painter, pictures by a hungry, *The Blithedale Romance*, chapter xxi.

Painters: British, *English Note-Books*, vol. ii., July 28, August 9, December 8, 1857; Dutch, *ibid.*, August 9, 1857, *French and Italian Journals*, vol. ii., June 8, 15, 1858, *The Marble Faun*, vol. ii., chapter xii.; Italian, *French and Italian Journals*, vol. i., February 25, 1858, *The Marble Faun*, vol. ii., chapter xii.; Old Masters, *English Note-Books*, vol. ii., August 2, 9, 30, 1857.

Painting: in oil, origin of the art, *French and Italian Journals*, vol. ii., October 5, 1858; not attractive to simplicity, *Mosses from an Old Manse*, vol. ii., The New Adam and Eve.

Pakenham, General, death of, *English Note-Books*, vol. ii., December 15, 1856.

Palace Beautiful, the, *Mosses from an Old Manse*, vol. i., The Celestial Railroad.

Palaces: Barberini, *French and Italian Journals*, vol. i., February 20, March 25, 1858; Blenheim, *Our Old Home*, Near Oxford; Borghese, *French and Italian Journals*, vol. i., February 25, 1858; Buckingham, *English Note-Books*, vol. i., September 8, 1855; Buonarotti, *French and Italian Journals*, vol. ii., July 2, 1858; Caffarelli, *The Marble Faun*, vol. i., chapter xviii.; Colonna, *French and Italian Journals*, vol. i., April 15, 1858; Conservators, *ibid.*, March 1, 1858; Corsini, *ibid.*, vol. ii., October 21, 1858; Crystal, *English Note-Books*, vol. ii., September 27, November 16, 1857, *Our Old Home*, Up the Thames; del Torre, see HILDA'S TOWER; Doria, *French and Italian Journals*, vol. i., March 10, 1858; Pargello, *ibid.*, vol. ii., June 28, July 16, 1858; Piccolomini, *ibid.*, October 14, 1858; Pitti, *ibid.*, June 10, 13, 21, July 27, September 10, 1858; Quirinal, *ibid.*, vol. i., April 10, 1858; Riccardi, *ibid.*, vol. ii., June 28, 1858; Roman, *ibid.*, vol. i., February 7, 1858, *The Marble Faun*, vol. i., chapter v.; Rospigliosi, *French and Italian Journals*, vol. i., February 20, 1858; St. James, *English Note-Books*, vol. i., September 8, 10, 1855, March 22, 1856; Sciarra, *French and Italian Journals*, vol. i., March 10, 1858; Siena, public, *ibid.*, vol. ii., October 2, 3, 4, 9, 1858; Spada, *ibid.*, vol. i., May 21, 1858; Vecchio, *ibid.*, vol. ii., June 21, July 2, 1858.

Palfrey, John G., *English Note-Books*, vol. ii., July 13, 1856.

Palfrey, Peter, *The Snow Image, etc.*, Main Street, *Twice-Told Tales*, vol. i, The Maypole of Merry Mount, *Grandfather's Chair*, part i., chapter ii.

Palmer, General, *The Dolliver Romance, etc.*, A Book of Autographs.

Pamfili, Cardinal, resemblance of, to the demon in Guido's picture of Michael and the Dragon, *The Marble Faun*, vol. i., chapter xv.

Pamfili Doria Palace, *French and Italian Journals*, vol. i., March 10, 1858.

Pamfili Villa, *French and Italian Journals*, vol. i., March 25, 1858.

Pan, *Tanglewood Tales*, The Pomegranate Seeds; statue of, *English Note-Books*, vol. ii., May 29, 1857.

Panacea for long life, a, *The Dolliver Romance, etc.*, Dr. Bullivant.

Pandora, *Wonder-Book*, The Paradise of Children, *The Blithedale Romance*, chapter iv.; statue of, *English Note-Books*, vol. ii., May 29, 1857.

Pansie, the pet name of a child in *The Dolliver Romance.*

Pantheon, the, *French and Italian Journals*, vol. i., February 21, May 1, 1858, *The Marble Faun*, vol. ii., chapter xxv.

Pantheon, the, London, *English Note-Books*, vol. i., September 28, 1855.

Papacy, Puritan horror of the, *Twice-Told Tales*, vol. ii., Endicott and the Red Cross. See CATHOLICISM.

Papists, expedition against, *The Snow Image, etc.*, A Bell's Biography.

Paracelsus *Mosses from an Old Manse*, vol. i., The Birthmark.

Paradise, in a rainy day, *Mosses from an Old Manse*, vol. i., The Old Manse, middle.

Paradise of Children, The, the story of Pandora's Box in the *Wonder-Book.*

Paralytic, description of a, *Our Old Home*, Pilgrimage to Old Boston.

Paraman, a seaman, *English Note-Books*, vol. i., February 20, 1854.

Pargello Palace, the, Florence, *French and Italian Journals*, vol. ii., June 28, July 16, 1858.

Paris, *French and Italian Journals*, January 8 to 12, 1858.

Parker, Mr., *English Note-Books*, vol. ii., August 31, 1856.

Parker, Rev. Thecdore, a frequent visitor at Brook Farm while living at West Roxbury, is mentioned in *The Blithedale Romance*, Preface.

Parker, Uncle, *Twice-Told Tales,* vol. ii., The Village Uncle.

Parker's Saloon, Boston, characters at, *American Note-Books,* vol. ii., May 7, 16, 1850.

Parliament Houses, the, *English Note-Books,* vol. i., September 10, 30, October 2, 1855, *Our Old Home,* Up the Thames.

Parnassus, Mount, *Tanglewood Tales,* The Dragon's Teeth.

Parr, Dr., church and preaching of, *Our Old Home,* Leamington Spa, about Warwick.

Parris, Mercy, *The Snow Image, etc.,* Main Street.

Parris, Rev. Mr., children of, *Grandfather's Chair,* part, ii., chapter ii.

Party, Political, a man who had lost his, *Mosses from an Old Manse,* vol. ii., The Christmas Banquet.

Passages from a Relinquished Work, *Mosses from an Old Manse,* vol. ii. A fragment of the story of a young man who resolved to spend his life as a traveling story-teller. It was apparently designed as a framework for a number of short stories.

Passignano, town of, *French and Italian Journals,* vol. i., May 29, 1858.

Past, burden left by the, *English Note-Books,* vol. i., March 27, 1856.

Pastimes of Old England, *Twice-Told Tales,* vol. i., The May-pole of Merry Mount.

Patch, Sam: last leap of, *The Dolliver Romance, etc.,* Rochester; an undertaking worthy of, *English Note-Books,* vol. i., September 5, 1855.

Patent Office, the, *Mosses from an Old Manse,* vol. i., The Hall of Fantasy.

Paternoster Row, *English Note-Books,* vol. i., September 8, 1855.

Patmore, Coventry, *English Note-Books,* vol. ii., January 3, 1858.

Patriot, an incorruptible, *Mosses from an Old Manse,* vol. i., A Select Party; ghost of a, *The Dolliver Romance, etc.,* Ghosts and Goblins.

Patriotism, *English Note-Books,* vol. ii., May 10, 1857; colonial, *The Snow Image, etc.,* Old News, part ii.; of Americans, *The Dolliver Romance, etc.,* A Book of Autographs.

Paul before Agrippa, picture of, *English Note-Books,* vol. ii., April 13, 1857.

Paul Pry, a spiritualized, *Twice-Told Tales,* vol. i., Sights from a Steeple.

Peabody, Mr., *English Note-Books,* vol. ii., April 8, 1856.

Peabody, Rev. W. B. O., life of Cotton Mather by, *Grandfather's Chair,* part ii., chapter v.

Peace, Temple of, in Rome, *The Marble Faun,* vol. i., chapter xvi.

Peace, universal, *Mosses from an Old Manse,* vol. ii., Earth's Holocaust.

Pearce, Mr., Vice-Consul at Liverpool, *English Note-Books,* vol. i., August 4, 10, 1853, *Our Old Home,* Consular Experiences.

Pearl, the child of Hester Prynne, in *The Scarlet Letter.* She is a child of great beauty, peculiar insight, and inexplicable temperament, the reflection of her mother's wayward moods and wild sorrows.

Pearl-diver, statue of a, by Paul Akers, *The Marble Faun,* Preface, and vol. i., chapter xiii.

Pearl of Great Price, the, *Mosses from an Old Manse,* vol. ii., The Intelligence Office.

Pearson, Tobias. See Tobias.

Pedigree of Monte Bene, the, *The Marble Faun,* vol. ii., chapter i.

Pedlers, trials and compensations of, *American Note-Books,* vol. i., July 27, 1838.

Peel, Sir Robert, *English Note-Books,* vol. i., March 25, 1856; incident of, *Our Old Home,* Civic Banquets; statue of, *English Note-Books,* vol. ii., May 24, 1856, Manchester.

Peerage, desire for the, *English Note-Books,* vol. i., February 18, 1856.

Pegasus, *Wonder-Book,* The Chimæra, *Mosses from an Old Manse,* vol. ii., A Virtuoso's Collection.

Pelasgic Race, the, *The Marble Faun,* vol. ii., chapter i.

Pelias, *Tanglewood Tales,* The Golden Fleece.

Pell, Mr., home of, *The Snow Image, etc.,* Old Ticonderoga, end.

Pemberton, Clara, a character in The Antique Ring, in the volume *The Dolliver Romance.*

Pembroke, Anne, Countess of, *English Note-Books,* vol. ii., April 10, 1857.

Pembroke, Earl, statue of, *English Note-Books,* vol. ii., August 31, 1856.

Penitents, masked, in Rome, *The Marble Faun,* vol. ii., chapter xviii.

Pennington, Mr., *True Stories,* Biographies, chapter ii. (Only in 16mo edition.)

Penobscot Bay, islands in, *American Note-Books,* vol. i., August 12, 1837.

Peony, pet name of a little boy in *The Snow Image.*

People, intolerably alike unless varied by circumstances, *The Blithedale Romance,* chapter xvii.

People, the, intuitions of, *The Scarlet Letter,* chapter ix., near the end; relations of, with the sovereign and nobility, *Our Old Home,* A London Suburb.

Pepperell, Lady, advice to, *American Note-Books,* vol. ii., 1842.

Pepperell, Sir William, biographical sketch of, included in the volume with *Fanshawe; Grandfather's Chair,* part ii., chapter vii., *American Note-Books,* vol. ii., August 30, 1852; family and death of, and gifts to, *ibid.,* 1842; portrait of, *ibid.,* vol. i., August 22, 1837.

Perception of truth and falsity, *American Note-Books,* vol. i., 1840.

Percival, Captain, Commander of the Charleston Navy-Yard, *American Note-Books,* vol. i., August 27, 1837.

Percy, Lord, *Twice-Told Tales,* vol. ii., Howe's Masquerade.

Percys, the, residence of, *English Note-Books,* vol. i., September 10, 1855.

Perfection: aiming at, *American Note-Books,* vol. i., January 4, 1839, suggestion of, The Birthmark; specimens of, *Mosses from an Old Manse,* vol. i., A Select Party.

"**Pergasus,**" *American Note-Books,* vol. i., July 29, 1838.

Periwinkle, name given to one of the children to whom the stories of the *Wonder-Book* and *Tanglewood Tales* were told.

Perjury, pious, *Fanshawe, etc.,* Sir William Pepperell, first paragraph.

Perkins, Benjamin D., *Fanshawe, etc.,* T. G. Fessenden, sixth paragraph.

Perkinsism, the theory of, *Fanshawe, etc.,* T. G. Fessenden.

Perpetual Motion, *Mosses from an Old Manse,* vol. ii., The Artist of the Beautiful.

Perry, Commodore, *English Note-Books,* vol. i., December 25, 1854.

Perseus, *Wonder-Book,* The Gorgon's Head.

Persico, bust by, *French and Italian Journals,* vol. i., June 4, 1858.

Perugia, *French and Italian Journals,* vol. i., May 28, 29, 1858, *The Marble Faun,* vol. ii., chapter ix.

Perugino, *French and Italian Journals,* vol. ii., July 27, 1858, *The Marble Faun,* vol. ii., chapter xxvi.; devoutness of, *ibid.,* vol. ii., chapter xii.; drawings by, *French and Italian Journals,* vol. ii., September 3, 1858; frescoes by, *ibid.,* vol. i., May 28, 1858; pictures by, *ibid.,* vol. ii., July 13, 1858; "Pietà" by, *ibid.,* June 17, 1858; St. Columba by, *ibid.,* vol. i., May 29, 1858; St. Michael by, *ibid.,* May 12, 1858.

Pestilence, horrors of, *Twice-Told Tales,* vol. ii., Lady Eleanore's Mantle, Edward Fane's Rosebud.

Peter Bell, *Mosses from an Old Manse,* vol. ii., A Virtuoso's Collection.

Peter Goldthwaite's Treasure, a story in vol. ii. of *Twice-Told Tales,* of a visionary whose buoyant faith in luck springs up unharmed after every fresh disappointment, See *American Note-Books,* vol. ii., May 6, 1850.

Peter, St.: dungeon of, *French and Italian Journals,* vol. i., February 23, 1858; mark of the fingers of, *Twice-Told Tales,* vol. ii., The Village Uncle; type for, *ibid.,* vol. i., Sunday at Home.

Peterborough, Town and Cathedral, *English Note-Books,* vol. ii., May 27, 1857.

Peters, Rev. Hugh, of Salem, *Grandfather's Chair,* part i., chapter iii., *The Snow Image, etc.,* Main Street, *Fanshawe, etc.,* Mrs. Hutchinson, third paragraph.

Pet-names of children, *The Dolliver Romance,* second fragment.

Petrarch: birthplace of, *French and Italian Journals*, vol. i., May 30, 1858; portraits of, and Laura, *ibid.*, vol. ii., September 7, 1858.

Petrifaction, *American Note-Books*, vol. i., September 7, 1835.

Petronilla. See GUERCINO.

Petty, the, mingling of with the noble, *The House of the Seven Gables*, chapter ii., end.

Pharaoh, relic of a, *English Note-Books*, vol. ii., July 26, 1857.

Phidias, statue by, *French and Italian Journals*, vol. i., February 10, 14, 1858.

Philadelphian, a curious, *Our Old Home*, Consular Experiences.

Philanthropist, a, *Mosses from an Old Manse*, vol. ii., The Christmas Banquet; made a monster, *The Blithedale Romance*, chapter xxv.

Philanthropists, *The Blithedale Romance*, chapter iii.; besetting sin of, *ibid.*, chapter xv., near the middle; danger of enslavement to their idea, *ibid.*, chapter vii.; lesson for, *The Snow Image*, title story; right of to drive mankind, *The Blithedale Romance*, chapter xii.; tendency of to egotism, *ibid.*, chapter ix., beginning.

Philanthropy: an Italian's idea of, *The Marble Faun*, vol. ii., chapter iv.; peril of, as a ruling passion, *The Blithedale Romance*, chapter xxviii.

Philemon, *Wonder-Book*, The Miraculous Pitcher.

Philip, King, *Grandfather's Chair*, part i., chapter viii.

Phillips, Mr., of Boston, *American Note-Books*, vol. i., July 27, 1838.

Philosopher's Stone, the, *Mosses from an Old Manse*, vol. ii., A Virtuoso's Collection.

Philosopher's use for beauty, a, *Twice-Told Tales*, vol. i., The Great Carbuncle.

Philosophy of life, a bitter, *The Blithedale Romance*, chapter ix., middle.

Phineas, *Tanglewood Tales*, The Golden Fleece.

Phips, Sir William: sketch of, published in the volume with *Fanshawe*; *Grandfather's Chair*, part i., chapters x., xi., part ii., chapter ii., *Twice-Told Tales*, vol. ii., Howe's Masquerade,

Old Esther Dudley; connection of with the witchcraft delusion, *The House of the Seven Gables,* chapter xiii.; wife of, *Twice-Told Tales,* vol. i., The Prophetic Pictures.

Phœbus, *Tanglewood Tales,* The Pomegranate Seeds.

Phœnix, *Tanglewood Tales,* The Dragon's Teeth.

Phrixus, *Tanglewood Tales,* The Golden Fleece.

Physical well-being, joy in mere, *The Blithedale Romance,* chapter xxiv.

Physicians, suggested tendency of, *The Scarlet Letter,* chapter ix.

Piazza del Campo, Siena, *French and Italian Journals,* vol. ii., October 3, 1858.

Piazza del Popolo, *The Marble Faun,* vol. i., chapter xii.

Piazza Navona, the, *French and Italian Journals,* vol. i., May 1, 1858.

Piccolomini, palace of the, *French and Italian Journals,* vol. ii., October 14, 1858.

Pickerel-flower, the, *American Note-Books,* vol. ii., August 13, 1842.

Pickering, Timothy, *Grandfather's Chair,* part iii., chapter vii., *The Dolliver Romance, etc.,* A Book of Autographs.

Picton, Mr., *English Note-Books,* vol. ii., April 19, 1857.

Picture-galleries, *English Note-Books,* vol. ii., August 2, 1856; emptiness of, *The Marble Faun,* vol. ii., chapter xii.; in England and Italy compared, *French and Italian Journals,* vol. i., March 1, 1851; Barberini, *French and Italian Journals,* vol. ii., February 20, March 25, May 15, 1859; Capitol, at Rome, *ibid.,* March 18, 1859, *The Marble Faun,* vol. i., chapter i.; Florence Academy, *French and Italian Journals,* vol. ii., June 17, July 13, 1858; Louvre, *ibid.,* vol. i., January 8, 10, 1858; Manchester Arts' Exhibition, *English Note-Books,* vol. ii., July 22 to September 6, 1857; National, London, *ibid.,* vol. i., March 26, 1856; St. Luke's Academy, Rome, *French and Italian Journals,* vol. ii., April 16, 1858; Siena Institute, *ibid.,* vol. ii., October 5, 1858; Taylor Institute, Oxford, *English Note-Books,* vol. ii., August 31, 1856; Uffizi, *French and Italian Journals,* vol. ii., June 8, 11, 16, 30, July 4, 16, September 3, 7, 21, 25, 28, 1858; Vernon, Marlborough House,

English Note-Books, August 2, 1856 ; Vatican, *French and Italian Journals,* vol. i., February 19, April 12, 1858.

Pictures : best observers of, *Twice-Told Tales,* vol. i., The Prophetic Pictures ; by a hungry painter, *The Blithedale Romance,* chapter xxi. ; collections of, *English Note-Books,* vol. i., March 24, 1856, vol. ii., July 26, 1857 ; criticisms on, *French and Italian Journals,* vol. ii., June 21, 1858 ; famous, *Mosses from an Old Manse,* vol. ii., A Virtuoso's Collection ; of a toper, *The Blithedale Romance,* chapter xxi. ; prejudice against, in the colonies, *Twice-Told Tales,* vol. i., The Prophetic Pictures ; prescriptive admiration for, *French and Italian Journals,* vol. i., April 22, 1858 ; rarity of good, *ibid.,* March 10, 1858 ; requirements for a full appreciation of, *The Marble Faun,* vol. ii., chapter xii. ; restoring, *French and Italian Journals,* vol. ii , June 10, 1858 ; shallow men often good critics of, *The Marble Faun,* vol. ii., chapter xii. ; subjects for, *American Note-Books,* vol. ii., June 1, 1842 and 1842 ; taste for, *English Note-Books,* vol. i., March 26, 1856, vol. ii., August 9, 16, 20, September 6, December 8, 1857, *The Marble Faun,* vol. ii., chapter xii.

Picturesque : fashion of the, *English Note-Books,* vol. ii., May 10, 1856 ; the moral, *Mosses from an Old Manse,* vol. ii., The Old Apple Dealer.

Picturesqueness, a symptom of decay, *The Marble Faun,* vol. ii., chapter vii.

Picus, King, *Tanglewood Tales,* Circe's Palace.

Pierce, Franklin, *American Note-Books,* vol. ii., August 30, September 5, 1852, *English Note-Books,* vol. ii., April 4, 1856, *French and Italian Journals,* vol. ii., March 11, 15, 23, April 19, 1859, *Our Old Home,* dedication.

Pierce, Franklin, The Life of, was written in the summer of 1852, when General Pierce was a candidate for the presidency ; a thin volume, published by Ticknor & Fields, long since out of print.

Pierpont, John, seal of, *The Dolliver Romance, etc.,* A Book of Autographs.

Pigsnort, Ichabod, a character in the Great Carbuncle, *Twice-Told Tales,* vol. i., seeking the stone from motives of avarice.

Pike, Dominicus, a gossipy traveling tobacconist in Mr. Higginbotham's Catastrophe, *Twice-Told Tales*, vol. i., and mentioned in *Mosses from an Old Manse*, vol. ii., Passages from a Relinquished Work, and in *The Dolliver Romance, etc.*, Journal of a Solitary Man, ii.

Pilgrimage to Old Boston, an article in *Our Old Home*, describing the English town of that name with St. Botolph's Church, Lincoln, and Lincoln Cathedral.

Pilgrims, the, *Grandfather's Chair*, part i., chapter ii.; characters of, *Twice-Told Tales*, vol. i., The Gray Champion; flowers brought over by, *Our Old Home*, Recollections of a Gifted Woman; enterprise of, carried beyond their own dreams, *The Blithedale Romance*, chapter xiv.

Pillory, the, *Twice-Told Tales*, vol. ii., Endicott and the Red Cross, *The Scarlet Letter*, chapter ii.

Pills, Poetical, Political, and Philosophical, etc., title of a volume of verse, *Fanshawe, etc.*, T. G. Fessenden.

Pilots, old-time, *Twice-Told Tales*, vol. ii., The Village Uncle.

Pincian Gardens, the, *French and Italian Journals*, vol. i., April 30, May 23, 1858.

Pincian Hill, the, description of, *The Marble Faun*, vol. i., chapter xii.

Pine-Tree Shillings, The, story in *Grandfather's Chair*, part i., chapter vi.

Pipes, famous, *Mosses from an Old Manse*, vol. ii., A Virtuoso's Collection.

Pique, lovers', *The Marble Faun*, vol. ii., chapter xvi.

Pirene, fountain of, *Wonder-Book*, The Chimæra.

Pitcairn, Major, pistol of, *Mosses from an Old Manse*, vol. ii., A Virtuoso's Collection.

Pitcher, Moll, *The Blithedale Romance*, chapter xxiv.

Pitt, William, statues of, *English Note-Books*, vol. i., September 7, 1855, vol. ii., July 13, 1856.

Pittheus, King, *Tanglewood Tales*, The Minotaur.

Pitti, Palace, the, *French and Italian Journals*, vol. ii., June 10, 13, 21, July 27, September 10, 1858.

Pittsfield, Mass., *American Note-Books*, vol. i., July 27, 1838.

Pius IX., *French and Italian Journals*, vol. i., March 27, vol. ii., August 3, 1858.

Place, danger of stepping aside from one's, *Twice-Told Tales*, vol. i., Wakefield; people out of, *Mosses from an Old Manse*, vol. ii., The Intelligence Office.

Place de la Concorde, *French and Italian Journals*, vol. i., January 8, 1858.

Plantagenet, Richard, statue of, *English Note-Books*, vol. i., September 5, 1855.

Plantain, name given to one of the children to whom the stories of the *Wonder-Book* and *Tanglewood Tales* were told.

Plate, design for a service of, *Mosses from an Old Manse*, vol. i., The Old Manse, near the beginning.

Platt, **stage-driver**, *American Note-Books*, vol. i., September 9, 1838.

Playfulness in despair, *The Dolliver Romance, etc.*, The Antique Ring.

Plays, seen by their authors, *English Note-Books*, vol. ii., April 5, 1856.

Pleasure-house, no site on earth for a, *American Note-Books*, vol. i., October 25, 1836.

Pluto, *Tanglewood Tales*, The Pomegranate Seeds.

Poet, a disappointed, a character in the story The Canterbury Pilgrims, in *The Snow Image, etc.*

Poet, a forgotten, *The Snow Image, etc.*, Old News, part ii.

Poetic insight, *The House of the Seven Gables*, chapter ii., end.

Poetry, and labor, *The Blithedale Romance*, chapter viii., near the end.

Poets: associations with, *Our Old Home*, Near Oxford, toward the end; choice of mates by, *The House of the Seven Gables*, chapter ix., toward the end; distaste of for their own work, *The Marble Faun*, vol. ii., chapter xvi.; fame of, *Our Old Home*, Up the Thames; in daily talk, *French and Italian Journals*, vol. ii., June 9, 1858; revealers of nature and humanity, *The Snow Image, etc.*, The Great Stone Face; some English, *Mosses from an Old Manse*, vol. ii., P.'s Correspondence.

Poets' Corner, the, *English Note-Books*, vol. i., September 30, 1855, *Our Old Home*, Up the Thames.

Poisons, theory of, *Mosses from an Old Manse*, vol. i., Rappaccini's Daughter.

Police, the Roman. See Rome.

Police Court, scenes in an English, *English Note-Books*, vol. i., January 6, February 20, 1854, June 2, 1855.

Political Ideas and Phrases, sameness of, *Twice-Told Tales*, vol. i., Dr. Heidegger's Experiment.

Political parties, conduct of, in victory, *The Scarlet Letter*, The Custom-House, near the end.

Political Strifes of 1838, *Twice-Told Tales*, vol. ii., The Sister Years.

Politicians, *American Note-Books*, vol. i., letter, March 15, 1840; culture of, *English Note-Books*, vol. i., September 29, 1854.

Polydectes, King, *Wonder-Book*, The Gorgon's Head.

Polygamist, a, *Twice-Told Tales*, vol. ii., Chippings with a Chisel.

Polyphemus, *Tanglewood Tales*, Circe's Palace.

Pomegranate Seeds, The, title of a story in *Tanglewood Tales*.

Pompey: bust of, *French and Italian Journals*, vol. ii., June 8, 1858; forum of, see Forums; statue of, *ibid.*, vol. i., May 21, 1858.

Pond Lily, the (row-boat), *American Note-Books*, vol. ii., September 2, 4, 1842.

Poor: and proud the, *The Blithedale Romance*, chapter iv.; real abasement of, *The House of the Seven Gables*, chapter iii., end.

Pope, Alexander: description of Stanton Harcourt by, *Our Old Home*, Near Oxford; MS. of Homer by, *English Note-Books*, vol. ii., December 7, 1857.

Pope Julius III., bronze statue of, in Perugia, *The Marble Faun*, vol. ii., chapters vi., ix., x.

Popularity, attributes essential to, *Mosses from an Old Manse*, vol. ii., The Christmas Banquet.

Porteous, place of execution of, *English Note-Books*, vol. ii., May 10, 1856, Edinburgh.

Porter, Mr., collection of antiquities of, *Our Old Home*, Pilgrimage to Old Boston.

Portinscale, *English Note-Books*, vol. i., July 21, 1855.

Portland Place, *English Note-Books*, vol. i., September 9, 1855.

Portrait-painting, value of, *English Note-Books*, vol. ii., July 30, August 2, 1857.

Portraits, *American Note-Books*, vol. ii., May 5, 1850; artists', of themselves, *The Marble Faun*, vol. i., chapter v.; English historical, *English Note-Books*, vol. ii., July 30, 1857; interest in our own, *Twice-Told Tales*, vol. i., The Prophetic Pictures; old family, *American Note-Books*, vol. i., August 22, 1837.

Portsoaken, Dr. Jabez, a villainous character in *Septimius Felton.*

Possessions, great, rights of, *The House of the Seven Gables*, chapter i., toward the end.

Posterity: best method of being known to, *Mosses from an Old Manse*, vol. i., A Select Party; building for, *The House of the Seven Gables*, chapter xii., near the end; the love of, *American Note-Books*, vol. i., 1840; the representative of, *Mosses from an Old Manse*, vol. i., A Select Party.

Pot-holes in rocks, *American Note-Books*, vol. i., August 31, 1838.

Poulton Hall, *English Note-Books*, vol. i., August 8, 1853.

Powers, Hiram, *French and Italian Journals*, vol. ii., June 16, 1858, *The Marble Faun*, vol. i., chapter xiii.; "America" of, *French and Italian Journals*, vol. ii., September 29, 1858; conversations with, *ibid.*, June 7, 27, July 8, 28, September 29, 1858; criticisms by, *ibid.*, June 13, 1858; criticisms on, *ibid.*, October 21, 1858; daughter of, *ibid.*, June 13, 1858; "Eve" of, *Mosses from an Old Manse*, vol. i., The Birthmark; first impressions of, *French and Italian Journals*, vol. i., May 30, 1858; Greek Slave of, *English Note-Books*, vol. ii., April 8, August 7, 1856; incidents told by, *French and Italian Journals*, vol. ii., June 27, September 11, 1858; on eyes, *ibid.*, June 27, 1858; on government patronage, *ibid.*, vol. i., June 4, 1858; on spiritualism, *ibid.*, vol. ii, September 1, 1858; Proserpine and Psyche of, *ibid.*, June 13, 1858; Webster of, *ibid.*, September 29, 1858; works of, *ibid.*, vol. i., June 4, 1858.

Pownall, Thomas, Governor of Massachusetts, *Twice-Told Tales*, vol. ii., Howe's Masquerade, *The Snow Image, etc.*, Old News, part ii., *Grandfather's Chair*, part ii., chapter x.

Practical Men, fantasies of, *Mosses from an Old Manse*, vol. i., The Hall of Fantasy.

Praise, torture of unmerited, *Mosses from an Old Manse*, vol. ii., Roger Malvin's Burial.

Praxiteles : faun of, *French and Italian Journals*, vol. i., April 30, 1858, *The Marble Faun*, vol. i., chapter i.; copy of the faun, *French and Italian Journals*, vol. i., April 18, 22, 1858; statue at a fountain by, *ibid.*, February 10, 14, 1858.

Prayer, *The Blithedale Romance*, chapter vi., beginning; extempore, *American Note-Books*, vol. i., September, 1836; of purity, the, *Mosses from an Old Manse*, vol. ii., A New Adam and Eve.

Preaching in England, *Our Old Home*, A London Suburb, Up the Thames.

Precocity of children, *American Note-Books*, vol. ii., April 14, 1844.

Prefaces, the antique fashion of, *The Marble Faun*, Preface.

Premonitions, *The Blithedale Romance*, chapter xvi., end, xxiv.

Pre-Raphaelites, the : Gibson's opinion of, *French and Italian Journals*, vol. i., March 14, 1858; pictures of, *English Note-Books*, vol. ii., July 28, 1857, *French and Italian Journals*, vol. ii., July 13, 1858; subject for one of, *French and Italian Journals*, vol. i., May 30, 1858, Incisa.

Prescott, George, *American Note-Books*, vol. ii., August 5, 1842.

Presidential candidates, like popes, *The Snow Image, etc.*, The Great Stone Face.

Preston, England, *English Note-Books*, vol. ii., June 28, 1857.

Preston family, the, *English Note-Books*, vol. i., July 13, 1855, end.

Preston, Captain, *Grandfather's Chair*, part iii., chapter v.

Pride, effects of different degrees of, *Fanshawe*, chapter v.

Prideaux, Bishop of Worcester, anecdote of, *American Note-Books*, vol. i., October 17, 1835.

Priest, an unworldly, *Mosses from an Old Manse*, vol. i., A Select Party.

Primrose, name given to one of the children to whom the stories of the *Wonder-Book* and *Tanglewood Tales* were told.

Prince, Miss Deborah, *Fanshawe, etc.*, Jonathan Cilley.

Pringle, names of the family in *Tanglewood Tales*.

Pringle family, a, tombs of, *English Note-Books*, vol. ii., May 10, 1856, Dryburgh.

Printing, no improvement in the art of, *English Note-Books*, vol. ii., April 8, 1856.

Prior, Matthew: monument to, *English Note-Books* vol. i., September 30, 1855; prefaces of, *Fanshawe, etc.*, Mrs, Hutchinson, beginning.

Priscilla, one of the principal characters in *The Blithedale Romance*, first appears in chapter iv. She is a delicate girl of highly nervous and susceptible temperament, and forms a complete contrast to Zenobia. Through the peculiarity of her temperament she has fallen into the power of a mesmerist whose control over her is complete until it comes in contact with the stronger power of her love for Hollingsworth. The character of her beauty is described in chapter xx., and some of the characteristics of her manner and feelings in the closing part of chapter xvi. A temporary resemblance to Margaret Fuller is alluded to in chapter vii., with a hint that it is due to her clairvoyant quality. The character is said to be drawn in part from the little seamstress mentioned in the *American Note-Books*, October 9, 1841.

Prisons, *Mosses from an Old Manse*, vol. ii., The New Adam and Eve; of Boston, *The Scarlet Letter*, chapter i.

Privateers, American, in the Revolution, *The Snow Image, etc.*, Old News, part iii.

Procession of Life, the, a sketch in *Mosses from an Old Manse*, vol. i., in which mankind are supposed to be classified by more real distinctions than the ordinary ones of wealth, rank, and so on. It first appeared in "The Democratic Review." A suggestion of the sketch will be found in the *American Note-Books*, vol. i., October 25, 1836.

Processions, dullness of, *The House of the Seven Gables*, chapter xi.

Procrustes, *Tanglewood Tales*, The Minotaur.

Procter, Bryan W. (Barry Cornwall), *English Note-Books*, vol. i., June 12, 1854, *Our Old Home*, Near Oxford, Up the Thames.

Proctor, John and Elizabeth, *The Snow Image, etc.*, Main Street.

Proctor, Mr., drive with, *American Note-Books*, vol. i., June 22, 1835.

Prodigal Son: engravings of the, *American Note-Books*, vol. i., August 12, 1837; statue of, *French and Italian Journals*, vol. i., April 3, 1858.

Profanity, a story of, *English Note-Books*, vol. i., February 28, 1858.

Profile Mountain, Franconia group, *The Snow Image, etc.*, The Great Stone Face.

Prometheus, fire of, *Mosses from an Old Manse*, vol ii., A Virtuoso's Collection.

Property in lands, abolition of, *Mosses from an Old Manse*, vol. ii., Earth's Holocaust.

Prophetic Pictures, The, a story in *Twice-Told Tales*, vol. i. The instinct of the true artist is made to see tendencies indicated by faint and transient expressions of the face, and by bringing them out clearly in the picture to foreshadow the future. The purpose of the story is perhaps to illustrate the view that foreknowledge of the results of their actions would not influence men in refraining from them. The plot is founded on an incident in Dunlap's "History of the Arts of Design in America."

Proselytes, a reformer's, *The Blithedale Romance*, chapter viii.. end.

Proserpina, *Tanglewood Tales*, The Pomegranate Seeds.

Prosperity: brief sunshine of, *American Note-Books*, vol. i., August 31, 1838; creatures of, *The Blithedale Romance*, chapter xxii., beginning.

Protestantism: discarding of pictures by, *French and Italian*

Journals, vol. ii., June 8, 1858; a need of, *ibid.,* vol. i., May 1, 1858.

Providence, *The House of the Seven Gables,* chapter xvi., middle; sign of a, *Twice-Told Tales,* vol. i., David Swan.

Providence, R. I., journey of Roger Williams to, *Grandfather's Chair,* part i., chapter iv.

Province House, the, *Grandfather's Chair,* part ii., chapter viii., part iii., chapter ix.; wooden Indian on, *Mosses from an Old Manse,* vol. ii., Drowne's Wooden Image. See LEGENDS OF THE PROVINCE HOUSE.

Provincial Muster, The, a sketch of the preparations for the siege of Louisburg, in *Grandfather's Chair,* part ii., chapter vii.

Prynne, Hester, one of the chief characters of *The Scarlet Letter.* She is a woman of strong character, and strong passions and affections. Her peculiar and isolated condition makes her a freethinker on religious and social topics, but disciplines her to self-sacrifice and sympathy with all suffering.

Psalms, poetic versions of, *The Snow Image, etc.,* Old News, part i.

P.'s Correspondence, a sketch in the form of a letter from a lunatic, describing what Byron, Shelley, and some of their literary contemporaries might have become under the conservative influence of age, if they had lived to that time (1845). The sketch is in *Mosses from an Old Manse,* vol. ii. It first appeared in "The Democratic Review."

"**Psyche,**" quotation from, *Fanshawe,* head of chapter ix.

Publishers, *American Note-Books,* vol. ii., September 16, 27, 1841, *The Snow Image, etc.,* The Devil in Manuscript.

Pue, Jonathan, *The Scarlet Letter,* The Custom-House, after the middle.

Pulpit, a natural, *The Snow Image, etc.,* The Great Stone Face.

Pulpit Rock, *American Note-Books,* vol. ii., October 22, 1841. See ELIOT'S PULPIT.

Punishment, future, what it may possibly be, *The Marble Faun,* vol. ii., chapter viii.

Puritanism in New England, *The Blithedale Romance,* chapter xxiii.

Puritans, the: appearance and dress of, *Twice-Told Tales,* vol. i., The Gray Champion; attitude toward mirth, and courtesy to women, of, *Twice-Told Tales,* vol. i., The Maypole of Merry Mount; characteristics of, *Grandfather's Chair,* Preface, *Septimius Felton,* pp. 11, 12 (12mo); churches and worship of, *The Snow Image, etc.,* Main Street; decay of the spirit of, *The Dolliver Romance, etc.,* Dr. Bullivant; descendants of, *The Snow Image, etc.,* Main Street; familiarity of with the designs of Providence, *Twice-Told Tales,* vol i., The Gentle Boy; merrymaking of, *The Scarlet Letter,* chapter xxi.; public discipline of, *Twice-Told Tales* vol. ii., Endicott and The Red Cross, *The Scarlet Letter,* chapter ii.; sermons of, *Twice-Told Tales,* vol. i., The Gentle Boy, *English Note-Books,* vol. ii., April 12, 1857, *The Dolliver Romance,* Dr. Bullivant; sketch of, *Grandfather's Chair,* part i., chapter ii.; treatment of Quakers by, *Twice-Told Tales,* vol. i., The Gentle Boy; what they lost, *The Snow Image, etc.,* Main Street; why they could not tolerate a diversity of sects, *Fanshawe, etc.,* Mrs. Hutchinson, fourth paragraph; women among, *The Scarlet Letter,* chapter ii.

Purpose: an engrossing, *Twice-Told Tales,* vol. i., The Prophetic Pictures, *The Blithedale Romance,* chapter vii., near the end, ix., beginning; too little and too much, *ibid.,* chapter xxix.

Purses, Priscilla's, suggestion of, *The Blithedale Romance,* chapters v., x.

Pusey, Dr., and the Puseyites, *English Note-Books,* vol. ii., August 31, 1856, Merton College.

Pygmalion, *Mosses from an Old Manse,* vol. i., The Birthmark, vol. ii., Drowne's Wooden Image.

Pygmies, The, a story in *Tanglewood Tales.*

Pyncheon, name of the family of *The House of the Seven Gables.* The portrait of a Pyncheon is mentioned in the *American Note-Books,* vol. i., August 22, 1837, as being in a collection of portraits of early New Englanders in the cabinet of the Essex Historical Society. **Colonel**, the first of the family in

America, and builder of the house, is described in chapter i. and alluded to frequently; the tradition concerning his portrait in chapter xiii. **Gervayse**, his grandson, appears as a child in chapter i., and is introduced into the story of his daughter in chapter xiii. **Alice**, mentioned in chapter i. and several other places in the book, is the subject of a romance in chapter xiii. **Judge Jeffrey**, the principal representative of the family at the time of the story. He repeats many of the traits of his ancestor, the colonel. His early life and character are described in chapter i and more fully in chapter viii. His connection with the incidents forming the groundwork of the plot is explained in chapter xxi. **Hepzibah**, one of the chief characters, is introduced in chapter ii. Notwithstanding her unfortunate personal appearance and ridiculous pride of pedigree, she gains the reader's sympathy by the real sweetness and humility of her character and her devotion to her brother. **Clifford**, brother of Hepzibah, is an example of a nature singularly adapted to enjoy beauty and luxury, but doomed to spend thirty years of his manhood in a prison. The circumstances of his trial are given in chapter i. He first appears in chapter vii., where his character is outlined. **Phœbe**, cousin of the other Pyncheons of the story. Her beauty and natural grace are sharply contrasted with the awkwardness of Hepzibah.

Pythagoras, thigh of, *Mosses from an Old Manse*, vol. ii., A Virtuoso's Collection.

Quakers, persecution of the, *Grandfather's Chair*, part i., chapter vii., *Twice-Told Tales*, vol. i., The Gentle Boy, *The Snow Image, etc.*, Main Street, *The Scarlet Letter*, The Custom-House.

Quebec, siege of, *Grandfather's Chair*, part ii., chapter ix., *The Snow Image, etc.*, Old News, part ii.

Queen of Spain, the, *French and Italian Journals*, vol. i., February 19, 1858.

Quicksilver. See MERCURY.

Quiet in emergencies, *Septimius Felton*, p. 151 (12mo).

Quirinal, pontifical palace on the, *French and Italian Journals*, vol. i., April 10, 1858.

R——, Captain, of Kentucky, *English Note-Books*, vol. ii., December 15, 1856.

Rabelais, *American Note-Books*, vol. ii., October 10, 1842, *Mosses from an Old Manse*, vol. i., The Hall of Fantasy.

Rachel, *Twice-Told Tales*, vol. i., A Rill from the Town Pump, end.

Rachel, a character in The Vision of the Fountain, *Twice-Told Tales*, vol. i.

Radicofani, mountain, castle, and town, *French and Italian Journals*, vol. ii., October 14, 1858.

Radley, Mr., landlord, *English Note-Books*, vol. ii., October 7, 1856.

Raglan, Lord, death of, *English Note-Books*, vol. i., February 18, 1856.

Raikes, Robert, *American Note-Books*, vol. i., October 25, 1836.

Railroad-car, scene in a, *The House of the Seven Gables*, chapter xvii.

Railways, views from, *Our Old Home*, Pilgrimage to Old Boston.

Rain, *Twice-Told Tales*, vol. ii., Night Sketches, *Mosses from an Old Manse*, vol. i., The Old Manse, middle, *American Note-Books*, vol. ii., August 28, 1842 ; in Paradise, *ibid.*, August 30, 1842.

Rainbow, The, *Twice-Told Tales*, vol. i., Sights from a Steeple, end.

Rainy days, best study for, *Twice-Told Tales*, vol. ii., Night Sketches.

Raleigh, Sir Walter : a fitting prison for, *Our Old Home*, Up the Thames ; room of, in the Tower, *English Note-Books*, vol. i., September 10, 1855.

Randal, Earl of Chester, *English Note-Books*, vol. i., October 13, 1853.

Randall, a wrestler, *American Note-Books*, vol. i., August 15, 1838.

Randolph, Edward, *Twice-Told Tales,* vol. ii., Edward Randolph's Portrait, vol. i., The Gray Champion, *The Dolliver Romance, etc.*, Dr. Bullivant.

Rank : decorations of, *Mosses from an Old Manse,* vol. ii., Earth's Holocaust; in America, *The House of the Seven Gables,* chapter ii., near the end.

Raphael, *The Marble Faun,* vol. ii., chapter xxiv. ; cartoons by, *English Note-Books,* vol. i., March 24, 1856 ; drawings by, *ibid.*, vol. ii., August 31, 1856, Taylor Institute, *French and Italian Journals,* vol. ii., September 3, 1858 ; frescoes by, *ibid.*, vol. i., April 12, 1858 ; Madonnas by, *ibid.*, vol. ii., June 10, 15, July 27, 1858 ; portraits of Julius II., *ibid.*, July 8, October 21, 1858 ; religious pictures of, *The Marble Faun,* vol ii., chapter xii. ; sketch by, *English Note-Books,* vol. ii., May 24, 1856, Manchester; the "Transfiguration" by, *French and Italian Journals,* vol. i., April 25, 1858 ; mosaic copy of the above, *ibid.*, February 9, 1858.

Rappaccini's Daughter, a story in *Mosses from an Old Manse,* vol. i., first published in "The Democratic Review" about 1844. The scene is laid in Padua. Its allegorical meaning is founded on the theory that poisons may be made to nourish human life by being used as the only food. It is one of the best known of the author's shorter stories. See quotation from Sir Thomas Browne, *American Note-Books,* vol. i., January 4, 1839.

Ratcliffe family, tomb of the, *English Note-Books,* vol. i., July 21, 1855.

Ratcliffe Library, the, *English Note-Books,* August 31, 1856.

Ravaillac, scene of the crime of, *French and Italian Journals,* vol. i., January 9, 1858.

Read, T. Buchanan, *English Note-Books,* vol. i., January 3, 1858, *French and Italian Journals,* vol. i., March 14, 1858.

Reade, Charles, *English Note-Books,* vol. ii., April 8, 1856, November 19, 1857.

Reading, desultory, *American Note-Books,* vol. i., September 7, 1835.

Realities of family life, where seen, *The Blithedale Romance,* chapter xvii.

Reality and anticipation, *Mosses from an Old Manse,* vol. ii., Passages from a Relinquished Work, A Fellow-Traveller.

Rear windows, view of, *American Note-Books,* vol. ii., May 7, 14, 16, 1850, *The Blithedale Romance,* chapter xvii.

Recluses, frankness of, *The House of the Seven Gables,* chapter v., near the end.

Recollections, long brooding over, *The Blithedale Romance,* chapter xii., end.

Recollections of a Gifted Woman, an article in *Our Old Home,* giving descriptions of Stratford, and personal recollections of Delia Bacon, the author of a work on the authorship of the plays of Shakspeare, the publication of which was managed for her by Hawthorne.

Recording Spirit, the, *Mosses from an Old Manse,* vol. ii., The Intelligence Office.

Red, the man in, *Mosses from an Old Manse,* vol. ii., The Intelligence Office.

Redcar, Yorkshire, where *The Marble Faun* was written, *The Marble Faun,* Preface.

Red Cross, story of the, *Grandfather's Chair,* part i., chapter iii., *Twice-Told Tales,* vol. ii., Endicott and the Red Cross.

Redfern's Curiosity Shop, *Our Old Home,* About Warwick, end.

Refinement, influence of, on the affections, *The Marble Faun,* vol. i., chapter xii.

Reflections in water, *American Note-Books,* vol. i., September 7, 1835, vol. ii., September 8, 1842, *Mosses from an Old Manse,* vol. i., The Old Manse, near the middle.

Reform, men devoted to one kind of, *Mosses from an Old Manse,* vol. i., The Procession of Life.

Reformation of the world, the, *The Blithedale Romance,* chapter iii., middle, chapter vi., beginning.

Reformatory, plan for a, *The Blithedale Romance,* chapter vii., end.

Reformers: an ideal, *Mosses from an Old Manse,* vol. i., A Select Party; female, nature of the attacks of, on society, *The Blithedale Romance,* chapter vi.; hint for a sketch of a, *American*

Note-Books, vol. i., September 7, 1835; tendency of, *Mosses from an Old Manse,* vol. i., The Hall of Fantasy.

Regent's Park, *English Note-Books,* vol. i., September 9, 1855.

Rejected Blessing, The, a story in *Grandfather's Chair,* part ii., chapter v.

Relics, classic, *Mosses from an Old Manse,* vol. ii., A Virtuoso's Collection.

Religion, change of, *French and Italian Journals,* vol. ii., October 10, 1858.

Religion: emblems of, *Mosses from an Old Manse,* vol. ii., Earth's Holocaust; in Italy, *The Marble Faun,* vol. i., chapter xvii.

Religious Books, *Mosses from an Old Manse,* vol. i., The Old Manse, at the middle.

Reminiscences, personal tendency of old men to, *Fanshawe, etc.,* T. G. Fessenden, near the end.

Remorse, *Twice-Told Tales,* vol. ii., The Haunted Mind, *The Scarlet Letter,* chapter xii.

Renovation, more sacrilegious than destruction, *Mosses from an Old Manse,* vol. i., The Old Manse, near the end.

Rensselaer School, Troy, students from, *American Note-Books,* vol. i., August 31, 1838.

Reporters, mark of, *English Note-Books,* vol. i., August 2, 1855.

Reputation after death, anxiety about, *Our Old Home,* Near Oxford.

Reputations, historical, *The Dolliver Romance, etc.,* A Book of Autographs.

Resolve, when complete, *Twice-Told Tales,* vol. i., Fancy's Show Box.

Respectability, force of false, *Our Old Home,* Outside Glimpses of English Poverty.

Resurrection, picture of the, *English Note-Books,* vol. i., March 24, 1856.

Retribution of Providence, supposed instance of, *Fanshawe, etc.,* Mrs. Hutchinson, end.

Revenge, effect of, *American Note-Books,* vol. i., October 25, 1836; a sweet morsel of, *The Blithedale Romance,* chapter xxv., near the end.

Revolution, the American. The scene of *Septimius Felton* is laid in Concord, and the story opens at about the time of the Battle of Lexington; attitude of British statesmen toward, *Grandfather's Chair*, part iii., chapter vi.; beginning of, *The Dolliver Romance, etc.*, A Book of Autographs; causes of, *Grandfather's Chair*, part iii., chapters ii., iii.; first omen of, *Twice-Told Tales*, vol. ii., Endicott and the Red Cross; generals and battles of, *Grandfather's Chair*, part iii., chapters vii., viii., x.; leaders of, *ibid.*, part iii., chapter vi.; newspapers and effect on morality of, *The Snow Image, etc.*, Old News, Part iii.; no classic folly in, and few men titled or intellectually distinguished, *The Dolliver Romance, etc.*, A Book of Autographs; spirit of, *American Note-Books*, vol. i., September 14, 1841.

Revolutionary iconoclasm in France and England, *French and Italian Journals*, vol. i., January 6, 1858.

Revolutionary Pensioner, a, *American Note-Books*, vol. i., September 3, 1838.

Reynolds, Sir Joshua: art of, *English Note-Books*, vol. ii., July 28, 1857; portrait of Johnson by, *Our Old Home*, Lichfield and Uttoxeter; window painted by, *English Note-Books*, vol. ii., August 31, 1856.

Rhode Island, settlement of, *Grandfather's Chair*, part i., chapter iv.; reason of toleration in, *Fanshawe, etc.*, Mrs. Hutchinson, sixth paragraph.

Rhone, the, *French and Italian Journals*, vol. i., January 15, 1858, vol. ii., June 1, 26, 11, 1859.

Rhyddlan Castle and Marsh, *English Note-Books*, vol. i., September 13, 20, 1854.

Rhyl, *English Note-Books*, vol. i., September 13, 1854.

Riccardi Palace, the, *French and Italian Journals*, vol. ii., June 28, 1858.

Richardson, *Mosses from an Old Manse*, vol. i., The Hall of Fantasy.

Ridley, place of martyrdom of, *English Note-Books*, vol. ii., August 31, 1856.

Rienzi, picture of, *French and Italian Journals*, vol. ii., June 2, 1859.

Rigby, Mother, a witch in Feathertop, *Mosses from an Old Manse,* vol. i.

Rill from the Town Pump, A, a sketch in *Twice-Told Tales,* vol. i., located in Salem. It has been widely copied, and was published by a London bookseller in pamphlet form to serve as a temperance tract. For allusions to, see *French and Italian Journals,* vol. i., May 30, 1858, *The Scarlet Letter,* The Custom-House, end.

Ripley, George, the originator of the Brook Farm Enterprise, *American Note-Books,* vol. ii., April 13, 14, 1841, *The Blithedale Romance,* Preface.

Ripley, Rev. Dr., *American Note-Books,* vol. ii., August 8, 9, 1842, April 8, 26, March 12, 1843, December 19, 1850, *Mosses from an Old Manse,* vol. i., The Old Manse, Fire Worship.

River scenery, description of, *Fanshawe,* chapter viii., near the close.

Rizzio, death of, *English Note-Books.* vol. ii., May 10, 1856, Edinburgh.

Robert, Son of William I., statue of, *English Note-Books,* vol. ii., June 29, 1856, Gloucester.

Roberts, President, of Liberia, *English Note-Books,* vol. ii., May 24, 1856.

Robin, name of a character in the story Major Molineux, in *The Snow Image and Other Twice-Told Tales.*

Robinson Crusoe, allusions to, *Twice-Told Tales,* vol. ii., Footprints on the Sea Shore, *English Note-Books,* vol. i., February 18, 1856.

Rob Roy: country of, *English Note-Books,* vol. ii., May 10, 1856; cave of, *ibid.,* July 4, 1857.

Robsart: Amy, needlework by, *Our Old Home,* About Warwick; tower of, *English Note-Books,* vol. ii., September 13, 1857.

Rochcliffe, Lady Eleanore, heroine of the tale Lady Eleanore's Mantle, *Twice-Told Tales,* vol. ii.

Rochester, N. Y., subject of one of the Sketches from Memory in the volume *The Dolliver Romance and Other Pieces.*

Rochester, the wicked Earl of, *Our Old Home,* Near Oxford.

Rock Ferry, near Liverpool, *English Note-Books*, vol. i., August 9, 10, 20, September 1, 1853.

Rock Park, *English Note-Books*, vol. i., September 2, 1853, June 11, 1855.

Roderic Dhu, dungeon of, *English Note-Books*, vol. ii., May 10, 1856.

Roger de Poictiers, castle built by, *English Note-Books*, vol. i., September 7, 1853.

Roger Malvin's Burial, a story in *Mosses from an Old Manse*, vol. ii. The scene is laid in the early days of the American colonies, and the story illustrates the development of a justifiable action into a sin through concealment. It first appeared in "The Democratic Review."

Rogers, John, a, in New England, *Twice-Told Tales*, vol. i., The Gray Champion.

Rogers, Randolph, sculptor, *The Marble Faun*, Preface.

Rogers, Rev. Mr., *The Snow Image, etc.*, A Bell's Biography.

Rogers, Rev. Nathanael, tomb of, at Ipswich, *American Note-Books*, vol. i., September 7, 1835.

Rogers, Samuel: articles from the collection of, *English Note-Books*, vol. ii., May 24, 1856, Manchester; residence of, *ibid.*, March 22, 1856.

Romance, phantom of, in the unromantic, *Twice-Told Tales*, vol. i., The Wedding Knell.

Romances, as distinguished from novels, *The House of the Seven Gables*, Preface; subjects for, *English Note-Books*, vol. i., April 12, November 28, 1855.

Romans, the: inherited dignity of, *The Marble Faun*, vol. ii., chapter xvi.; life of, in winter, *ibid.*; remains of, in England, *English Note-Books*, vol. ii., June 18, 1856, *Our Old Home*, Pilgrimage to Old Boston (Lincoln); solidity of the buildings of, *French and Italian Journals*, vol. i., April 25, 1858; uncleanliness of, *The Marble Faun*, vol. ii., chapter xvii.

Rome: the scene mainly of *The Marble Faun; French and Italian Journals*, vol. i., January 24 to May 24, 1858, vol. ii., October 17, 1858, to May 29, 1859; affection for, *French and Italian Journals*, vol. i., May 24, 1858, *The Marble Faun*, vol. ii., chapter xi.; atmosphere of, *ibid.;* at the present day, *ibid.*, vol. i., chapter xii.; attractions of, for artists, *ibid.*, vol. i., chapter xv.; cookery of, *ibid.*, vol. ii., chapter xi.; dreariness of, *ibid.*, vol. ii., chapter xx.; feeling commonest in, *ibid.*, vol. i., chapter i.; filth of, *French and Italian Journals*, vol. i., February 19, 1858, *The Marble Faun*, vol. ii., chapter xi.; first impressions of, *French and Italian Journals*, vol. i., February 3, 7, 1858; the Ghetto, *The Marble Faun*, vol. ii., chapter xvii.; inherited evil of, *ibid.*, vol. ii., chapter xx.; malaria of, *French and Italian Journals*, vol. i., March 25, 26, 1858, *The Marble Faun*, vol. ii., chapter xi.; morality of, *ibid.*, vol. ii., chapter ix.; number of dwarfs in, *French and Italian Journals*, vol. i., April 16, 1858; pavements of, *The Marble Faun*, vol. ii., chapter xi.; pilgrims in, *French and Italian Journals*, vol. i., April 3, 1858; police of, *The Marble Faun*, vol. ii., chapter xix.; ruins of, *The Marble Faun*, vol. i., chapter xvii.; spring in, *French and Italian Journals*, vol. i., March 25, 1858; summer in, *The Marble Faun*, vol. i., chapter xxiv.; tradesmen of, *French and Italian Journals*, vol. i., May 21, 1858; wall of, *ibid.*, February 23, 1858; winter in, *ibid.*, February 7, 1858, *The Marble Faun*, vol. ii., chapter xvi.

Romeli, Robert de, builder of Skipton Castle, *English Note-Books*, vol. ii., April 10, 1857; escutcheon of, *ibid.*, April 11, 1857.

Romulus, *The Marble Faun*, vol. i., chapter i.

Rooks, tradition among, *English Note-Books*, vol. i., March 23, 1854.

Rosa, Salvator: landscape by, *French and Italian Journals*, June 13, 1858; a namesake of, *ibid.*, January 24, 1858.

Rosamond, Fair, place of seclusion and well of, *Our Old Home*, Near Oxford, toward the end.

Roscoe, William, grave of, *English Note-Books*, vol. i., March 13, 1854.

Rosina, the wife of Roderick Elliston, in the story of Egotism, in *Mosses from an Old Manse*, vol. ii. She also appears in connection with the story The Christmas Banquet.

16

Rospigliosi Palace, the, *French and Italian Journals*, vol. i., February 20, 1858.

Rothay, the River, *English Note-Books*, vol. i., July 19, 1855.

Rousseau, J. J., "Julie" of, *French and Italian Journals*, vol. ii., June 12, 1859.

Routledge, publishing firm of, *English Note-Books*, vol. ii., August 2, 1856

Rows of Chester, the, *English Note-Books*, vol. i., October 1, 1853.

Royal Society, Transactions of the, *Mosses from an Old Manse*, vol. i., The Birthmark.

Royalty: distinguishing look of, *French and Italian Journals*, vol. ii., June 13, 1858; impressiveness of, *English Note-Books*, vol. i., March 24, 1856; insignia of, *Mosses from an Old Manse*, vol. ii., Earth's Holocaust; relics of, *ibid.*, A Virtuoso's Collection.

Rubens, a Bacchus by, *French and Italian Journals*, vol. ii., June 15, 1858.

Rugg, Peter, *Mosses from an Old Manse*, vol. ii., A Virtuoso's Collection.

Ruggles, John, *Fanshawe, etc.*, Jonathan Cilley.

Ruin, various guises and kinds of, *American Note-Books*, vol. i., October 25, 1836.

Ruins: impression of antiquity made by Roman and Gothic, *French and Italian Journals*, vol. i., April 15, 1858; impressiveness of, *English Note-Books*, vol. i., July 13, 1855; in England and Italy, *French and Italian Journals*, vol. i., February 7, 1858; in Rome, *ibid.*, February 23, 1858; need of neglect of, *English Note-Books*, vol. ii., April 11, 1857.

Rules of life, *Septimius Felton*, p. 126 *et seq.* (12mo).

Runcorn, *English Note-Books*, vol. ii., August 21, 1856.

Russell, Captain, *English Note-Books*, vol. i., March 6, 1856.

Russell, Lord John, *English Note-Books*, vol. ii., April 8, 1856, *Our Old Home*, Consular Experiences.

Russians, hatred of foreigners by, *English Note-Books*, vol. i., September 26, 1855.

Rusticity, *The Blithedale Romance*, chapter xxiii.

Ruthin, *English Note-Books*, vol. i., September 20, 1854.

Ruthven, Lord, breastplate of, *English Note-Books*, vol. ii., May 10, 1856, Edinburgh.

Rydal Lake, *English Note-Books*, vol. i., July 19, 1855.

Sabbath: a New England, *The House of the Seven Gables*, chapter xi.; connection of, with faith, *Twice-Told Tales*, vol. i., Sunday at Home.

Sabbath-breakers, a community of, *American Note-Books*, vol. i., June 22, 1835. See SUNDAY.

Sacheverell, Dr., *Our Old Home*, Lichfield and Uttoxeter.

Saco, valley of the, *Mosses from an Old Manse*, vol. ii., Sketches from Memory, The Notch of the White Mountains.

Sadness: of the world, its growing heaviness, *The Marble Faun*, vol. ii., chapter i.; that cannot be dealt with, *The Blithedale Romance*, chapter xviii.

Sagacity of animals, *American Note-Books*, vol. i., September, 1836.

Sailors: conduct of, toward women, *English Note-Books*, vol. i., January 1, 1856; examination of, *ibid.*, April 24, 1855; kidnapping of a, *ibid.*, May 18, 1855; murder of a, *ibid.*, September 22, 1853; on the lakes, *The Dolliver Romance, etc.*, The Inland Port; superstition of, *American Note-Books*, vol. ii., September 10, 1852; treatment of, *English Note-Books*, vol. i., November 16, 22, 1855.

Saint Angelo, Castle of, *French and Italian Journals*, vol. i., March 25, 1858, *The Marble Faun*, vol. i., chapter xii., vol. ii., chapter xv.

Saint Asaph, *English Note-Books*, vol. i., September 20, 1854.

Saint Bartholomew, Island of, *French and Italian Journals*, vol. i., February 23, 1858.

Saint Bernard, dogs of, *English Note-Books*, vol. ii., September 17, 1857.

Saint Clair, General, *The Snow Image, etc.*, Old Ticonderoga.

Saint James Palace, Park, and Place, *English Note-Books*, vol. i., September 8, 10, 1855, March 22, 1856.

Saint John, Feast of, *French and Italian Journals*, vol. ii., June 28, 30, 1858.

Saint John, River, Vale, and Castle, *English Note-Books*, vol. i., July 21, 1855.

Saint John's School-house, *Our Old Home*, About Warwick.

Saint's Chamber, the, *Mosses from an Old Manse*, vol. i., The Old Manse, at the middle.

Saints, mediation of the, *The Marble Faun*, vol. ii., chapters xiii., xiv., xxv.

Salem, Mass., the scene of *The House of the Seven Gables*, Endicott and the Red Cross, Young Goodman Brown, and others of the short stories and sketches. Some incidents of its early history are given in Main Street, in *The Snow Image, etc*, and some notes concerning it in The Sister Years, *Twice-Told Tales*, vol. ii. The Custom-House is described in the introduction to *The Scarlet Letter*, where the author alludes also to the residence of his ancestors in Salem and his feeling toward the place; chamber of Hawthorne in, *American Note-Books*, vol. ii., March, 1843; dealings of Satan in, *Fanshawe, etc.*, Sir William Phips, third paragraph; first settlers of, *Grandfather's Chair*, part i., chapter ii., *The Snow Image, etc.*, Main Street; a hill and house in, *The Dolliver Romance, etc.*, Browne's Folly; made capital, *Grandfather's Chair*, part iii., chapter vii.; old family names of, *The Dolliver Romance, etc.*, Time's Portraiture; old merchants of, *The Scarlet Letter*, The Custom-House, middle; reminder of the Custom-House of, *Our Old Home*, About Warwick; visit to, *American Note-Books*, vol. ii., March 31, 1843; walks about, *ibid.*, vol. i., June 15, 18, 1835, August 31, 1836, August 22, 1837.

Salisbury, City, Cathedral, and Plain of, *English Note-Books*, vol. ii., June 17, 1856.

Salisbury, Countess, garter of, *Mosses from an Old Manse*, vol. ii., A Virtuoso's Collection.

Sallust, gardens of, *French and Italian Journals*, vol. i., March 26, 1858.

Salt, *American Note-Books*, vol. i., letter, October 4, 1840; manufacture of, by Indians, *The Dolliver Romance, etc.*, A Book of Autographs.

Saltonstall, Sir Richard, *Grandfather's Chair,* part i., chapter ii., *The Snow Image, etc.,* Main Street.

Salvator Rosa. See Rosa.

Samphire, *American Note-Books,* vol. i., June 18, 1835.

Sand, George (Madame Dudevant), allusion to one characteristic of her writings, *The Blithedale Romance,* chapter vii.

Sanguinea Sanguinissima, *Septimius Felton,* pp. 131–3, 157 (12mo).

Sanguinetto, the, *French and Italian Journals,* vol. i., May 30, 1858.

San Lorenzo, old and new towns of, *French and Italian Journals,* vol. ii., October 15, 1858.

San Miniato, convent of, *French and Italian Journals,* vol. ii., September 25, 1858.

San Paolo, the gate of, *French and Italian Journals,* vol. i., March 27, 1858.

San Querico, *French and Italian Journals,* vol. ii., October 13, 14, 1858.

Sarcophagi, significance of the carvings on, *The Marble Faun,* chapters ii., x.

Sarto, Andrea del, *French and Italian Journals,* vol. ii., July 13, September 10, 25, 1858.

Satan, *Mosses from an Old Manse,* vol. i., Young Goodman Brown; characteristics of, *Twice-Told Tales,* vol. ii., The Seven Vagabonds; reputed portrait of, *ibid.,* Edward Randolph's Portrait.

Satirist, a bitter, *American Note-Books,* vol. ii., December 19, 1850.

Satyrs, the, *Tanglewood Tales,* The Pomegranate Seeds.

Saurians, theory concerning extinct, *American Note-Books,* vol. i., September, 1836.

Savonarola, convent of, *French and Italian Journals,* vol. ii., July 10, 1858.

Scarecrows, *Wonder-Book,* The Gorgon's Head, *Mosses from an Old Manse,* vol. i., Feathertop.

Scarlet Letter, The, A Romance. This novel was written in Salem, Mass., in 1849, and published in Boston by Ticknor,

Reed & Fields, in 1850. It was published in London the same year. The scene is laid in Boston, near the middle of the seventeenth century. An allusion to the punishment which gives the story its name, and which the author says he saw mentioned in the town records of Boston, is made in the story Endicott and the Red Cross, in *Twice-Told Tales.* An opera founded on it is mentioned in the Note-Books. For allusions to it see the *American Note-Books,* vol. ii., May 6, 1850, *English Note-Books,* vol. i., September 7, 14, 1855, *Our Old Home,* Near Oxford.

Scarlet, Old, portrait of, *English Note-Books,* vol. ii., May 27, 1857.

Scenery: American and British, *English Note-Books,* vol. ii., July 5, 1857; description of, *ibid.,* vol. i., July 21, 1855; most exquisite, *ibid.,* vol. ii., June 7, 1857; represented in art, *ibid.,* July 5, 1857; seen from water, *ibid.,* May 10, 1856; taste in, *ibid.,* July 2, 1857; views of noted, *ibid.,* July 7, 1857.

Schaefer, Miriam. See MIRIAM.

Schaefer, Monsieur. See FRENCHMAN, the little.

Schlemihl, Peter, *Mosses from an Old Manse,* vol. ii., The Intelligence Office, A Virtuoso's Collection.

Scholar, the ideal, *Mosses from an Old Manse,* vol. i., A Select Party.

Schoolmasters, characteristics of, *Twice-Told Tales,* vol. ii., The Shaker Bridal.

Schoolmistress, name for a, *American Note-Books,* vol. ii., June 1, 1842.

Schools, old, *Our Old Home,* About Warwick.

Schuyler, General, letter from, *The Dolliver Romance and Other Pieces,* A Book of Autographs.

Sciarra Palace, *French and Italian Journals,* vol. i., March 10, 1858.

Science, expectations from, in the last century, *Mosses from an Old Manse,* vol. i., The Birthmark, at the beginning.

Scientists, a common wish of, *Mosses from an Old Manse,* vol. ii., The Intelligence Office.

Scinis, the robber, *Tanglewood Tales,* The Minotaur.

Scipio, a black servant in the story Egotism, vol. ii., *Mosses from an Old Manse.*

Scipios, tomb of the, *French and Italian Journals,* vol. i., March 3, 1858.

Scituate, *Twice-Told Tales,* vol. ii., The Village Uncle.

Scorn of humanity, *Twice-Told Tales,* vol. ii., Lady Eleanore's Mantle.

Scotch, the: drunkenness of, *English Note-Books,* vol. ii., May 10, 1856, Melrose; features of, *ibid.*, May 10, 1856; speech of, *ibid.*, July 11, 1857.

Scotland: interest of the world in, *English Note-Books,* vol. ii., May 10, 1856, Abbotsford; mountains of, *ibid.*, May 10, 1856; regalia of, *ibid.*, July 9, 1857; view of battle-fields of, from Stirling, *ibid.*, May 10, 1856; women of, *ibid.*, July 1, 1857.

Scott, Captain, *American Note-Books,* vol. i., August 27, 1837.

Scott, Lady, portrait of, *English Note-Books,* vol. ii., May 10, 1856, Abbotsford.

Scott, Michael, the wizard: allusion to, *The Blithedale Romance,* chapter vi.; magic of, *English Note-Books,* vol. ii., May 10, 1856, Dryburgh; tomb of, *ibid.*, May 10, 1856, Melrose, July 11, 1857.

Scott, Sir Walter, *English Note-Books,* vol. ii., May 10, 1856, Abbotsford; change in the estimation of, *ibid.*; description of Melrose by, *ibid.*, May 10, 1856, Melrose; evening with Major Burns, *ibid.*, vol. i., October 3, 1853; fame of, *Mosses from an Old Manse,* vol. ii., P.'s Correspondence; inn named after, *English Note-Books,* vol. i., July 19, 1855; Kenilworth manuscript, *ibid.*, vol. ii., December 7, 1857; monuments to, *ibid.*, May 10, 1856, July 10, 1857; monuments of the family of, *ibid.*, May 10, 1856, Dryburgh; places celebrated by, *ibid.*, vol. i., July 21, 1855, vol. ii., May 10, 1856, July 5, 9, 1857, *Our Old Home,* Near Oxford; plaster cast of, *English Note-Books,* vol. ii., May 10, 1856, Abbotsford; quotation from, *Fanshawe,* head of chapter vii.; real nature of, *English Note-Books,* vol. ii., May 10, 1856, Abbotsford; statue of, *ibid.*, May 10, 1856, Glasgow, July 1, 1857; tombstone erected by, *ibid.*, May 10, 1856, Melrose.

Scottish Chiefs, The, *Twice-Told Tales,* vol. ii., The Seven Vagabonds.

Scribbler, a, *Twice-Told Tales,* vol. ii., The Village Uncle.

Scrofula, the royal touch for, *True Stories,* chapter iv. of Biographies. (Only in 16mo ed.)

Scroope, Lord, story of a daughter of, *English Note-Books,* vol. ii., June 28, 1857.

Sculptors, American and English in Rome, *French and Italian Journals,* vol. i., May 9, 1858; characteristics of American, *The Marble Faun,* vol. i., chapter xv.; criticism on Powers by a, *French and Italian Journals,* vol. ii., October 21, 1858; government patronage of, in America, *ibid.,* June 4, 1858; lack of originality in modern, *The Marble Faun,* vol. i., chapter xiv.; studio of a, *ibid.,* vol. i., chapter xiii.; what they should be, *ibid.,* vol. i., chapter xv.

Sculpture: classic, *English Note-Books,* vol. ii., December 7, 1857; costume in, *French and Italian Journals,* vol. i., May 9, vol. ii., June 16, 1858; first American to attempt, *Mosses from an Old Manse,* vol. ii., Drowne's Wooden Image; immortality of, *The Marble Faun,* vol. i., chapter xv.; in the Capitol at Rome, *ibid.,* vol. i., chapter i.; more genuine than painting, *Mosses from an Old Manse,* vol. ii., The New Adam and Eve.

Sea, the: air of, *American Note-Books,* vol. i., letter, April, 1841; companionship of, *Twice-Told Tales,* vol. ii., Footprints on the Sea Shore; views of, *American Note-Books,* vol. i., August 31, 1836, August 22, 1837; walk to, *ibid.,* October 16, 1837; weeds of, *ibid.,* June 15, 1835.

Sea-anemones, *English Note-Books,* vol. ii., May 10, 1857.

Sea Nymphs, the, *Tanglewood Tales,* The Pomegranate Seeds.

Sea service, the American, miserable condition of, *Our Old Home,* Consular Experiences.

Sealsfield, *Mosses from an Old Manse,* vol. i., A Select Party.

Seamstress, the, *American Note-Books,* vol ii., October 9, 1841. See PRISCILLA.

Sebastopol: reported fall of, *English Note-Books,* vol. i., October 6, 1854; representation of the storming of, *ibid.,* October 3, 1855; rejoicings at the fall of, *ibid.,* October 14, 1855.

Seclusion, instinctive avoidance of, in certain moods, *The Marble Faun*, vol. ii., chapter x.

Secrets, instinct to betray guilty, *Twice-Told Tales*, vol. i., Mr. Higginbotham's Catastrophe; love for petty, *ibid.*, Wakefield.

Sects, hedges around, *Messes from an Old Manse*, vol. i., The Procession of Life.

Sedgwick, C. M., *Wonder-Book*, Bald-Summit (authoress in Lenox, name not given).

Seeker, the, a character in The Great Carbuncle, *Twice-Told Tales*, vol. i., a representation of ambition become an irresistible fate after its objects have ceased to be alluring.

Sefton, Lord, *English Note-Books*, vol. i., November 14, 1854; residence of, *ibid.*, March 23, 1854.

Select Party, A, a fanciful sketch of a gathering of ideal and representative characters, surrounded by unrealities of imagination and hope, *Mosses from an Old Manse*, vol. i. It was first published in "The Democratic Review."

Selectmen of Boston, the, *Twice-Told Tales*, vol. ii., Edward Randolph's Portrait.

Self, from an outside point of view, *American Note-Books*, vol. i., July 13, 1838.

Self-contemplation, morbid, *Mosses from an Old Manse*, vol. ii., Egotism.

Selfishness: induced by absorbing secrets, *Mosses from an Old Manse*, vol. ii., Roger Malvin's Burial; in philanthropy, *The Blithedale Romance*, chapter xxv.; inspiring love, *American Note-Books*, vol. i., 1840. (This idea is carried out, perhaps, in Hollingsworth.)

Self-knowledge, incapacity for, in certain characters, *The House of the Seven Gables*, chapter xv., middle.

Self-made men: a type of, *The House of the Seven Gables*, chapter xii; in England and America, *English Note-Books*, vol. ii., April 8, 1856.

Sensations on coming back to an old way of life, *The Blithedale Romance*, chapter xvii.

Sensuality, the mystic, of the age, *The Blithedale Romance*, chapter xxiii.

September Afternoon, a, *The Dolliver Romance, etc.,* Journal of a Solitary Man, ii.

Septimius Felton; or, The Elixir of Life, a novel only roughly completed, founded on the same idea as *The Dolliver Romance.* It was found among the author's papers after his death, deciphered by his daughter Una with the assistance of Robert Browning, and published in 1872. The scene is laid in Concord, Mass., at the time of the Revolution. A suggestion of the subject is given in a letter in which the author mentions a legend of a former inhabitant of "The Wayside," his house at Concord, who believed himself to have found the secret Septimius was seeking, the elixir of life. The idea of the Bloody Footstep, referred to on page 111 *et seq.*, may be found in the account of Smithell's Hall in the *English Note-Books,* vol. i, April 7 and August 25, 1855.

Septimius Severus. See SEVERUS.

Sepulchres, magnificent, fatality about, *Our Old Home,* About Warwick.

Seriphus, island of, *Wonder-Book,* The Gorgon's Head.

Sermons, *Mosses from an Old Manse,* The Old Manse, near the beginning, *Twice-Told Tales,* vol. i., Sunday at Home; Puritan, *ibid.,* The Gentle Boy; in England and America, *English Note-Books,* vol. i., November 5, 1853; quantity of, in the world, *American Note-Books,* vol. ii., August 30, 1842; subject for a, *English Note-Books,* vol. i., November 28, 1855.

Serpent, The Brazen, image of, *The Dolliver Romance,* first fragment.

Serpentine River, the, *English Note-Books,* vol. i., September 24, 1855.

Servitude, *Mosses from an Old Manse,* vol. ii., The New Adam and Eve.

Set Phrases, *Mosses from an Old Manse,* vol. i., Feathertop.

Sette Vene, *French and Italian Journals,* vol. ii., October 17, 1858.

Seven Vagabonds, The, one of the *Twice-Told Tales,* vol. ii., the vagabonds being vagrants of different kinds on their way to a camp-meeting. There is an allusion to it in *Mosses from* *an Old Manse,* vol. ii., Passages from a Relinquished Work, At Home.

Severn, the, *English Note-Books,* vol. i., September 5, October 14, 1855.

Severus, Septimius, the Emperor: death of, *English Note-Books,* vol. ii., May 10, 1856, York; triumphal arch of, *The Marble Faun,* vol. i., chapter i.

Sewall, Judge, *American Note-Books,* vol. ii., 1842, anecdotes of the Pepperells.

Seward, Miss Anna, *Our Old Home,* Lichfield and Uttoxeter.

Sewell, Samuel, *Grandfather's Chair,* part i., chapter vi.

Shadow Brook, *Wonder-Book.*

Shadows of life, comfort in, *Twice-Told Tales,* vol. ii., Chippings with a Chisel.

Shafton, Sir Piercy, wardrobe of, *Mosses from an Old Manse,* vol. ii., Passages from a Relinquished Work, A Fellow-Traveller.

Shakejoint, *Wonder-Book,* The Gorgon's Head.

Shaker Bridal, The, a sketch in *Twice-Told Tales,* vol. ii. It was published as original in the London "Metropolitan," in 1850. See *American Note-Books,* vol. ii., May 6, 1850.

Shakers, the, *Twice-Told Tales,* vol. ii., The Shaker Bridal, *The Snow Image, etc.,* The Canterbury Pilgrims.

Shakspeare: autograph of, *English Note-Books,* vol. ii., December 7, 1857; Crown Inn, Oxford, *ibid.,* August 31, 1856; description of a wounded stag by, *Our Old Home,* Recollections of a Gifted Woman; face of, *ibid.;* home and grave of, *ibid.;* Imogen, *ibid.,* About Warwick; inexhaustibleness of, *ibid.,* Recollections of a Gifted Woman; quotations from, *Fanshawe,* head of chapters i., ii., v.; stag shot by, and Prospero's wand, *Mosses from an Old Manse,* vol. ii., A Virtuoso's Collection; story of the death of, *English Note-Books,* vol. i., January 9, 1855; Vincentio in "Taming of the Shrew," *Twice-Told Tales,* vol. i., Sights from a Steeple; works of and commentaries on, *Mosses from an Old Manse,* vol. ii., Earth's Holocaust.

Shallow, Justice, *English Note-Books,* vol. i., September 15,

1855; orchard of, *American Note-Books*, vol. ii., August 9, 1842.

Shallowness of character, different manifestations of, *The Blithedale Romance*, chapter xxii.

Shame, *Twice-Told Tales*, vol. ii., The Haunted Mind.

Sharpe, Archbishop, relic of, *English Note-Books*, vol. ii., May 10, 1856, Abbotsford.

Shaw, Lieutenant, *English Note-Books*, vols. i., ii., April 1, 4, 1856.

Shays's Rebellion, *Grandfather's Chair*, part iii., chapter x.

Sheep, *American Note-Books*, vol. i., July 31, September 9, 1838.

Sheffield, appearance of, *Our Old Home*, Pilgrimage to Old Boston.

Shelburne Falls, *American Note-Books*, vol. i, August 31, 1838.

Shelley, *Mosses from an Old Manse*, vol. ii., Earth's Holocaust; poetry and imagined old age of, *ibid.*, P.'s Correspondence.

Shells, explosion of, *American Note-Books*, vol. i., October 25, 1836.

Shenstone, *Mosses from an Old Manse*, vol. ii., A Virtuoso's Collection.

Shepard, Miss, a traveling companion of the Hawthorne family, mentioned often in the *French and Italian Journals.*

Sherwood Forest, *English Note-Books*, vol. ii., May 29, 1857, *Our Old Home*, Pilgrimage to Old Boston.

Shibboleth, an American, *Our Old Home*, Consular Experiences.

Shillings, Pine-Tree, *Twice-Told Tales*, vol. i., The Great Carbuncle, *Fanshawe, etc.*, Sir William Phips, fourth paragraph. See PINE-TREE SHILLINGS.

Shipmasters, American, *Our Old Home*, Consular Experiences, *English Note-Books*, vol. i., May 22, September 24, 1855.

Ships: finery in, *English Note-Books*, vol. i., November 22, 1855; toy, *American Note-Books*, vol. ii., June 1, 1842.

Shirley, William, Governor of Massachusetts, *Twice-Told Tales*, vol. ii., Howe's Masquerade, Edward Randolph's Portrait,

Grandfather's Chair, part ii., chapters vii., viii., ix., *Fanshawe, etc.*, Sir William Pepperell, first paragraph; wife of, *American Note-Books*, vol. ii., September 16, 1841.

Shoes, famous, *Mosses from an Old Manse*, vol. ii., A Virtuoso's Collection.

Short, Captain, *Fanshawe, etc.*, Sir William Phips, fifth paragraph.

Shovel, Sir Cloudesley, monument of, *English Note-Books*, vol. i., September 26, 1855.

Show, an itinerant, *Twice-Told Tales*, vol. ii., The Seven Vagabonds.

Showmen, *American Note-Books*, vol. i., July 13, 1838, *English Note-Books*, vol. i., September 14, 1855.

Shrewsbury, *English Note-Books*, vol. i., June 21, September 5, 1855, *Our Old Home*, Pilgrimage to Old Boston.

Shrewsbury, The Countess of, introduced into the Legend in The Antique Ring, in *The Dolliver Romance, etc.*

Shrine, The Virgin's, *The Marble Faun*, vol. i., chapter vi.

Shrines, wayside, *French and Italian Journals*, vol. i., May 26, 28, 1858, *The Marble Faun*, vol. ii., chapter vii.

Shrubs, old age of, *Mosses from an Old Manse*, vol. i., Buds and Bird Voices.

Shute, Governor, *Twice-Told Tales*, vol. ii., Howe's Masquerade, Lady Eleanore's Mantle, *Grandfather's Chair*, part ii., chapter v.

Shuttleworth, Sir J. K., friendship of, with Miss Bronté, *English Note-Books*, vol. ii., April 19, 1857.

Shy, the, admiration of, for the active, *The House of the Seven Gables*, chapter v., after the middle.

Sibylline Responses, *The Blithedale Romance*, chapter i.

Sickles, Daniel E., afterwards general, *English Note-Books*, vol. i., October 19, 1853.

Siddons, Mrs., the actress, *Mosses from an Old Manse*, vol. ii., P.'s Correspondence.

Siena, *French and Italian Journals*, vol. ii., October 2–12, 1858.

Sights from a Steeple, a short sketch in *Twice-Told Tales*, vol. i. It first appeared in "The Boston Token."

Signet, the devil's, on the human face, *The Blithedale Romance*, chapter xviii.

Sigourney, Mrs., quotation from, *American Note-Books*, vol. i., October 25, 1835.

Silk Manual, The, newspaper, *Fanshawe, etc.*, T. G. Fessenden.

Silliman, Benj., "Journal of Science" of, *English Note-Books*, vol. ii., August 31, 1856, Ratcliffe Library.

Silsbee, Mr., of Salem, *English Note-Books*, vol. ii., November 15, 16, 19, 1857.

Silver Hills, Indian story of the, *Mosses from an Old Manse*, vol. ii., Sketches from Memory, Our Evening Party among the Mountains.

Silvery Veil, The, Zenobia's legend, *The Blithedale Romance*, chapter xiii.

Simplicity of character: its growing rarity, *The Marble Faun*, vol. ii., chapter i.; rarity of, among Yankees, *Twice-Told Tales*, vol. ii., Chippings with a Chisel.

Sin: emblem of cherished, *American Note-Books*, vol. ii., 1842; fatality of the results of, *The Scarlet Letter*, chapters xiv., end, xviii., xx.; power of, over its slaves, *The Snow Image, etc.*, John Inglefield's Thanksgiving, end; searched out by the Puritans, *Twice-Told Tales*, vol. ii., Endicott and the Red Cross; secret, *ibid.*, vol. i, The Minister's Black Veil; sympathy for, *Mosses from an Old Manse*, vol. i., Young Goodman Brown; theory of, see EVIL; the unpardonable, *The Snow Image, etc.*, Ethan Brand, *The Blithedale Romance, etc.*, chapter vii.; untried cure for, *Mosses from an Old Manse*, vol. ii., The New Adam and Eve.

Sinclair, Catharine, *English Note-Books*, vol. ii., July 9, 1856.

Sisera, *The Blithedale Romance*, chapter v., end. See JAEL.

Sister Years, The, a short New Year's sketch for 1838, in *Twice-Told Tales*, vol. ii.

Sistine Chapel, the, *French and Italian Journals*, vol. i., May 15, 1858.

Skeletons, at the board, *Mosses from an Old Manse*, vol. ii., The Christmas Banquet.

Skeptics, result of intercourse with, *The Blithedale Romance*, chapter xii.

Sketches and Stories, suggestions for. See SUGGESTIONS.

Sketches: artists', *French and Italian Journals*, vol. ii., September 3, 1858; first of old masters, *The Marble Faun*, vol. i., chapter xv.; Miriam's, *ibid.*, vol. i., chapter v.

Sketches from Memory, notes of an excursion to the White Mountains and a ride on the Erie Canal, in vol. ii. of *Mosses from an Old Manse.*

Sketches from Memory, second series, in the volume with *The Dolliver Romance*, includes The Inland Port (Burlington, Vt.), Rochester (N. Y.), and A Night Scene (on Lake Erie).

Skiddaw, Mount, *English Note-Books*, vol. i., July 21, 1855.

Skipper, a dejected, *American Note-Books*, vol. ii., September 11, 1852.

Skipton, town and castle, *English Note-Books*, vol. ii., April 10, 1857.

Skulls, put to base uses, *English Note-Books*, vol. ii., May 29, 1857.

Slade, Ellen, *American Note-Books*, vol. ii., May 4, 1841.

Slang-term, an old Cheshire, *English Note-Books*, vol. i., December 1, 1853.

Sleep: periodic, of a whole village, *The Dolliver Romance, etc.*, An Old Woman's Tale; talking in, *Mosses from an Old Manse*, vol. i., The Birthmark, near the beginning; truth in, *ibid.*; the moment after waking from, *Twice-Told Tales*, vol. ii., The Haunted Mind; the world's need of, *ibid.*, The Old Manse, toward the end.

Sleepy Hollow, Concord, *American Note-Books*, vol. ii., August 22, November 8, 1842.

Slide, a mountain, *Twice-Told Tales*, vol. ii., The Ambitious Guest.

Slough of Despond: a, *Twice-Told Tales*, vol. ii., Night Sketches; the, *Mosses from an Old Manse*, vol. i., The Celestial Railroad.

Small-pox, *Twice-Told Tales*, vol. ii., Lady Eleanore's Mantle; ravages of, in New England, *Grandfather's Chair*, part ii., chapter v.

Smith, Albert, lecture of, *English Note-Books,* vol. ii., April 8, 1856.

Smith, Captain John, *Twice-Told Tales,* vol. i., The Great Carbuncle ; incident of, *American Note-Books,* vol. i., October 25, 1836 ; monument of, *ibid.,* vol. ii., September 8, 1852 ; tradition of, *ibid.*, August 30, 1852.

Smith, Daniel, a sailor, death of, *English Note-Books,* vol. i., May 11 and 18, 1855.

Smith, Miss, trial of, *English Note-Books,* vol. ii., July 9, 1857.

Smith, Mr., hero of the sketch Fancy's Show Box, *Twice-Told Tales,* vol. i.

Smith, Mr., a character in The Christmas Banquet, *Mosses from an Old Manse,* vol. ii.

Smith, Sydney, Pennsylvania bonds of, *Mosses from an Old Manse,* vol. ii., Earth's Holocaust.

Smithell's Hall, *English Note-Books,* vol. i., August 25, September 30, 1855 ; tradition of, *ibid.*, April 7, 1855, *Septimius Felton,* last page.

Smithfield, *English Note-Books,* vol. ii., September 15, November 15, 1857.

Smoke, from cannon, appearance of, *American Note-Books,* vol. i., September 7, 1835.

Smollett, Tobias, tomb of, *French and Italian Journals,* vol. i., January 24, 1858.

Smooth-it-Away, Mr., a character in The Celestial Railroad, *Mosses from an Old Manse,* vol. i.

Smutty Nose, Isles of Shoals, *American Note-Books,* vol. ii., September 11, 1852.

Sneyd, Honoria, *Our Old Home,* Lichfield and Uttoxeter.

Snoring, *Mosses from an Old Manse,* vol. ii., Sketches from Memory, The Canal Boat.

Snow: illuminating quality of, *American Note-Books,* vol. ii., March 11, 1851 ; the great, 1717, *The Snow Image, etc.,* Main Street.

Snowball Fights, *Twice-Told Tales,* vol. ii., Snow Flakes.

Snow-Birds, *Twice-Told Tales,* vol. ii., Snow Flakes.

Snowdon, Mount, *English Note-Books,* vol. i., July 19, 1854.

Snowdrops, model for a statue, *The Marble Faun*, vol. ii., chapter xvi.

Snow Flakes, title of a short description of a snow storm in vol. ii. of *Twice-Told Tales*.

Snow Image, The, and Other Twice-Told Tales, a collection of short stories first published in 1852. It was dedicated to Horatio Bridge, a classmate of the author.

Snow Image, The, A Childish Miracle, first story in the volume to which it gives its name, illustrating the fate of ideals in contact with the hard common sense of the world.

Snowy days favorable to thought, *Twice-Told Tales*, vol. ii., Snow Flakes.

Soap-bubbles, *The House of the Seven Gables*, chapter xi., end.

Socialists of Brook Farm, the, *The Blithedale Romance*, Preface.

Society, a new classification of, *American Note-Books*, vol. i., October 25, 1836, *Mosses from an Old Manse*, vol. i., The Procession of Life.

Sodoma, "Christ Bound" by, *French and Italian Journals*, vol. ii., October 5, 21, 1858, *The Marble Faun*, vol. ii., chapter xii.; "Judith" by, *French and Italian Journals*, vol. ii., October 5, 1858; "Madonna" by, *ibid.*, October 9, 1858.

Soldiers: care of government for old, *Our Old Home*, A London Suburb; moral influence of, *English Note-Books*, vol. i., April 1, 1856.

Solitude: in city and in forest, *Mosses from an Old Manse*, vol. ii., The New Adam and Eve; necessity of, *Twice-Told Tales*, vol. ii., Footprints on the Sea Shore.

Solomon, legend of, *American Note-Books*, vol. ii., 1842.

Some of the Haunts of Burns, an article in *Our Old Home*, describing his home in Dumfries, his birthplace at Ayr, the farm of Moss Giel, the monument, and the scenes of some of the poems.

Somerset family, monument of the, *English Note-Books*, vol. ii., June 17, 1856.

Somerset House, *English Note-Books*, vol. ii., November 12, 1857.

Somma, Monte, *French and Italian Journals*, vol. i., May 26, 1858.

Songs, *Fanshawe*, chapter v. ; description of, *The Marble Faun*, vol. ii., chapter iv.

Sophistry, peculiar, often used by oppressors, *Fanshawe*, chapter viii., near the close.

Soracte, Mount, *French and Italian Journals*, vol. i., May 24, 1858, *The Marble Faun*, vol. i., chapter xii.

Sorrow, *Twice-Told Tales*, vol. ii., The Haunted Mind, The Lily's Quest; classification by, *Mosses from an Old Manse*, vol. i., The Procession of Life; influence of, on artistic insight, *The Marble Faun*, vol. ii., chapter xvi. ; refining influence of, *Twice-Told Tales*, vol. ii., Chippings with a Chisel; varieties of, *Mosses from an Old Manse*, vol. ii., The Christmas Banquet.

Souls : our, not our own, *The Blithedale Romance*, chapter xxiii.; the dullest, *American Note-Books*, vol. ii., August 7, 1842. See HUMAN SOUL.

Southampton, *English Note-Books*, vol. i., October 11, 1855, vol. ii., June 15, 1856.

Southey, Robert : character of, grave and house of, *English Note-Books*, vol. i., July 21, 1855; friendship with Byron imagined, *Mosses from an Old Manse*, vol. ii., P.'s Correspondence; "Curse of Kehama," *American Note-Books*, vol. i., July 10, 1838, *Mosses from an Old Manse*, vol. i., Monsieur du Miroir; Nelson's life by, *Our Old Home*, A London Suburb.

Southport, England, *English Note-Books*, vol. ii., August 21, September 13 to 21, October 26, 1856, February 27, May 10, June 21, July 14, 1857.

Southwick, Cassandra, *The Snow Image, etc.*, Main Street.

Spada Palace, the, *French and Italian Journals*, vol. i., May 21, 1858.

Spaniards, shipwrecked on the Isles of Shoals, *American Note-Books*, vol. ii., September 11, 1852.

Spanish boys at Brook Farm, *American Note-Books*, vol. ii., September 28, 1841.

Sparhawk, Colonel, *American Note-Books,* vol. ii., 1842.

Sparks, Jared, two busts of, *French and Italian Journals,* vol. i., June 4, 1858.

Sparrow's nest, mysteriousness of a, *American Note-Books,* vol. i., 1840.

Spectre of the Catacomb, the, *The Marble Faun,* vol. i., chapter iv. See MIRIAM'S MODEL.

Speculations in religion, *Mosses from an Old Manse,* vol. ii., The Christmas Banquet.

Speech-making, *English Note-Books,* vol. i., August 5, 15, 1853, October 5, 1854, April 24, 1855, vol. ii., April 4, 21, 1856, April 19, 1857, *Our Old Home,* Civic Banquets, middle and end.

Speed, John, bust of, *English Note-Books,* vol. i., March 25, 1856.

Spello, town of, *French and Italian Journals,* vol. i., May 28, 1858.

Spendthrift, his money's worth, *American Note-Books,* vol. ii., June 1, 1842.

Spenser, *Mosses from an Old Manse,* vol. i., The Hall of Fantasy, A Select Party.

Spiers, Mr., of Oxford, *English Note-Books,* vol. ii., August 31, September 9, 1856.

Spirit: the, renewing power of, *Mosses from an Old Manse,* vol. i., Buds and Bird Voices; truest state of, *ibid.,* vol. ii., Drowne's Wooden Image.

Spirits: argument for the existence of, *Mosses from an Old Manse,* vol. i., Monsieur du Miroir; of famous men, fancy about, *American Note-Books,* vol. ii., June 1, 1842; of modern spiritualism, what kind of existences, *The Blithedale Romance,* chapter xxiii.

Spiritual bodies, *American Note-Books,* vol. i., October 4, 1840.

Spiritual capacity of the earthliest, *Mosses from an Old Manse,* vol. i., The Old Manse, near the beginning.

Spiritualism, *American Note-Books,* vol. ii., September 27, 1841, *English Note-Books,* vol. ii., December 20, 1857; Robert Browning on, *French and Italian Journals,* vol. ii., June 9,

1858; Mrs. Browning on, *English Note-Books,* vol. ii., July 13, 1856; discussed, *French and Italian Journals,* vol. ii., September 1, 1858; indications of its phenomena, and materialism of, *The Blithedale Romance,* chapter xxiii.; interview with a medium, *French and Italian Journals,* vol. ii., August 12, 1858; stories of, *French and Italian Journals,* vol. ii., September 11, 1858.

Spiritualist, a, *English Note-Books,* vol. i, July 4, 6, 1855.

Spirituality, a poet's idea of, *The Blithedale Romance,* chapter v.

Spoleto, *French and Italian Journals,* vol. i., May 26, 1858.

Spring: approach of, *Mosses from an Old Manse,* vol. i., Buds and Bird Voices; effect of the sunshine of, *American Note-Books,* vol. i., letter April 30, 1840; impression of, *ibid.,* vol. ii., March 31, May 22, 1851; in New England, *The Blithedale Romance,* chapter viii.; leisurely progress of, in Rome, *The Marble Faun,* vol. i., chapter xii.; observation of, *American Note-Books,* vol. ii., April 25, 26, 1843.

Squarey, Mr., *English Note-Books,* vol. i., November 5, 1853.

Squash Blossom, name given to one of the children to whom the stories of the *Wonder-Book* and *Tanglewood Tales* were told.

Squashes, summer, beautiful shapes of, *Mosses from an Old Manse,* vol. i., The Old Manse, near the middle.

Squaw Sachem, the, *The Snow Image, etc.,* Main Street.

Squirrel, observation of a, *American Note-Books,* vol. ii., October 18, 1841.

Stable, description of a, *American Note-Books,* vol. ii., May 14, 1850.

Staff, a magic, *Mosses from an Old Manse,* vol. i., Young Goodman Brown.

Stafford House, *English Note-Books,* vol. i., September 8, 1855.

Stage-coaches, *Mosses from an Old Manse,* vol. ii., Sketches from Memory, The Notch of the White Mountains; agent for, *The Snow Image, etc.,* Ethan Brand; drivers of, *American Note-Books,* vol. i., July 26, September 9, 1838; traveling in, *ibid.,* July 27, 1838, *English Note-Books,* vol. i., July 30, 1855.

Stamford, *Twice-Told Tales,* vol. ii., The Seven Vagabonds.

Stanley, the House of, *English Note-Books*, vol. ii., April 19, 1857.

Stanley, Lord, *English Note-Books*, vol. ii., April 19, 1857 (name in blank), *Our Old Home*, Civic Banquets.

Stanley, Sir John, tower built by, *English Note-Books*, vol. i., September 7, 1853.

Stanton Harcourt, *Our Old Home*, Near Oxford; Pope's description of, *ibid*.

Staples Inn, London, *English Note-Books*, vol. i., September 8, 1855.

Star Island, Isles of Shoals, *American Note-Books*, vol. ii., September 4, 13, 1852.

Statesmen: faces of, compared with heroes', *Our Old Home*, A London Suburb; some English, *Mosses from an Old Manse*, vol. ii., P.'s Correspondence.

Station, people out of their true, *Mosses from an Old Manse*, vol. i., The Procession of Life.

Statuary: allegoric figures in, *French and Italian Journals*, vol. ii., September 29, 1858; costume in, *ibid*., June 19, September 29, 1858; in the Louvre, *ibid*., vol. i., January 10, 1858; nude, *ibid*., April 22, 1858; Thorwaldsen's analogy, *The Marble Faun*, vol. ii., chapter xvi. See SCULPTURE.

Statues: how cut in marble, *The Marble Faun*, vol. i., chapter xiii.; famous, *Mosses from an Old Manse*, vol. ii., A Virtuoso's Collection; necessary law for, *Our Old Home*, Up the Thames.

Staves of famous men, *Mosses from an Old Manse*, vol. ii., A Virtuoso's Collection.

Steam-engine, fancy about a, *American Note-Books*, vol. i., July 31, 1838.

Steamers, Collins and Cunard, *English Note-Books*, vol. i., September 1, 1853.

Stebbing, Mr., *English Note-Books*, vol. ii., August 31, 1856.

Steele, Mr., of Rock Ferry, *English Note-Books*, vol. i., January 20, 1855.

Steeple of a church, impression made by, *Twice-Told Tales*, vol. i., Sunday at Home.

Stephen, King, *English Note-Books*, vol. i., July 13, 1855.

Sterne, Lawrence: MS. of "The Sentimental Journey," *English Note-Books,* vol. ii., December 7, 1857; portraits of, *Our Old Home*, Pilgrimage to Old Boston.

Steuben, Baron, *The Dolliver Romance, etc.*, A Book of Autographs.

Stevens, Henry, *English Note-Books,* vol. ii., April 8, July 9, 1856. (Name in blank.)

Stick-to-the-right, Mr., *Mosses from an Old Manse,* vol. i., The Celestial Railroad.

Stirling, Town and Castle, *English Note-Books,* vol. ii., May 10, July 7, 1857.

Stirling, Sir William, *French and Italian Journals,* vol. ii., May 17, 1860.

Stockings, *Twice-Told Tales,* vol. i., Sunday at Home.

Stocks, the, *Twice-Told Tales,* vol. ii., Endicott and the Red Cross.

Stone, Rev. Mr., *Grandfather's Chair,* part i., chapter iv.

Stonehenge, *English Note-Books,* vol. ii., June 17, 1856.

Stone-wall, effect of a, *American Note-Books,* vol. ii., October 22, 1841.

Stony Phiz, Old, the popular name of a candidate for the presidency in The Great Stone Face, in *The Snow Image, etc.*

Stories, impulse to write, *American Note-Books,* vol. i., letter November, 1840, *Twice-Told Tales,* vol. i., Sights from a Steeple; rapid growth of in traveling, *ibid.*, Mr. Higginbotham's Catastrophe; suggestions for, see SUGGESTIONS.

Storms, *American Note-Books,* vol. ii., September 18, 1852.

Story, William W., *English Note-Books,* vol. i., September 14, 1855, *French and Italian Journals,* vol. i., March 25, May 23, 1858, vol. ii., October 4, 1858, *The Marble Faun,* Preface; conversation with, *French and Italian Journals,* vol. ii., August 3, 1858; spiritualism and, *English Note-Books,* vol. ii., July 13, 1856; statues by, *French and Italian Journals,* vol. i., February 14, April 22, 1858, *The Marble Faun,* vol. i., chapter xiv.

Story-tellers, *Tanglewood Tales,* introduction; wandering, *Mosses from an Old Manse,* vol. ii., Passages from a Relinquished Work, At Home; qualifications requisite for, *ibid.*, A Fellow-Traveller.

Story-writer, fantasy about a, *American Note-Books*, vol. i., October 25, 1835.

Stoves, *American Note-Books*, vol. ii., November 8, 1842, *Mosses from an Old Manse*, vol. i., Fire Worship.

Stowell, Lieutenant-Colonel, *English Note-Books*, vol. i., April 1, 1856.

Strafford family, tombs of the, *English Note-Books*, vol. ii., April 13, 1857.

Stratford-on-Avon, *Our Old Home*, Recollections of a Gifted Woman.

Street-life, charm of, *Our Old Home*, Outside Glimpses of English Poverty.

Strength, in nervous excitement, *The Blithedale Romance*, chapter xv., end.

Strozzi family, chapel of, *French and Italian Journals*, vol. ii., July 4, 1858.

Struggle, a great, *The Blithedale Romance*, chapter xxv.

Strutt's Book of English Sports and Pastimes, *Twice-Told Tales*, vol. i., The Maypole of Merry Mount.

Stuart, Gilbert C.: an anecdote of, suggested the story The Prophetic Pictures, *Twice-Told Tales*, vol. i.; picture of Washington by, *English Note-Books*, vol. i., September 14, 1855.

Stuart, Professor, of Andover, *American Note-Books*, vol. i., August 12, 1837.

Stuarts, the, *Twice-Told Tales*, vol. i., The Gray Champion; monument to, in St. Peter's, *French and Italian Journals*, vol. i., February 9, 1858; temporary residence of, *English Note-Books*, vol. i., September 5, 1855. See Charles, James, and Mary.

Students, college, *English Note-Books*, vol. ii., June 11, 1856; middle-aged, *American Note-Books*, vol. i., August 31, 1838.

Studio: a painter's, suggestions of, *The Marble Faun*, vol. i., chapter v.; a sculptor's, *ibid.*, vol. i., chapter xiii.

Stumps, of trees, fancy about, *Fanshawe, etc.*, Mrs. Hutchinson, third paragraph.

Sturgis, Russell, *English Note-Books*, vol. i., September 14, October 6, 1855. (Name in blank.)

Stuyvesant, Peter, wooden leg of, *Mosses from an Old Manse,* vol. ii., A Virtuoso's Collection.

Sublegras, Maria, *French and Italian Journals,* vol. i., March 1, 1858.

Sublimity, sensations of, from humble sources, *Twice-Told Tales,* vol. ii., Night Sketches.

Success of the wrong kind, *Mosses from an Old Manse,* vol. i., The Procession of Life.

Sue, Eugene, success of, *Mosses from an Old Manse,* vol. i., Rappaccini's Daughter.

Suffering, influence of, *English Note-Books,* vol. i., May 20, 1854.

Sugar Hill, *The Snow Image, etc.,* Old Ticonderoga.

Suggestions, for sketches and stories, *American Note-Books,* vol. i., August 31, September 7, October 17, 1835, September, October 25, 1836, August 22, October 16, December 6, 1837, June 15, July 13, 26, October 24, 1838, January 4, 1839, 1840, letter of May 30, 1840, vol. ii., 1842, March 11, October 27, 1851, August 20, 1852, *English Note-Books,* vol. i., December 13, 1853, August 8, November 14, 1854, vol. ii., October 10, 1857.

Suicide, *The Marble Faun,* vol. ii., chapter xxii.

Suicide, burial of a, *English Note-Books,* vol. i., March 16, 1854.

Summer-house, at "The Wayside," *Tanglewood Tales,* introduction.

Summons, a mysterious, *The Marble Faun,* vol. ii., chapters iv., xii.

Sumner, Charles, *French and Italian Journals,* vol. i., May 22, 1858.

Sunday: attire of, *Twice-Told Tales,* vol. i., Sunday at Home; Blithedale on, *The Blithedale Romance,* chapter xiv.; mode of spending, *American Note-Books,* vol i., June 22, 1835; observance of, *Our Old Home,* A London Suburb.

Sunday at Home, sketch in *Twice-Told Tales,* vol. i., describing the outside view of a church on Sunday.

Sunderland, Lord, heir to the Marlborough estate, *Our Old Home,* Near Oxford.

Sunken Treasure, The, story in *Grandfather's Chair,* part i., chapter x.

Sunlight, contrasted with moonlight, *American Note-Books*, vol. i., October 24, 1838.

Sunset: in Italy, a, *The Marble Faun*, vol. ii., chapter iv.; in June, *American Note-Books*, vol. i., June 15, 1838; in winter, *ibid.*, vol. ii., February 12, 1851.

Sunshine: an effect of morning, *American Note-Books*, vol. i., July 26, 1837; reflected, *ibid.*, October 7, 1837; Sabbath, *Twice-Told Tales*, vol. i., Sunday at Home; time marked by, *American Note-Books*, vol. i., October 25, 1836; wasted, *ibid.*

Sunshine of Monte Beni (wine), *The Marble Faun*, vol. i., chapter xxv.

Superficiality of character, different manifestations of, *The Blithedale Romance*, chapter xxii.

Superstitions: popular, *English Note-Books*, vol. ii., May 10, 1856, Abbotsford; instances of, *Twice-Told Tales*, vol. ii., The Ambitious Guest, *The Marble Faun*, vol. i., chapter xxi.

Surrey, *English Note-Books*, vol. i., October 3, 1855.

Surrey, Earl of, original of the "Geraldine" of, *English Note-Books*, end of vol i., Battle Abbey.

Susan, a character in The Village Uncle, *Twice-Told Tales*, vol. ii., the original of which is said to have been the daughter of a fisherman in Salem.

Sussex, the Duke of, friendship for Colonel Wildman, *English Note-Books*, vol. ii., May 29, 1857.

Sutherland, the Duke of, residence of, *English Note-Books*, vol. i., September 8, 1855.

Swain, Charles, *English Note-Books*, vol. ii., May 24, 1856, Manchester, August 20, 1857.

Swallows, *Mosses from an Old Manse*, vol. i., Buds and Bird Voices.

Swans, *English Note-Books*, vol. i., August 12, 1854; moral drawn from, *Our Old Home*, Leamington Spa.

Swedenborg, *Mosses from an Old Manse*, vol. i., The Hall of Fantasy.

Swedenborgians, *American Note-Books*, vol. ii., May 5, 1850.

Sweet Fern, name given to one of the children to whom the stories of the *Wonder-Book* and *Tanglewood Tales* were told.

Swift, Dean, *American Note-Books*, vol. i., June 15, 1835, vol. ii., 1842; character of his satire, *Fanshawe, etc.*, T. G. Fessenden, middle; invitation to the Chester clergy by, *English Note-Books*, vol. ii., November 30, 1856.

Swine: allusion to Swift in connection with, *American Note-Books*, vol. i., June 15, 1835; drove of, *ibid.*, September 9, 1838; independence of, *ibid.*, vol. ii., October 1, 1841; interest in, *ibid.*, October 1, 1841, August 9, 1842; on a march, *ibid.*, vol. i., August 31, 1838; the only happy, *The Blithedale Romance*, chapter xvi., end.

Swineferd, Catherine, tomb of, *Our Old Home*, Pilgrimage to Old Boston (Lincoln).

Swinnerton, Dr. John, a physician in Salem in the early days of the settlement, mentioned in *The House of the Seven Gables*, chapter i., and *The Dolliver Romance*, first fragment; grave of, *American Note-Books*, vol. i., July 4, 1838.

Swiss, a colony of, *Mosses from an Old Manse*, vol. ii., Sketches from Memory, The Canal Boat.

Switzerland, *French and Italian Journals*, vol. ii., June 11 to 14, 1859.

Swords: ancient, *English Note-Books*, vol. ii., October 30, 1857; famous, *Mosses from an Old Manse*, vol. ii., A Virtuoso's Collection.

Sybaritic character, the, *The House of the Seven Gables*, chapter vii.

Sympathy, *The Blithedale Romance*, chapter xix.; best, for the morbid, *Our Old Home*, Outside Glimpses of English Poverty; effect of, *The House of the Seven Gables*, chapter iii., beginning; need of, *Mosses from an Old Manse*, vol. i., Monsieur du Miroir; nervous, *The Blithedale Romance*, chapter xvi.; right of, to minister, *ibid.*, chapter xxvi.; to solitary people, *Mosses from an Old Manse*, vol. ii., The Artist of the Beautiful; turned to account, *The Blithedale Romance*, chapter xxvi.; unintelligent most grateful, *ibid.*, chapter ix., near the end.

Synod, the first in New England, *Fanshawe and Other Pieces*, Mrs. Hutchinson, fourth and fifth paragraphs.

T ——, Mr., of Newburyport, *American Note-Books*, vol. ii., September 4, 1852.

T ——, Mr., an American traveler, *English Note-Books*, vol. ii., September 17, 1857.

T ——, Mr., an English gentleman, *French and Italian Journals*, vol. i., May 23, 1858.

T ——, Mrs., mentioned in *French and Italian Journals*, vol. i., February 13, 1858.

Tabitha Porter, an old servant in Peter Goldthwaite's Treasure, *Twice-Told Tales*, vol. ii.

Tableaux vivants, *The Blithedale Romance*, chapter xiii

Taciturnity, natural in the dark, *Twice-Told Tales*, vol. i., The Vision of the Fountain.

Taconic, Mount, *American Note-Books*, vol. ii., February 12, March 11, October 27, November 3, 1851, *Wonder-Book*, beginning, Bald-Summit.

Take-it-easy, Mr., *Mosses from an Old Manse*, vol. i., The Celestial Railroad.

Talby, Dorothy, punishment of, *The Snow Image, etc.*, Main Street.

Talents, superficial and versatile, *Fanshawe*, chapter iv.

Talfourd, Field, *French and Italian Journals*, vol. ii., May 17, 1860..

Talk out of nothing, *Our Old Home*, beginning of Consular Experiences.

Talus, *Tanglewood Tales*, The Minotaur.

Tam O'Shanter's Ride, scene of, *Our Old Home*, Some of the Haunts of Burns.

Tangibility, desire for, *The Dolliver Romance, etc.*, A Book of Autographs.

Tanglewood, country house, and children at, *Wonder-Book*, beginning.

Tanglewood Tales for Girls and Boys, being a Second Wonder-Book, a volume of classical stories retold for children. It was written in Concord in 1852–3, and published in 1853. The purpose to write it is mentioned in the *American Note-Books*, vol. ii., March 16, 1843; the order in which the stories were written, March 9, 1853.

Tantalus, a cistern of, *American Note-Books*, vol. ii., August 6, 1842.

Tapestry, *English Note-Books*, vol. i., March 24, 1856, vol. ii., April 10, 1857; at Blenheim, *Our Old Home*, Near Oxford; in Coventry, *ibid.*, Civic Banquets; the Gobelin, *French and Italian Journals*, vol. i., April 10, 1858.

Tarleton, General Bannastre, *American Note-Books*, vol. i., October 25, 1836.

Tarpeian Rock, the, *French and Italian Journals*, vol. i., May 22, 1858, *The Marble Faun*, vol. i., chapter xviii.

Tasso, translation of, by James, *French and Italian Journals*, vol. ii., May 29, 1859.

Tattershall, tower of, *Our Old Home*, Pilgrimage to Old Boston.

Tavern-haunter, a young, *American Note-Books*, vol. i., July 29, 1838.

Tavern-keepers, *American Note-Books*, vol. i., July 5, 1837, September 9, 1838.

Taylor Institute, the, Oxford, *English Note-Books*, vol. ii., August 31, 1856.

Taylor, Jeremy: "Ductor Dubitantium," *Mosses from an Old Manse*, vol. ii., Egotism; marriage sermon by, *Twice-Told Tales*. vol. i., The Wedding Knell.

Taylor, Tom, *English Note-Books*, vol. ii., April 4, 8, July 10, 1856.

Taylor, William, prophetic dream of, *English Note-Books*, vol. ii., July 6, 1856.

Taylor, Zachary, portrait of, *Our Old Home*, Consular Experiences, beginning.

Tecumseh, death of, *English Note-Books*, vol. ii., December 15, 1856.

Tediousness, charm of, *Our Old Home*, Leamington Spa.

Telegraph, the, *The House of the Seven Gables*, chapter xvii., near the end; a disadvantage of, *English Note-Books*, vol. ii., August 14, 1857.

Telephassa, Queen, *Tanglewood Tales*, The Dragon's Teeth.

Telford, Thomas, statue of, *English Note-Books*, vol. i., October 5, 1855.

Tells, the, legend of, *English Note-Books*, vol. i., June 30, 1854.
Temperance : in England, *Our Old Home*, Civic Banquets ; emblem for writers on, *The Marble Faun*, vol. ii., chapter vii. ; reformers, *Our Old Home*, Outside Glimpses of English Poverty ; when it will prevail, *The Blithedale Romance*, chapter xxi.
Temple, name of the family in which the Biographies (of the volume *True Stories*) in the 16mo edition were told.
Temple, the, and gardens of, *English Note-Books*, vol. i., September 10, 25, 1855, vol. ii., November 12, 1857, *Our Old Home*, Up the Thames.
Temple of Happiness, the, *Twice-Told Tales*, vol. ii., The Lily's Quest.
Temptation to wine, *The Blithedale Romance*, chapter xxi.
Tenderness, want of, in men, *The Blithedale Romance*, chapter vi.
Teniers, pictures by, *French and Italian Journals*, vol. ii., September 25, 1858, *The Marble Faun*, vol. ii., chapter xii.
Tennent, Sir Emerson, *English Note-Books*, vol. ii., July 9, 1856.
Tennyson, Alfred : best poem of, *English Note-Books*, vol. ii., July 10, 1856 ; friendship with Allingham, *ibid.*, vol. i., February 23, 1854 ; looks of, *ibid.*, vol. ii., July 30, 1857 ; scenery described by, *Our Old Home*, Leamington Spa.
Terni, town and falls of, *French and Italian Journals*, vol. i., May 25, 1858.
Terrible Tractoration, poem, *Fanshawe, etc.*, T. G. Fessenden.
Terrors of childhood and youth, *Mosses from an Old Manse*, vol. i., A Select Party.
Test of the noble in an individual, *The Blithedale Romance*, chapter xix., near the end.
Testaccio, Monte, *French and Italian Journals*, vol. i., March 27, 1858, *Septimius Felton*, p. 202 (12mo).
Teucer behind the shield of Ajax, *Fanshawe*, chapter vii.
Thackeray, *English Note-Books*, vol. i., August 12, September 14, 1855, vol. ii., April 8, 1856 ; in America, *ibid.*, April 5, 1856 ; note from, *French and Italian Journals*, vol. i., March 25, 1858.

Thames, the. *English Note-Books*, vol. i., September 7, 10, 25, 1855, vol. ii., April 8, 1856, *Our Old Home*, Near Oxford, toward the end, Up the Thames; antiquities from, *English Note-Books*, vol. ii., December 7, 1857.

Thanets, portraits of the, *English Note-Books*, vol. ii., April 10, 1857.

Thanksgiving Day, *American Note-Books*, vol. ii., November 24, 1842; description of a dinner on, *ibid.*, vol. i., October 25, 1836.

Thasus, *Tanglewood Tales*, The Dragon's Teeth.

Thaxter, Mr., *American Note-Books*, vol. ii., August 30, September 4, 13, 1852.

Theatre, the National, visit to, *American Note-Books*, vol. ii., May 8, 1850.

Theodore, a character in Zenobia's story of The Veiled Lady, *The Blithedale Romance*, chapter xiii.

Theological Libraries, *Mosses from an Old Manse*, vol. i., The Old Manse, at the middle.

Theories, wild, underlying sentiment of, *Mosses from an Old Manse*, vol. i., The Hall of Fantasy.

Theorists, *Mosses from an Old Manse*, vol. ii., The Christmas Banquet; conformity of, to custom, *The Scarlet Letter*, chapter xiii., near the end.

Theseus, *Tanglewood Tales*, The Minotaur.

Thinkers, original, followers of, *Mosses from an Old Manse*, vol. i., The Old Manse, near the end.

Thirlmere, *English Note-Books*, vol. i., July 21, 1855.

Thom, Rev. Mr., chapel of, *English Note-Books*, vol. i., March 13, 1854.

Thomas Thumb, story of, *Twice-Told Tales*, vol. ii., The Seven Vagabonds, *Mosses from an Old Manse*, vol. ii., Earth's Holocaust.

Thompson, C. G.: Hawthorne's portrait by, *American Note-Books*, vol. ii., May 5, 6, 7, 1850; other pictures by, *French and Italian Journals*, vol. i., February 14, March 11, May 9, 1858, *The Marble Faun*, vol. i., chapter vii.

Thomson, James, quotation from, *Fanshawe*, head of chapter iii.

Thoreau, H. D., *American Note-Books,* vol. ii., August 5, September 1, 1842, April 7, 8, 11, 1843, *English Note-Books,* vol. ii., April 5, 1856, *Mosses from an Old Manse,* vol. i., The Old Manse, *The Scarlet Letter,* The Custom-House, middle.

Thornhill, Sir James, paintings by, *Our Old Home,* Near Oxford, A London Suburb.

Thorwaldsen, analogy about art by, *The Marble Faun,* vol ii., chapter xvi.; statue of Byron, *Mosses from an Old Manse,* vol. ii., P.'s Correspondence.

Thrasymêne, Lake, *French and Italian Journals,* vol. i., May 29, 30, 1858.

Three Golden Apples, the, story of the Search of Hercules in the *Wonder-Book.*

Threefold Destiny, The, A Fairy Legend, in *Twice-Told Tales,* vol. ii., illustrates the folly of seeking happiness and greatness in things distant and hardly attainable. For suggestion of, see *American Note-Books,* August 22, 1837. It was first published in "The American Monthly Magazine" for March, 1838.

Throne, the English, in Parliament, *English Note-Books,* vol. i., September 30, 1855.

Thumpcushion, Parson, a New England clergyman of the old school, guardian of the wandering story-teller in Passages from a Relinquished Work, *Mosses from an Old Manse,* vol. ii.

Thursday Lecture, the, *The Snow Image, etc.,* Main Street.

Tiber, the, *French and Italian Journals,* vol. i., February 9, 21, March 18, May 28, 1858, *The Marble Faun,* vol. i., chapter xv.

Tickell, Thomas, source of the lines on Addison, *Our Old Home,* Up the Thames.

Ticknor, George, author of "History of Spanish Literature," *American Note-Books,* vol. ii., May 5, 1850, *English Note-Books,* vol. i., October 1, 1853, vol. ii., July 13, 1856, August 30, 1857.

Ticonderoga, Fort, *The Snow Image, etc.,* Old Ticonderoga, Old News, ii., *Twice-Told Tales,* vol. ii., Edward Randolph's Portrait.

Tidy Man, the, *The Snow Image, etc.*, Main Street.

Tieck, Ludwig, reading of, *American Note-Books*, vol. ii., April 8, 9, 10, 11, 1843.

Tiffany, Bela, *Twice-Told Tales*, vol. ii., Legends of the Province House.

Tiles, *American Note-Books*, vol. i., September 7, 1835, October 16, 1837.

Time: apart from man's life, *Twice-Told Tales*, vol. i., Sunday at Home; compensations of, *American Note-Books*, vol. i., October 25, 1836, emblems of, *Mosses from an Old Manse*, vol. ii., A Virtuoso's Collection; nature's measurement of, *ibid.*, The New Adam and Eve; trifling with, *ibid.*, The Artist of the Beautiful.

Time, Father, mistakes about, *The Dolliver Romance and Other Pieces*, Time's Portraiture.

Time's Portraiture, the New Year's Address for 1838 of the carriers of the " Salem Gazette," included in the volume with *The Dolliver Romance*.

Times, the London, *English Note-Books*, vol. i., October 6, 1854, vol. ii., April 4, 1856; an exponent of English feeling, *ibid.*, May 24, 1856, Manchester; ghost in the office of, *ibid.*, July 16, 1856; grievances in, *ibid.*, vol. i., January 6, 1854; manager of, *ibid.*, vol. ii., April 4, 1856.

Tippecanoe, incident of the battle of, *English Note-Books*, vol. ii., December 15, 1856.

Titcomb, B. B., *American Note-Books*, vol. ii., September 4, 10, 1852.

Titian: Bella Donna of, *French and Italian Journals*, vol. i., March 10, 1858; coloring of, *ibid.*, April 16, 1858; Magdalen of the Pitti Palace, *ibid.*, vol. ii., June 21, 1858, *The Marble Faun*, vol. ii., chapter iii.; Venus by, *French and Italian Journals*, vol. ii., June 8, 1858.

Tituba, *The Snow Image, etc.*, Main Street.

Titus, Arch of, *The Marble Faun*, vol. i., chapter xvii.

Tobias Pearson, a character in The Gentle Boy, *Twice-Told Tales*, vol. i., who suffers for loyalty to his convictions without being upheld by the enthusiasm of the fanatic.

Toil, *American Note-Books,* vol. i., letter July 3, 1839, April, 1841, bread earned by, *Mosses from an Old Manse,* vol. i., The Old Manse, near the middle.

Toil, Mr., a school-master, *The Snow Image, etc.,* Little Daffydowndilly.

Toleration, why the Puritans of New England could not exercise, *Fanshawe, etc.,* Mrs. Hutchinson, fourth paragraph.

Toll-Gatherer's Day, The, A Sketch of Transitory Life, a sketch in *Twice-Told Tales,* vol. i., of life as seen passing a toll-house, on a bridge. The description answers to that of a bridge between Salem and Beverly.

Tomaso, butler of the Count of Monte Beni, type of the devoted and affectionate family servant, first appears in chapter xxv., *The Marble Faun,* vol. i.

Tomb, a, in every heart, *Twice-Told Tales,* vol. ii., The Haunted Mind.

Tombs, *American Note-Books,* vol. i., July 4, 1838; of the Appian Way, *The Marble Faun,* vol. ii., chapter xxi.; of the Popes, in St. Peter's, *ibid.,* chapter xiii.; other, *French and Italian Journals,* vol. i., May 8, 1858.

To-morrow, *Mosses from an Old Manse,* vol. ii., The Intelligence Office.

Toothaker, Widow, character in Edward Fane's Rosebud, *Twice-Told Tales,* vol. ii.

Toper, picture of a, *The Blithedale Romance,* chapter xxi.

Tophet, *Mosses from an Old Manse* vol. i., The Celestial Railroad; way of sending a letter to, *English Note-Books,* vol. i., October 22, 1853.

Tories, the, of the Revolution, *The Snow Image, etc.,* Old News, part iii.

Torment, bodily, uses of, *American Note-Books,* vol. i., letter April 7, 1840.

Torres, town of, *French and Italian Journals,* vol. i., May 30, 1858.

Tortures, inflicted by nature and by men, *American Note-Books,* vol. i., August 22, 1837.

Tory, The Old. See OLD TORY.

Tory's Farewell, The, a sketch in *Grandfather's Chair,* part iii., chapter ix., representing the departure of Peter Oliver from Boston.

Toulmin, Camilla (Mrs. Newton Crosland), *English Note-Books,* vol. i., March 25, 1856; criticism of, on *The Scarlet Letter, ibid.*

Tourists, names of, in celebrated places, *Our Old Home,* Recollections of a Gifted Woman.

Tower of London, the, *English Note-Books,* vol. i., September 10, 1855, vol. ii., November 11, 1857, *Our Old Home,* Up the Thames.

Tower Hill, London, *English Note-Books,* vol. ii., November 15, 1857.

Town-Pump, the, Salem. See RILL FROM THE TOWN-PUMP.

Towns: of Italy, *The Marble Faun,* vol. ii., chapter vii.; should be rebuilt every half century, *ibid.,* vol. ii., chapter viii.

Toy-shop, a, *Twice-Told Tales,* vol. i., Little Annie's Ramble.

Trades, marks of, *American Note-Books,* vol. i., August 31, 1838.

Traditions, *Septimius Felton,* p. 111 (12mo); verisimilitude of, *The House of the Seven Gables,* chapter viii., middle.

Trafalgar Square, *English Note-Books,* vol. i., September 10, 1855.

Trainband, the, *Twice-Told Tales,* vol. ii., Endicott and the Red Cross, *Fanshawe, etc.,* Sir William Phips, last paragraph.

Traitor's Gate, the, *Our Old Home,* Up the Thames.

Trajan's Forum. See FORUMS.

Tramp, ruse of a, *American Note-Books,* vol. i., October 17, 1835.

Tranmere, village and hall, *English Note-Books,* vol. i., March 7, May 30, August 17, 1855.

Transcendentalist, Giant, *Mosses from an Old Manse,* vol. i., The Celestial Railroad.

Transcendentalists, the, *Mosses from an Old Manse,* vol. i., Rappaccini's Daughter.

Transformation. See MARBLE FAUN.

Translations, why not satisfactory, *American Note-Books,* vol. i., October 25, 1835.

Travel: bad influence of, *Our Old Home,* Consular Experiences; books of, *Twice-Told Tales,* vol. ii., Night Sketches; longing for, *The Dolliver Romance, etc.,* Journal of a Solitary Man, i.

Traveler, a, *Twice-Told Tales,* vol. ii., The Threefold Destiny; heroism of an English, *The Dolliver Romance, etc.,* My Visit to Niagara; lingering reluctance of, *Twice-Told Tales,* vol. ii., Night Sketches.

Treasure, buried, *Twice-Told Tales,* vol. ii., The Threefold Destiny; seekers of, *American Note-Books,* vol. ii., September 5, 1852.

Tredagh, incident at the storming of, *English Note Books,* vol. i., October 22, 1853.

Trees: agreeable kinds of, *Mosses from an Old Manse,* vol. i., Buds and Bird Voices; set out by authors, *English Note-Books,* vol. ii., April 8, 1856.

Treja River, the, *French and Italian Journals,* vol. i., May 24, 1858.

Trelawny, Captain E. J., *French and Italian Journals,* vol. ii., August 12, 1858.

Tremont House, Boston, sketches of people seen there, *American Note-Books,* vol. i., June 16, 1838.

Trevi, City of, *French and Italian Journals,* vol. i., May 26, 1858.

Trevi, Fountain of, *French and Italian Journals,* vol. i., April 25, 1858; tradition about, *The Marble Faun,* vol. i., chapter xvi.

Trial for life, a, *The Blithedale Romance,* chapter xxv.

Trinity Church, New York, model for the wings of the cherubim, *American Note-Books,* vol. ii., September 10, 1852.

Trœzene, *Tanglewood Tales,* The Minotaur.

Trollope, T. Adolphus, *French and Italian Journals,* vol. ii., June 27, 1858.

Trosachs, the, *English Note-Books,* vol. ii., May 10, 1856, July 5, 6, 1857.

Troubles: acting like intoxication, *Fanshawe,* chapter v.; earthly, *Wonder-Book,* The Paradise of Children.

True Stories from History and Biography. See GRANDFATHER'S CHAIR.

Trumbull, John, pictures by, *The Dolliver Romance and Other Pieces,* A Book of Autographs.

Truth : intoxicating quality of, *Mosses from an Old Manse,* vol. i., The Procession of Life ; search for, *ibid.,* vol. ii., The Intelligence Office ; tendency to pervert, *American Note-Books,* vol. ii., May 1, 1841.

Tucke, Rev. Mr., monument to, *American Note-Books,* vol. ii., September 5, 1852.

Tucker, Beverly, successor of Hawthorne at Liverpool, *Our Old Home,* Consular Experiences. (Name not given.)

Tuckerman, Henry T., his "Month in England," *Our Old Home,* Up the Thames.

Tufton, Sir R., property of, *English Note-Books,* vol. ii., April 10, 1857.

Tuileries, gardens of the, *French and Italian Journals,* vol. i., January 12, 1858.

Tunbridge Wells, *English Note-Books,* end of vol. i., Battle Abbey.

Tunnel, the Thames, suggested use for, *Our Old Home,* Up the Thames.

Tupper, Martin F., *English Note-Books,* vol. i., March 27, April 1, 1856, Wooton, vol. ii., April 4, 1856.

Turner, J. M. W., pictures of, *English Note-Books,* vol. i., September 26, 1854, March 26, 1856, vol. ii., July 28, August 9, December 8, 20, 1857.

Turtle-Soup, the fountain-head of, *Our Old Home,* Civic Banquets.

Tuscany, the Grand Duchess of, *French and Italian Journals,* vol. ii., June 28, 30, 1858.

Tutors, position of, *English Note-Books,* vol. i., August 2, 1855.

Tuttle, Miss Lydia, *Fanshawe, etc.,* T. G. Fessenden.

Tweed, the, *English Note-Books,* vol. ii., May 10, 1856, Melrose, Berwick, July 11, 1857.

Twice-Told Tales, a collection of stories and sketches in two volumes, the first of which was published in Boston in 1837, the second in 1842. Most of the tales had previously appeared in magazines. See allusions to the book in the *English Note-Books*, vol. i., August 24, 1854, vol. ii., October 10, 1857.

Twilight, midsummer, *American Note-Books*, vol. ii., June 23, 1843.

Twining, John Maggott, *English Note-Books*, vol. i., May 20, 1854.

Twins, venerable, *American Note-Books*, vol. ii., 1842.

Tyburn, *English Note-Books*, vol. i., September 24, 1855.

Uffizi Palace and Gallery, *French and Italian Journals*, vol. ii., June 8, 11, 16, 30, July 4, 16, September 3, 7, 21, 25, 28, 1858.

Ullswater, Lake, *English Note-Books*, vol. i., July 21, 1855.

Ulverton, *English Note-Books*, vol. i., July 13, 1855.

Ulysses, *Tanglewood Tales*, Circe's Palace; dog of, *Mosses from an Old Manse*, vol. ii., A Virtuoso's Collection.

Umbrian Valley, description of the, *The Marble Faun*, vol. ii., chapter iii.

Una, the lamb of, *Mosses from an Old Manse*, vol. ii., A Virtuoso's Collection.

Unexpected, the, how to bring it about, *The Marble Faun*, vol. ii., chapter vii.

Union Village, near North Adams, *American Note-Books*, vol. i., July 31, 1838.

Unitarian Chapel in London, a, *English Note-Books*, vol. ii., July 29, 1856.

Unitarians in Liverpool, *English Note-Books*, vol. i., March 13, 1854.

University of Glasgow, *English Note-Books*, vol. ii., May 10, 1856.

Unreality: appearance of, *Septimius Felton*, p. 121–2 (12mo); of earthly things, *American Note-Books*, vol. i., December 6, 1837; of nature, *Mosses from an Old Manse*, vol. ii., The Christmas Banquet; reality of, *ibid*, vol. i., A Select Party.

Upham, Hon. N. G., mention of, *American Note-Books*, vol. ii., September 5, 1852.

Up the Thames, an article in *Our Old Home* describing views from the river,—Greenwich, the Tunnel, Wapping, the Tower,

Chelsea, with the Hospital, the Crystal Palace, and Westminster Abbey, and concluding with a sketch of an interview with Leigh Hunt.

Ursula, Lady, *American Note-Books*, vol. ii., 1842.

Uttoxeter, see LICHFIELD AND UTTOXETER.

Vagrancy, the primeval instinct, *Twice-Told Tales*, vol. ii., The Seven Vagabonds.

Vagrants, liking for, *American Note-Books*, vol. ii., August 30, 1842.

Valence, *French and Italian Journals*, vol. ii., June 11, 1859.

Vale of the Deadly Nightshade, the, *English Note-Books*, vol. i., July 13, 1855.

Valley of Humiliation, the, *Mosses from an Old Manse*, vol. i., The Celestial Railroad.

Valley of the Shadow of Death, the, *Mosses from an Old Manse*, vol. i., The Celestial Railroad.

Vandyke, pictures of, *English Note-Books*, vol. i., March 24, 25, 1856, vol. ii., July 30, 1857, *French and Italian Journals*, vol. i., April 16, 1858.

Vane, Alice, a character in Edward Randolph's Portrait, *Twice-Told Tales*, vol. ii.

Vane, Sir Henry, *Twice-Told Tales*, vol. ii., Howe's Masquerade, *The Snow Image, etc.*, Main Street, *Grandfather's Chair*, part i., chapter iv., *Fanshawe, etc.*, Mrs. Hutchinson, third paragraph.

Vanity Fair, *Mosses from an Old Manse*, vol. i., The Celestial Railroad ; clergymen of, *ibid.*

Van Mieris, art of, *The Marble Faun*, vol. ii., chapter xii.

Vatican, the, *French and Italian Journals*, vol. i., February 19, April 12, 1858 ; sculptures in, *ibid.*, March 10, 23, 1858.

Vaughan, Edgar, or Edward Hamilton, a character in the story Sylph Etherege, in *The Snow Image, etc.*

Vaughan, William, *Fanshawe, etc.*, Sir William Pepperell, first paragraph.

Vegetables, garden, beauty of, *American Note-Books*, vol. ii., October 8, 1841, August 10, 1842.

Veil, The Silvery, Zenobia's Legend, *The Blithedale Romance,* chapter xiii.

Veiled Lady, the, a mesmeric phenomenon, introduced into the *The Blithedale Romance.* She is first alluded to in chapter i. See PRISCILLA.

Vendôme, Place and Column, *French and Italian Journals,* vol. i., January 9, 1858.

Vengeance of a woodman, a sailor, and a governor, *Fanshawe, etc.,* Sir William Phips, fifth paragraph.

Venner, Uncle, a character in *The House of the Seven Gables,* introduced in chapter iv. He is an old man who lives by doing odd jobs for families, has been regarded in his youth as a little lacking in intellect, but has acquired some homely wisdom in the course of his long life. He has no influence on the movement of the story.

Venus : and Cupid, curious picture of, *French and Italian Journals,* vol. ii., June 15, 1858; by Titian, *ibid.,* June 8, 1858.

Venus de' Medici, the, *French and Italian Journals,* vol. ii., June 8, 11, 13, 15, September 3, 1858; Powers's criticism on, *ibid.,* June 13, 1858; supposed original of, *ibid.,* April 14, 1859.

Venus of the Tribune, the, *The Marble Faun,* vol. ii., chapter xxi.

Vermont, a walk into, *American Note-Books,* vol. i., September 5, 1838.

Vermont House, English residence of Mr. Stevens, *English Note-Books,* vol. ii., April 8, 1856.

Veronese, Paul, "The Rape of Europa," *French and Italian Journals,* vol. i., March 1, April 22, 1858.

Verrio, frescoes by, *English Note-Books,* vol. i., March 24, 1856.

Very, Jones, *Mosses from an Old Manse,* vol. ii., A Virtuoso's Collection.

Vessels, famous, *Mosses from an Old Manse,* vol. ii., A Virtuoso's Collection.

Vesta, the Temple of, *French and Italian Journals,* vol. i., March 18, 1858.

Vetturini : Constantine Bacci, *French and Italian Journals,* vol. ii., October 17, 1858; Gaetano, *ibid.*, vol. i., May 24–30, 1858.

Vices, precocious, of a boy, *Fanshawe*, chapter iv.

Victoria, Queen: American relatives of, and photographs sent to, *Our Old Home*, Consular Experiences; bust of, *English Note-Books*, vol. i., March 25, 1856.

Victory, trophies of, *Our Old Home*, Up the Thames.

Vigwiggie, the cat, *American Note-Books*, vol. ii., March 12, April 9, 1843.

Village Theatre, The, One of the Passages from a Relinquished Work in *Mosses from an Old Manse*, vol. ii. The theatre is the scene of a performance by the wandering story-teller, the author of the work.

Village Uncle, The, An Imaginary Retrospect, title of a sketch in *Twice-Told Tales*, vol. ii.

Villages: a fishing, *Twice-Told Tales*, vol. ii., The Village Uncle; in New England, *ibid.*, vol. ii., The Threefold Destiny, *The Marble Faun*, vol. i., chapter xii.; meddling tendency in, *Fanshawe*, chapter vii.

Villeneuve, Town and Castle of, *French and Italian Journals*, vol. ii., June 6, 1859.

Vines, *French and Italian Journals*, vol. i., May 30, 1858, Incisa.

Vintage, the: in Italy, *French and Italian Journals*, vol. i., September 21, 1858; in Italy and New England, *The Marble Faun*, vol. ii., chapter v.

Violet, a little girl in the *The Snow Image, etc.*, title story.

Virgil, quotation from, *The Blithedale Romance*, chapter viii.

Virgin: the beauty of the Catholic faith in, *The Blithedale Romance*, chapter xiv., *The Marble Faun*, vol. ii., chapter vii.; pictures of, and their defects, *ibid.*, vol. ii., chapters xii., xiii.; shrine of, *ibid.*, vol. i., chapter vi. See MADONNAS.

Virginia, death of, *The Marble Faun*, vol. i., chapter xviii.

Virtuoso, collection of a, *Our Old Home*, Pilgrimage to Old Boston.

Virtuoso's Collection, a, a description of an imaginary collection of historic and literary curiosities, *Mosses from an Old Manse*, vol. ii.

Vision of the Fountain, The, a sketch in vol. i. of *Twice-Told Tales.*

Visions, the realm of, *Septimius Felton,* p. 121 (12mo).

Viterbo, *French and Italian Journals,* vol. ii., October 15, 1858.

Volsinii, *French and Italian Journals,* vol. ii., October 15, 1858.

Voltaire: "Candide" of, *American Note-Books,* vol. ii., April 8, 1843, *The Blithedale Romance,* chapter viii.; on the Louisburg expedition, *Fanshawe, etc.,* Sir William Pepperell, last paragraph; works of, *Mosses from an Old Manse,* vol. ii., Earth's Holocaust.

Vow, a Pythagorean, *American Note-Books,* vol. ii., April 7, 1843.

Vulcan, *Tanglewood Tales,* The Minotaur.

W ——, Mr., a Manchester merchant, *English Note-Books,* vol. ii., May 24, 1856, Manchester.

Waite, Thomas, keeper of the old Province House, *Twice-Told Tales,* vol. ii., Howe's Masquerade.

Wakefield, the hero of a story of that name in *Twice-Told Tales,* vol. i. It is an analysis of the possible character that may have led to a strange freak, which was an actual occurrence.

Wakefulness, the best hour for, *Twice-Told Tales,* vol. ii., The Haunted Mind.

Walcott, Edward, a character in *Fanshawe,* described in chapter i., introduced in chapter ii. He is brave and generous, but not very unusual in any way.

Walden Pond, *American Note-Books,* vol. ii., August 15, 1842, October 6, 1843.

Waldoborough, Maine, Knox's claim in, *American Note-Books,* vol. i., August 12, 1837.

Waldo County, Maine, claim of the Pyncheons in, *The House of the Seven Gables,* chapter i.

Wales, North, tour in, *English Note-Books,* vol. i., July 19, 1854; lakes and mountains of, *ibid.;* village in, *ibid.,* September 13, 1854.

Walker, John, D. D., citation from, *American Note-Books,* vol. i., September, 1836.

Wallace, William, site of monument to, *English Note-Books*; vol. ii., July 6, 1857; sword of, *ibid.*, July 2, 1857.

Walmesley, Gilbert, tomb of, *Our Old Home*, Lichfield and Uttoxeter.

Walpole, Horace: house of, *English Note-Books*, vol. i., March 24, vol. ii., May 10, 1856, Abbotsford; incident in "The Castle of Otranto," *ibid.*, July 30, 1857; statue in memory of the mother of, *ibid.*, vol. i., October 5, 1855.

Walpole, Sir Robert, *The Dolliver Romance and other Pieces*, The Antique Ring.

Wanderers, instincts of, *Our Old Home*, Leamington Spa, beginning.

Wandering, dreams of, *Mosses from an Old Manse*, vol. ii., Roger Malvin's Burial.

Wandering Jew, the, *Mosses from an Old Manse*, vol. i., A Select Party, vol. ii., A Virtuoso's Collection.

Want, the hardest, to satisfy, *Mosses from an Old Manse*, vol. ii., The Intelligence Office.

Wanton Gospeller, a, *Twice-Told Tales*, vol. ii., Endicott and The Red Cross.

Wappacowett, Indian priest, *The Snow Image*, etc., Main Street.

Wapping, *Our Old Home*, Up the Thames.

War: a country in time of, *English Note-Books*, vol. i., January 1, 1856; development of character by, *Septimius Felton*, p. 185 (12mo); influence of, *ibid.*, pp. 20, 80; weapons and munitions of, *Mosses from an Old Manse*, vol. ii., Earth's Holocaust.

War of 1812, a soldier of the, *English Note-Books*, vol. ii., December 15, 1856.

War, the American Civil, *Our Old Home*, dedication.

Ward, Lord, pictures belonging to, *English Note-Books*, vol. ii., August 7, 1856.

Ward, Rev. Nathanael, of Ipswich, *The Snow Image, etc.*, Main Street, *Fanshawe, etc.*, Mrs. Hutchinson, third paragraph.

Ware, William, a criticism of, on Michael Angelo, *French and Italian Journals*, vol. ii., June 30, 1858.

Warland, Owen, hero of the story The Artist of the Beautiful, *Mosses from an Old Manse,* vol. ii. He is a man with the artistic temperament, and without force of character to assert himself against the sensual and worldly spirit of his surroundings.

Warren, Joseph, *Grandfather's Chair,* part iii., chapters vi., vii.; letter from, *The Dolliver Romance and other Pieces,* A Book of Autographs.

Warren, Samuel, author of "Ten Thousand a Year," *English Note-Books,* vol. i., March 27, 1855.

Warren, Sir Peter, *Grandfather's Chair,* part ii., chapter vii., *Fanshawe and other Pieces,* Sir William Pepperell, third and fourth paragraphs, *Our Old Home,* Up the Thames.

Warwick, Earl of, relic of, *English Note-Books,* vol. ii., October 30, 1857.

Warwick, Castle and Town, *English Note-Books,* vol. i., June 21, 1855, *French and Italian Journals,* vol. ii., November 14, 1859, *Our Old Home,* About Warwick.

Washington, D. C., first visit to, *American Note-Books,* vol. ii., April 14, 1853.

Washington, George, *Grandfather's Chair,* part iii., chapter viii.; an officer of the 28th British Regiment, *English Note-Books,* vol. i., February 23, 1854; at table, *The Dolliver Romance, etc.,* A Book of Autographs; expression of face of, *French and Italian Journals,* vol. ii., June 13, 1858; in the first Congress, *The Dolliver Romance, etc.,* A Book of Autographs; letter from, *ibid.;* personality of, *ibid.;* picture of, by Stuart, *English Note-Books,* vol. i., September 14, 1855; visit of, to Salem, *The Snow Image, etc.,* A Bell's Biography; with Braddock, *Grandfather's Chair,* part ii., chapter viii.

Washington Monument, Crawford's, *French and Italian Journals,* vol. i., March 11, 1858.

Washington, Mount, *Twice-Told Tales,* vol. i., The Prophetic Pictures, vol. ii., The Ambitious Guest, *Mosses from an Old Manse,* vol. ii., Sketches from Memory, The Notch of The White Mountains; sonnet on, *ibid.,* Our Evening Party among the Mountains.

Washingtons, the, supposed old home of, *English Note-Books*, vol. ii., May 10, 1856, Newcastle.

Water, among the mountains, *American Note-Books*, vol. i., September 9, 1838.

Water-drinking, custom of, *American Note-Books*, vol. i., September, 1836.

Water-lilies, *American Note-Books*, vol. ii., August 6, 13, 1842, *Mosses from an Old Manse*, vol. i., The Old Manse, near the beginning.

Waterston, Robert C., *American Note-Books*, vol. i., August 27, 1837.

Watt, James, statues of, *English Note-Books*, vol. i., October 5, 1855, vol. ii., July 1, 1857.

Watts, Isaac, incident told by, *English Note-Books*, vol. ii., July 6, 1856.

Wax Figures, a show of, *American Note-Books*, vol. i., July 13, 1838 ; suggestion about, *ibid.*

Wayside, The, the home of Hawthorne at Concord, Mass., bought in 1852, formerly owned by A. B. Alcott. The house and scenery about it are described in *Septimius Felton*, pp. 4, 5 (12mo), and in the Preface to *Tanglewood Tales.*

Weak men, in power, *French and Italian Journals*, vol. i., March 23, 1858.

Wealth, desire for, *Mosses from an Old Manse*, vol. ii., The Intelligence Office.

Weapons: collection of, *English Note-Books*, vol. ii., July 7, 1857 ; famous, *Mosses from an Old Manse*, vol. ii., A Virtuoso's Collection.

Wear River, the, *English Note-Books*, vol. ii., July 11, 1857, Durham.

Weather, Clerk of the, *Mosses from an Old Manse*, vol. i., A Select Party.

Webster, Daniel: an ox like, *American Note-Books*, vol. ii., December 19, 1850; Powers' statue of, *French and Italian Journals*, vol. ii., June 16, September 29, 1858.

Webster, Noah, letter from, *The Dolliver Romance, etc.*, A Book of Autographs.

Webster family, the, *English Note-Books,* end of vol. i., article Battle Abbey.

Wedding journeys, *American Note-Books,* vol. i., July 26, 1838, *Twice-Told Tales,* vol. i., The Toll-Gatherer's Day.

Wedding Knell, The, story in *Twice-Told Tales,* vol. i. The scene is laid at an old church in New York, probably Trinity, perhaps St. Paul's, one hundred years ago. It was first published in "The Boston Token and Atlantic Souvenir," about 1835.

Weddings: among the poor, *Our Old Home,* Outside Glimpses of English Poverty, near the end; in Florence, *French and Italian Journals,* vol. ii., July 27, 1858; interest in, *English Note-Books,* vol. ii., August 14, 1857.

Weeds: *Septimius Felton,* p. 91 (12mo); mystery of the hardiness of, *American Note-Books,* vol. ii., June 23, 1843.

Weiss, John, *American Note-Books,* vol. ii., August 30, September 4, 1852.

Wellesley, Marquis of, portrait of the, *English Note-Books,* vol. ii., August 31, 1856, Christ Church.

Wellington, Duke of: funeral canopy of, *English Note-Books,* vol. i., March 24, 1856; statue of, *ibid.,* vol. ii., November 11, 1859.

Welsh, the, *English Note-Books,* vol. i., July 19, 1854.

Welsh language, the, *English Note-Books,* vol. i., September 20, 1854.

West, Benjamin: paintings of, *Our Old Home,* A London Suburb; sketch of, *True Stories* (only in 16mo edition).

Westervelt, Professor, a character in *The Blithedale Romance,* introduced in chapter xi., where his appearance and manner are described. He is a mesmerist and exhibitor of the Veiled Lady, his first connection with whom is explained in chapter xxii. He stands in a close and unexplained relation to Zenobia.

Westmacott, statuary by, *English Note-Books,* vol. ii., September 13, 1857.

Westminster Abbey, *English Note-Books,* vol. i., September 10, 26, 30, October 5, 1855, vol. ii., August 7, 1856, November 12, December 27, 1857, *Our Old Home,* Up the Thames.

Westminster Hall, *English Note-Books*, vol. i., September 30, 1855.

Weston, Miss, *French and Italian Journals*, vol. i., March 25, 1858.

Whale, use for the jaw-bones of a, *Twice-Told Tales*, vol. ii., The Village Uncle.

Wharf, scene at a, *Twice-Told Tales*, vol. i., Sights from a Steeple.

Wharfe River, the, *English Note-Books*, vol. i., April 11, 1857.

Wheatley, Mr., death of, *English Note-Books*, vol. ii., December 15, 1856.

Wheelock, President, of Dartmouth College, *Fanshawe and other Pieces*, T. G. Fessenden.

Whipping-post, the, *Twice-Told Tales*, vol. i., The Maypole of Merry Mount, vol. ii., Endicott and the Red Cross.

Whipple, Colonel, *American Note-Books*, vol. ii., 1842.

Whispers, expressive of moods, *The Blithedale Romance*, chapter ix., near the close.

White, Joseph Blanco, grave of, *English Note-Books*, vol. i., March 13, 1854.

White, Thomas, landlord, *English Note-Books*, vol. i., July 27, 1855.

Whitefield, George: a friend of, *Mosses from an Old Manse*, vol. i., The Old Manse, middle; oracular response of, *Fanshawe, etc.*, Sir William Pepperell, first paragraph.

White Mountains, the, *Twice-Told Tales*, vol. i., The Great Carbuncle, vol. ii., The Ambitious Guest, *Mosses from an Old Manse*, vol. ii., Sketches from Memory, The Notch of the White Mountains, Our Evening Party, *English Note-Books*; vol. i., July 21, 1855.

White Old Maid, The, a story in *Twice-Told Tales*, vol. ii.

White-weed, *American Note-Books*, vol. i., June 18, 1835.

Whitnash, village and church, *Our Old Home*, Leamington Spa, *Septimius Felton*, p. 35 (12mo).

Whitsuntide, festival of, *English Note-Books*, vol. i., May 30, 1855, vol. ii., June 7, 1857.

Whittier, J. G., *Mosses from an Old Manse*, vol. ii., P.'s Correspondence.

Wicked Earl of Rochester, the. See ROCHESTER.
"Wicked Lord" Byron, the, *English Note-Books*, vol. ii., May 29, 1857.
Widowers: anecdote of, *French and Italian Journals*, vol. i., May 8, 1858; grief of, compared with that of widows, *American Note-Books*, vol. i., August 11, 1838, *Twice-Told Tales*, vol. ii., Chippings with a Chisel.
Wigglesworth, Mr., *Twice-Told Tales*, vol. ii., Chippings with a Chisel.
Wigglesworth, President, *The Snow Image, etc.*, Old News, part i.
Wigs, *The Snow Image, etc.*, Old News, part ii.; of English judges, *English Note-Books*, vol. i., August 21, 1854.
Wilberforce, statue of, *Our Old Home*, Up the Thames.
Wilde, Mr., pictures of, *French and Italian Journals*, vol. i., April 27, 1858.
Wilding, Mr., clerk of the Consulate, *English Note-Books*, vol. i., May 11, November 16, 22, 1855, *Our Old Home*, Consular Experiences.
Wildman, Colonel, *English Note-Books*, vol. ii., May 29, 1857.
Wilkie, Sir David, pictures by, *English Note-Books*, vol. ii., August 2, 1856.
Wilkins, Sergeant, *Our Old Home*, Civic Banquets.
Willard, John, *The Snow Image, etc.*, Main Street.
Willey Family, story of the, *Twice-Told Tales*, vol. ii., The Ambitious Guest.
William of Wickham, crosier of, *English Note-Books*, vol. ii., August 31, 1856.
William the Conqueror: carved face of, *English Note-Books*, end of vol. i., article Battle Abbey; castle built by, *Our Old Home*, Pilgrimage to Old Boston (Lincoln).
William III.: New England under, *Grandfather's Chair*, part ii., chapter ii.; relic of, *English Note-Books*, vol. i., March 24, 1856.
Williams, Roger, *Twice-Told Tales*, vol. ii., Endicott and the Red Cross, *The Snow Image, etc.*, Main Street, *Grandfather's Chair*, part i., chapters iii., iv.

Williamstown, on Commencement Day, *American Note-Books*, vol. i., August 15, 1838.

Willis, N. P., *Mosses from an Old Manse*, vol. ii., P.'s Correspondence, A Virtuoso's Collection.

Willoughby d'Eresby, Lord, hotel of, *English Note-Books*, vol. ii., July 5, 1857.

Willows, *American Note-Books*, vol. ii., April 27, 1843, *Mosses from an Old Manse*, vol. i., Buds and Bird Voices.

Wilmot, John, Earl of Rochester. See ROCHESTER.

Wilson, Rev. John, *The Scarlet Letter*, chapters iii., viii., xii.

Windermere, Lake, *English Note-Books*, vol. i., July 13, 16, 1855.

Windows, Painted. See PAINTED WINDOWS.

Windsor, Mass., *American Note-Books*, vol. i., July 27, 1838.

Wine: effects of the use of, *Fanshawe*, chapters iv., v., vii.; temptation with, *The Blithedale Romance*, chapter xxi.

Wine-press, the. See VINTAGE.

Wines: Est and Montefiascone, *French and Italian Journals*, vol. ii., October 15, 1858; of Monte Beni, see SUNSHINE.

Wine-shops, the bush before, *French and Italian Journals*, vol. i., May 30, 1858, Incisa.

Wine-vaults of the London Docks, *English Note-Books*, vol. ii., July 6, 1856.

Winslow, John, *Twice-Told Tales*, vol. i., The Prophetic Pictures.

Winter: fancies for, *Mosses from an Old Manse*, vol. i., Buds and Bird Voices; in New England, see NEW ENGLAND; walks in, *American Note-Books*, vol. ii., February 12, 18, 1851.

Winthrop, John, Governor of Massachusetts, *Grandfather's Chair*, part i., chapter ii., *Fanshawe, etc.*, Mrs. Hutchinson, fifth paragraph, *Twice-Told Tales*, vol. i., A Rill from the Town Pump, vol. ii., Howe's Masquerade, Endicott and the Red Cross, *The Snow Image, etc.*, Main Street, *The Scarlet Letter*, chapter xii.

Wisdom: foolish, *Twice-Told Tales*, vol. ii., The Seven Vagabonds; relations of, with gayety, *The Marble Faun*, vol. ii., chapter xxiii.; true, *The Dolliver Romance, etc.*, Journal of a

Solitary Man, i.; when a delightful pastime, *The Blithedale Romance*, chapter xvi., near the end.

Wise, Mr., *Fanshawe, etc.*, Jonathan Cilley.

Wishes, best test of character, *Mosses from an Old Manse*, vol. ii., The Intelligence Office.

Witchcraft, the miracles of, *Mosses from an Old Manse*, vol. i., Feathertop.

Witchcraft, Salem, the, *Grandfather's Chair*, part ii., chapter ii.; lingering feeling about, *The House of the Seven Gables*, chapter i., toward the end; teachings of, *ibid.*

Witches: feasts produced by, *American Note-Books*, vol. ii., December 19, 1850; meeting of, *Mosses from an Old Manse*, vol. i., Young Goodman Brown; prosecution of, *The Scarlet Letter*, The Custom-House; of Salem, *The Snow Image, etc.*, Main Street.

Witham River, the, *Our Old Home*, Pilgrimage to Old Boston.

Wives, choosing, *American Note-Books*, vol. i., October 25, 1836, *Mosses from an Old Manse*, vol. i., Mrs. Bullfrog.

Wives of the Dead, The, a story of curious coincidences in *The Snow Image and Other Twice-Told Tales*. The scene is laid in a seaport of Massachusetts in the time of the French and Indian War. The story first appeared in "The Democratic Review."

Woe, long communion with, *Twice-Told Tales*, vol. ii., Edward Fane's Rosebud.

Wolfe, General, *Grandfather's Chair*, part ii., chapter ix., *Fanshawe, etc.*, Sir William Pepperell, third paragraph; an early station of, *English Note-Books*, vol. ii., July 5, 1857; cloak of, *ibid.*, vol. i., September 10, 1855; death of, *The Snow Image, etc.*, Old News, part ii.

Wollaston, Mount, *Twice-Told Tales*, vol. i., The Maypole of Merry Mount.

Wolsey, Cardinal: hall built by, *English Note-Books*, vol. i., March 24, 1856; hat of, *ibid.*, vol. ii., July 26, 1857.

Wolverhampton, *English Note-Books*, vol. ii., June 29, 1856.

Wolves, famous, *Mosses from an Old Manse*, vol. ii., A Virtuoso's Collection.

Womanhood, the type that centuries have been spent in making, *The Blithedale Romance*, chapter xiv.

Woman's Rights advocate, a, *Mosses from an Old Manse*, vol. ii., The Christmas Banquet.

Women: American, see AMERICA; appreciation of the heroic by, *The Blithedale Romance*, chapters ix., xix., end; apprehensions of danger by, *The Marble Faun*, vol. ii., chapter xvii.; as ministers of religion, *The Blithedale Romance*, chapter xiv.; changes in the habits and feelings of, *Fanshawe, etc.*, Mrs. Hutchinson, first page; characteristic of, refined away, *The Blithedale Romance*, chapter iii.; choice of names by literary, *ibid.*, chapter v.; command of composure by, *Fanshawe*, chapter v.; conservative view of the place of, *The Blithedale Romance*, chapter xiv., middle; criticism on independent, *ibid.*, chapter xxii., near the end; development of, in New England, *ibid.*, chapter xxiii.; easy proselytes, *ibid.*, chapter viii., end; effect of unusual circumstances on, *Septimius Felton*, p. 22 (12mo); English, see ENGLAND; faults and virtues of, *The Blithedale Romance*, chapter xxv.; French, see FRANCE; government by, *The Blithedale Romance*, chapter xiv.; happiness of, *ibid.*, chapter viii.; heart admiration of, *The Dolliver Romance, etc.*, The Antique Ring; homage of young girls to brilliant, *The Blithedale Romance*, chapter v.; husbands of celebrated, *Fanshawe, etc.*, Mrs. Hutchinson, sixth paragraph; idea that love is the only resource of, *The Blithedale Romance*, chapter xxviii.; in literature, *Fanshawe, etc.*, Mrs. Hutchinson, first paragraph, *The Blithedale Romance*, chapter xiv.; in public life, *Fanshawe, etc.*, Mrs. Hutchinson, first paragraph; in poverty, *Our Old Home*, Outside Glimpses of English Poverty; in trade, *The Snow Image, etc.*, Old News, part ii.; in war time, *Septimius Felton*, p. 67 (12mo), *The Snow Image, etc.*, Old News, part iii.; in emergencies, *The House of the Seven Gables*, chapter xv., near the beginning; Italian, see ITALY; judgment-seat dreaded by, *The Blithedale Romance*, chapter xxv.; linked with emotionless men, *ibid.*, chapter xii.; love of, for others' children, *Fanshawe*, chapter i.; misery of, *Septimius Felton*, pp. 200–201

(12mo); morality of, *Fanshawe, etc.*, Mrs. Hutchinson, first paragraph; need of love of, *The Marble Faun*, vol. i., chapter xiii.; not natural reformers, *The Blithedale Romance*, chapter xii.; of genius, *Fanshawe, etc.*, Mrs. Hutchinson, first paragraph; of young men's dreams, *Mosses from an Old Manse*, vol. i., A Select Party; possible eloquence of, *The Blithedale Romance*, chapter xiv.; rebukes of, *ibid.*, chapter xviii., end; Scotch, see SCOTLAND; tendency to speculation of, *The Scarlet Letter*, chapter xiii., near the end; who would exercise the rights of, *The Blithedale Romance*, chapter xvi., near the close.

Women, the three gray, *Wonder-Book*, The Gorgon's Head.

Wonder-Book for Girls and Boys, A, a collection of classic stories told for children. It was written in Lenox, Mass., in 1851, and published the same year. A French translation of it is spoken of in the *French and Italian Journals*, vol. ii., June 1, 1859.

Wonders of the World, the, *Twice-Told Tales*, vol. ii., The Seven Vagabonds.

" **Wooden Booksellers**," a poem, *Fanshawe, etc.*, T. G. Fessenden, near the end.

Wood-piles, *American Note-Books*, vol. ii., September 7, 1850, *The Blithedale Romance*, chapter xxiv.

Woodside, walk to, *English Note-Books*, vol. i., February 27, 1854.

Woodstock, *Our Old Home*, Near Oxford.

Woolsack, the, *English Note-Books*, vol. i., September 30, 1855.

Wooton, residence of Evelyn, *English Note-Books*, vol. i., April 1, 1856.

Worcester, Town and Cathedral, *English Note-Books*, vol. i., October 14, 1855; relics of the battle of, *ibid.*

Words, *American Note-Books*, vol. i., letters of May 19, 1840, and April, 1841.

Wordsworth, William: home and grave of, *English Note-Books*, vol. i., July 19, 1855; sketch for portrait of, *ibid.*, September 28, 1855; statue of, *ibid.*, vol. ii., August 7, 1856; "The Excursion" and "Laodamia," *Mosses from an Old Manse*, vol.

ii., P.'s Correspondence; vaults referred to by, *English Note-Books*, vol. ii., April 11, 1857.

Work: on the farm, *American Note-Books*, vol. ii., April and May, 1841; quantity of, in the world, *ibid.*, April 22, 1841. See LABOR.

Work-house, visit to a, *English Note-Books*, vol. i., February 28, 1856, *Our Old Home*, Outside Glimpses of English Poverty.

World: the, fitness to enjoy, *Septimius Felton*, p. 138 (12mo); inexhaustibleness of, *ibid.*, pp. 13, 14.

Worship, in England and America, *English Note-Books*, vol. i., August 25, 1855.

Wragg, Charles, *English Note-Books*, vol. i., September 26, 1855.

Wrekin, the, *English Note-Books*, vol. i., June 21, 1855.

Wren, Sir Christopher, church designed by, *Our Old Home*, About Warwick.

Wrong-doing, effects of, on successive generations, *The House of the Seven Gables*, Preface, chapter i.

Wycherly, Widow, an old woman in Dr. Heidegger's Experiment, *Twice-Told Tales*, vol. i.

Wynn, Sir Watkins Williams, *English Note-Books*, vol. i., March 22, 1856.

Yahoos in Ceylon, *Our Old Home*, Consular Experiences.

Yankee effusion, a, *Fanshawe, etc.*, T. G. Fessenden, second paragraph.

Yankees: intolerance of holidays of, *The Blithedale Romance*, chapter xvi.; investigating propensity of, *ibid.*, chapter xix.; two, *American Note-Books*, vol. ii., August 30 to September 5, 1852.

Years, the, spoils and gifts of, *Twice-Told Tales*, vol. ii., The Sister Years.

Yeoman, a remarkable, *American Note-Books*, vol. ii., August 15, 1842.

Yews: ancient, *English Note-Books*, vol. i., March 23, 1854; longevity of, *Our Old Home*, Leamington Spa.

York, City and Minster, *English Note-Books*, vol. ii., May 10, 1856, April 11 to 13, July 11, 1857; St. Mary's Abbey and St. William's College, *ibid.*, April 11, 12, 1857.

Yorkshire, faces in, *English Note-Books*, vol. ii., April 11, 1857.

Young Goodman Brown, a story in *Mosses from an Old Manse*, vol. i. It is a parable, setting forth the result of yielding even temporarily to the powers of evil, — the penalty of carrying through life the perception that sees kindred evil everywhere, even in the holiest places.

Youth: the genuine condition, *The Dolliver Romance*, first fragment; the loss of, *The House of the Seven Gables*, chapter xiv.; the perpetual, of enthusiasm, *Twice-Told Tales*, vol. ii., Peter Goldthwaite's Treasure.

Zeal for temperance, intemperate, *Twice-Told Tales*, vol. i., A Rill from the Town Pump, near the end.

Zenobia, statue of, by Harriet Hosmer, *The Marble Faun*, Preface.

Zenobia, a character in *The Blithedale Romance*, introduced in chapter ii. Descriptions of her character and dress are given in chapters iii. and vi. Zenobia is her name in literature, the character of her contributions to which is described in chapter vi. The mystery of her past life is alluded to in many places, especially in the latter part of chapter vi. It is nowhere definitively explained, but is easily inferred in the course of the story. She is a woman of great personal power and imposingness, her intellectual force needing for its full impression to be united with the splendid force of her personality. Coverdale's fancy about the flower she wore is given near the end of chapter vi.; suggestions about her of a great actress, chapter xix.; question as to her true attitude, chapter xix.; a prophetic jest of her own, near the beginning of chapter v.; scene between her and her father, end of chapter xxii.; possibilities of her life, chapter xxviii. It has been thought that Zenobia was drawn from Miss Margaret Fuller, and by some that her prototype was a lady who lived at Brook Farm; others have traced resemblances in different points to several women. It is probable that traits were drawn from various sources, while the character is intended as the perfect embodiment of one type, the woman of original force; Priscilla being that of the opposite type, an essentially dependent nature, as expressed in her clairvoyant powers. The incident described in chapter xxvii. is taken from one which occurred in Concord while Hawthorne was living at the Old Manse.

Zoölogical Gardens: of Liverpool, *English Note-Books,* vol. i.. April 8, 1854; of London, *ibid.,* September 9, 1855; of Surrey, *ibid.,* October 3, 1855.

THE END.